C000141387

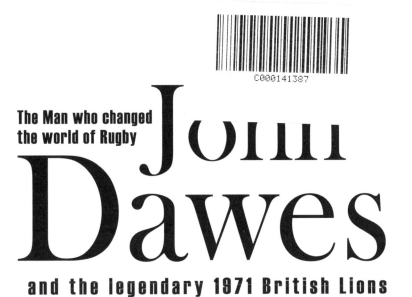

The Man who changed the world of Rugby

John Dawes

and the legendary 1971 British Lions

Ross Reyburn

y Lolfa

First impression: 2013

© Copyright Ross Reyburn and Y Lolfa Cyf., 2013

The contents of this book are subject to copyright, and may
not be reproduced by any means, mechanical or electronic,
without the prior, written consent of the publishers.

The publishers wish to acknowledge the support of
Cyngor Llyfrau Cymru

Cover design: Y Lolfa
Cover photograph: Courtesy of Colorsport

ISBN: 978 184771 706 1

FSC
Published and printed in Wales
on paper from well maintained forests by
Y Lolfa Cyf., Talybont, Ceredigion SY24 5HE
website www.ylolfa.com
e-mail ylolfa@ylolfa.com
tel 01970 832 304
fax 832 782

'The only ambition I ever had was that everyone would like to play the type of game we played at London Welsh. And this happened.'

John Dawes interviewed by *Hampstead & Highgate Express* journalist Ross Reyburn in 1973.

'The foundation of the 1970s (Wales) team was undeniably London Welsh and the influence of John Dawes was immense. When you played against these guys at the Gnoll or Old Deer Park, it was like meeting the Harlem Globetrotters with studs on. They ran everything.'

The great Welsh flanker Dai Morris in his autobiography *Shadow* (2012) describing the significance of the London Welsh side in the John Dawes era.

'The London Welsh team of the Dawes era not only played spectacular rugby at a time when the sport was leaden... the club were the driving force behind a colossal expansion of rugby. John Dawes, a clever yet unspectacular centre, became club captain. He may not have been pyrotechnic with his hands and feet but he was a cutting-edge professor of the game and he helped transform it. Dawes led the first and so far the only Lions team to win a series in New Zealand... That tour galvanised rugby in Britain and Ireland clean out of sight.'

***Sunday Times* rugby correspondent Stephen Jones recalling the Dawes era in 2012.**

'It is somewhat ironic that the Welsh back who rarely grabbed the spotlight just happened to the one who held everything together. That man was John Dawes... If the public address man announced John Dawes was missing through injury, the crowd would not bat an eyelid. In the dressing room, however, there would be a mood of panic because we knew just how important his presence was to the way we played.'

The mesmeric Wales and Lions fly-half Barry John in his 2000 autobiography describing the influence of 'the greatest captain' he ever encountered.

'Dawes concealed his great skills as a player and his high virtues as a leader by the quietness of his methods. It is impossible to recall an action, on the field or off it, which could have suggested he was momentarily out of control. You can put it most simply by saying that he was absolutely essential to the best functioning of the Lions backline.'

New Zealand rugby writer Sir Terry McLean's tribute to John Dawes guiding the 1971 Lions to glory.

'The Barbarians captain John Dawes, the man who guided the destiny of the 1971 (Lions) side, a tactical genius, a man of immense talent, superbly balanced player.'

Television match commentator Cliff Morgan pays tribute to Dawes as he takes the field leading the Barbarians against the 1973 All Blacks.

'The 1971 Lions tour was the biggest wake-up call in New Zealand rugby history. After '71 the coaching culture in New Zealand changed, from the grass roots upwards – mini rugby, schools and youth. By the mid Eighties and going into the 1987 World Cup, New Zealand boasted a generation of outstanding modern-thinking, quick-witted players.'

Graham Henry, coach of the World Cup winning All Blacks side in 2011, voicing his country's debt to John Dawes' 1971 Lions in a newspaper interview in 2001.

Contents

Foreword

WALES HAS A proud rugby tradition and, generally, due tribute is paid to the great players of our past. However there is a glaring exception in the case of John Dawes.

The legendary heroes of the 1970s Third Welsh Golden Era, Gareth Edwards, Barry John, Gerald Davies, JPR Williams and the late Mervyn Davies, are vividly remembered in print and film.

But not Dawes and this was amusingly highlighted when English rugby writer Mark Reason wrote: "John Dawes, the Welshman who captained the Lions in 1971, was almost a mythical person. It would be no great surprise to find out that he actually didn't exist."

John Dawes very much exists and Ross Reyburn's biography *The Man who changed the world of Rugby* is an inspirational story relating how a son of the Welsh Valleys with his vision of attacking rugby had a worldwide influence.

As a youthful sports editor with the *Hampstead & Highgate Express*, Reyburn first interviewed Dawes when he became a North London Polytechnic lecturer after returning from the historic 1971 tour. The result was a feature entitled 'The Unknown Giant of British Rugby' published on January 28, 1972 reflecting the fact that Dawes had been recognized only twice on the Tube while the tour's other Welsh heroes were bombarded with adulation in his native Wales.

Reyburn continued interviewing Dawes, completing an insightful biography in 1973 after Dawes' final playing triumph leading the Barbarians to their famous 23–11 win against Ian Kirkpatrick's All Blacks.

But it remained unpublished as Reyburn was not prepared to lose its objectivity by turning it into yet another sporting autobiography.

Today the book is more significant than ever as it provides the only detailed account of the greatest Lions tour and how rugby was transformed from the sterile days of the 1950s and early 1960s.

To the original biography entitled 'The Quiet Welshman', Reyburn has added a reflective postscript on Dawes' achievements including an assessment of his post-playing career, with its mixed results.

A freelance journalist who worked for 29 years with *The Birmingham Post*, primarily as a feature writer and also latterly as the regional daily's literary editor, Reyburn avoided a career in sports journalism so he could play club rugby and cricket at weekends.

But his sports writing credentials are far from limited. His lifelong interest in rugby history was inherited from his late father, New Zealand-born writer Wallace Reyburn.

Reyburn senior stayed north of the equator after reporting the 1935–36 All Blacks tour for the *New Zealand Herald*, was awarded the OBE as a Canadian war correspondent for his coverage of the ill-fated Dieppe Raid in 1942, worked as a magazine editor in Canada in the early post-war years and moved to England in 1950 as London columnist for the *Toronto Telegram*.

His nine rugby books included *The Unsmiling Giants* on the 1967 All Blacks tour hailed as "a minor miracle as sports books go" by *Punch* magazine, and *The Lions* (Stanley Paul, 1967), the first history of the British & Irish Lions.

Ross Reyburn, covering the history of international rugby, co-wrote his father's A–Z of the game *World of Rugby* (Elek, 1967). In the 'swinging' London of the late 1960s, it hardly ranked as a social plus but Reyburn junior may well have been the only man in the capital capable of naming all 30 players in the famous 1905 Wales v New Zealand match. In the early

1970s he was also a regular contributor to *The Game*, the full-colour A–Z of sport published by Marshall Cavendish.

His work for the *Post* included sports features as well as creating and editing a monthly sports books' page for the paper. In 1982 with Michael Emery, he co-wrote *Jonah*, the authorized biography of Jonah Barrington who created the world squash boom.

More recently, in 2010, he wrote *The Great Rivals – Oxford versus Cambridge*, the Pitkin Guide that detailed the vast Oxbridge contribution to the world of sport that includes the Boat Race, providing the rules of association football, Roger Bannister's four-minute mile, 32 England cricket captains and more than 600 Blues becoming rugby internationals.

With 2013 marking the 40th anniversary of the famous Barbarians victory and the 50th anniversary of his arrival at London Welsh, it is a highly appropriate time to finally publish a perceptive biography acknowledging the largely forgotten debt the game of rugby union owes John Dawes.

Lefi Gruffudd
Y Lolfa
June 2013

The Quiet Welshman

(1973)

CHAPTER 1

Into a New Era

It seems remarkable that so many doubted
the wisdom of sending Dawes to New Zealand.

FOR THE BRITISH rugby union man, the summer of 1971 was an unforgettable experience. It provided the many thousands who turned on their radios in the early hours of the morning with the unique experience of hearing a British touring team defeat New Zealand in a Test series for the first time.

The significance of this achievement went far beyond the victory over the All Blacks that summer. For almost seven decades, the awesome New Zealanders had dominated British rugby but now at long last, it seemed the balance of power had been shifted from the southern hemisphere back to the northern hemisphere where the game was created.

The 1971 Lions were led by a Welshman called John Dawes. After covering the tour for the BBC, Cliff Morgan was to describe Dawes as 'the greatest captain the game has seen for the past 50 years.' And he added: 'If there was one better before, then I'll bow. But during my lifetime, there has never been a captain who inspired so much effort and admiration and loyalty.'

And the veteran Irish forward Willie John McBride said of him: 'I have been on four Lions tours and never met anyone like him. You'd die for him.' After the tour, Dawes was awarded the OBE for his services to British rugby.

Sydney John Dawes, known to many simply as 'Syd', is the

son of a colliery blacksmith. He was born in a small mining village on the slopes of the Western Valley of Wales in 1940. Despite the tremendous hold the game of rugby has on the people of the valleys of south Wales, the young Dawes did not enjoy playing rugby until he was well into his teens. His academic talents earned him a place at Lewis School, labelled 'The Eton of Wales', and it was there Dawes was to show his exceptional talents both as a rugby player and leader in his two years playing for the school's exceptionally strong 1st XV.

Although he never gained a Welsh schools' cap, he had proved an outstanding wing forward. But he was small by forward standards and his future lay at centre where his early club rugby days with the valley side Newbridge revealed a rock-like defence and superb pass that made up for his apparent lack of true speed. After gaining a Chemistry degree at Aberystwyth University and a Physical Education qualification at Loughborough Colleges, Dawes was to move to London, working as a teacher, and the turning point of his career came when he joined London Welsh rugby club in 1963.

Condescendingly regarded back in the homeland as a collection of anglicised Welshmen unable to withstand the strong Welsh clubs, London Welsh was just an average first-class club where some 1st XV members barely bothered even to turn up to training. But all this was to change dramatically. Dawes was appointed club captain in the 1965–66 season.

In the six years he captained the Exiles, Dawes transformed London Welsh into the most glamorous rugby union club in Britain. Firstly he adopted the near revolutionary yardstick of picking only players with football ability, ignoring the convention that you had to play large forwards, and secondly, with his vice-captain Roger Michaelson he created a training regime that became legendary for the fitness levels achieved.

London Welsh were daubed 'The Robin Hoods of Rugby' when they amazed everyone by beating major clubs through lightweight packs that won little ball but reigned supreme in the loose because they were so much fitter than sides they played. Their forwards had handling skills and an awareness of the benefits of passing the ball not normally associated with the men inhabiting rugby's engine room.

This policy did have its limitations against sides with formidable large packs which could close down a match. But from these beginnings Dawes was to take the club gradually to new heights as large forwards with football ability joined the club and the Exiles, with their exhilarating style of play, showed they were capable of running up cricket scores against the best clubs.

Eventually the London Welsh concept of playing rugby, with its emphasis on fitness, running rugby, support using the full-back as an attacker, creating a man over in the backline and playing with width, ensuring the fastest runners on a rugby field were supplied with good ball, could not be ignored and was to transform the fortunes of British rugby.

Back home in south Wales, the people of the valleys had always found reasons to explain away the success of London Welsh. In the words of one Welsh club captain, the Exiles were 'a bunch of fairies' a real Welsh club had no right to lose to. But results were to come that could no longer be explained away.

Neath, the Welsh club champions, were humiliated 45–3 at Old Deer Park on February 4, 1968, and the result was received with shocked disbelief back in Wales.

The following season Newport, the great Newport club – sole conquerors of the formidable 1963–64 All Blacks, were put to the sword 31–5 at Old Deer Park on November 28, 1968, in a game hailed by critics as one of the most brilliant exhibitions of club rugby ever seen. Again the reaction in Wales was one of disbelief.

Under Dawes' inspirational leadership, Wales were to become European champions, winning the Grand Slam in the International Championship in the 1970–71 winter and then the 1971 Lions became the first British side to win a series on New Zealand soil, thus halting the southern hemisphere's only occasionally interrupted dominance of the game throughout the 20th century.

But Dawes' climb to world class stature took a long time, and for many years the Welsh selectors failed to realise his greatness as a leader, tactician and player, mistakenly judging his apparent lack of true speed as a handicap. Despite his 22 appearances for Wales, he was constantly in and out of the Welsh side. It wasn't until 1968 that he captained Wales for the first time and was promptly dropped after this match against Ireland was lost. That match saw Dawes wait in vain for his full-back to stop kicking the ball into touch and play the London Welsh style of counterattack that had been practised on the training ground again and again before the Test.

Unrealistically, the Welsh selectors had expected Dawes to convert Wales to the London Welsh style overnight. Two years later, Dawes was again made captain of Wales, this time with memorable results. After taking Wales to five successive wins, he led the Lions on their historic triumph in New Zealand. In view of what happened subsequently, it seems remarkable that so many doubted the wisdom of sending Dawes to New Zealand. His critics – and there was no shortage of them – argued he was too old and too slow and wouldn't be worth a place in the Test side.

There was also the fact that he was a Welshman. One of the major problems confronting a Lions captain is the fact he has to handle four nationalities – Englishmen, Scotsmen, Irishmen and Welshmen. This was a potentially disastrous situation even allowing for the game of rugby's ingrained sense of brotherhood. Just one Welshman, AF Harding in 1908, had led the Lions tour in the past. The Welsh, it was argued, were too moody, insular and bad tourists. But Dawes had outstanding credentials – and the universal respect rugby men, in general, had for the man, suggested that he could successfully unite the various nationalities.

Many believed the Lions faced an impossible task in New Zealand. From 1904 to 1968, Britain had sent twelve touring teams to New Zealand and South Africa and never managed to win a Test series. While the best players failed abroad, individual countries did little better at home. A long succession of All Black and Springbok touring teams came to Britain and were rarely defeated despite the arduous demands of these long tours. The only country to get the better of either of these two teams with any regularity was Wales, with three close-fought victories over New Zealand in 1905, 1935 and 1953. But the Welsh were destroyed when the All Blacks, for once, had home advantage on the 1969 Welsh tour of New Zealand. With this historical background, British sides understandably developed an inferiority complex facing these two rugby giants.

The crucial difference lay in forwards. The British seemed unable to produce packs of the same standard as those produced by the southern hemisphere giants of the game. The mere sight of a New Zealand or South African eight was enough to produce a shudder of expectancy among British crowds. It was true in the 1960s that the Springboks' dominance ended with two British tours that both ranked as a disaster by their high standards. But the aura of invincibility remained with the All Blacks, whose pack in the 1960s, ranked as arguably the greatest set of rugby forwards in the history of the game, centred around the legendary Colin 'Pinetree' Meads, the King Country farmer rumoured to have trained running up hillsides with a sheep under each arm.

But the 1971 Lions astonishingly won their four-match series against a New Zealand side led by Meads 2–1, and all their provincial matches. Just one game was lost on their 24-match tour of the Land of the Long White Cloud. The beneficial implications of this triumph seemed endless. No longer was there any need for an inferiority complex. The arrival of a new era for British rugby seemed confirmed in the summer of 1972 when England, the side humbled so often by Wales in their recent encounters, emerged unbeaten from their seven-match short tour in South Africa and won their single Test match against the Springboks 18–9.

The reason for the 1971 Lions triumph was that they were the best prepared, best drilled and best led side ever fielded by the British Isles. The prime architects of this triumph were the triumvirate who headed the tour party: Dawes the captain, Carwyn James the coach and Dr Doug Smith the manager. And it isn't unreasonable to argue that Dawes was the key figure in this trio. Through his unflappable and astute leadership and skills as a master passer of the rugby ball, the preparation and coaching were not wasted and the Lions at their explosive best elevated the London Welsh game to the highest stage.

The transformation of London Welsh was reflected in the high gates they came to draw, their new £100,000 pavilion and the fact that no less than seven members of the club – Dawes, JPR Williams, Gerald Davies, John Taylor, Mervyn Davies, Geoff Evans and Mike Roberts – were among the history-making 1971 Lions tour party captained by Dawes. His qualities as a leader are a reflection of the way he played the game. He is a soft-spoken man with a lilting Welsh accent which would provide a better answer for insomnia than counting sheep but for the fact that there are few things he says that don't make sense. As a captain he didn't lose his temper. He wasn't a shouter because he didn't need to raise his voice for players to respond to him. He was essentially the quiet man who got things done.

Doubts about his ability as a player proved totally unfounded on the tour. The hallmark of his game was his wonderful pass. Strongly built, he was without equal as a distributor of the ball to rugby's most lethal runner, the wing three-quarter. But he was also a magnificent defender and support player. Unselfishness was the essence of his game, enabling others to benefit from his talents.

Two years after the Lions tour, the All Blacks toured Britain in the winter of 1972–73. The British public waited expectantly for Ian Kirkpatrick's side to be humbled. But although their record was marginally worse than any of their predecessors, they still managed to remain undefeated in their four internationals with only a 10–10 draw against

Ireland preventing a whitewash of the Home Unions. It was against this background that Dawes, who had retired from international rugby, was summoned to captain the Barbarians against the All Blacks in the last match of their British tour.

The game turned out to be a sensational comeback for Dawes. Under his leadership, the 1971 Lions came to life again and defeated the New Zealanders 23–11 in what ranks as one of the greatest matches in rugby history.

Dawes, already something of a legendary figure, had done it again and this famous Barbarians victory re-emphasised his stature as one of the greatest figures in the history of the game.

In many respects, his supreme qualities as a leader, tactician and player have been submerged in the smokescreen created by his more spectacular contemporaries such as the scrum-half Gareth Edwards, hailed by many as the greatest rugby player of them all, idolised Welsh fly-half Barry John, the electrifying Gerald Davies and John Williams, the full-back who plays rugby like a Kamikaze pilot. But those who know their rugby will long remember John Dawes, the man who enabled British rugby to get rid of its inferiority complex.

CHAPTER 2

The Billy Goat and Other Stories

'If you were the captain of the school XV,
you were just one step away below God!'

CHAPEL OF EASE stands on the slopes of the Western Valley of Wales about nine miles from Newport. A typical small Welsh mining village, it consisted in the early 1940s of three or four streets, a Baptist chapel, some forty houses and a population of no more than 150 people.

It was at No. 4 Oak Street – one of a trio of little terraced houses – that Sydney John Dawes was born on June 29, 1940. He was the first child of colliery blacksmith, Reginald John Dawes, and his wife, Gladys.

By modern standards, the Dawes family lived in somewhat spartan conditions. The outside toilet was shared with the house next door. Inside the four-roomed house there was no hot water – just a cold water tap. Next to the open hearth fire was the iron stove where the cooking was done and the water boiled. Dawes senior earned £2.50p a week and out of this 40p was paid in rent other landlord. Even by war standards, this was not a high wage but the Dawes family was able to afford all the essentials.

The Western Valley lacks the satanic industrial darkness of its more famous neighbour, the Rhondda Valley. But the imprint of the coal industry is there for all to see. The small rear garden of the Dawes' home looked right across the valley towards the west. Down below Chapel of Ease lies the South Celynen Colliery. The gaunt shaft still stands there with its two giant wheels – the head gear pulleys. Leading away from this scene of industrial desolation is the long aerial ropeway taking the endless rotation of cages carrying coal dust high up to the giant coal tip – a long awesome black slag heap spread along the top of the next peak along from the village. Beyond the main road in the valley is another village, West End, with the coal-blackened River Ebbw sneaking its way through the streets into open country. And beyond West End lies the opposite slope of the valley – an impressive sight with its forests and farms. A little further south in the valley itself is the main village of the district, Abercarn, with it town hall and municipal offices. And above, on the same slope where Chapel of Ease stands is another village, Llanfach.

The visual effects created by the coal industry in the urban district of Abercarn are not so dramatic as those presented in Richard Llewellyn's classic account of life in the Welsh valleys, *How Green Was My Valley*. But you can understand why the young boy in Llewellyn's novel sadly asks 'Is the pit allowed to do this to us?' There exists this sheer contrast between the inherent beauty of the land and the things created by man – the colliery, the coal tip, the blackened river and the harsh stone buildings.

Life for the young Dawes was very much the same as for any other youngster in a small village community in a Welsh valley. In his early years, he and his terrier, Toby, were inseparable. Off they would wander on the slopes of the valley and if Dawes' parents wanted to find their son, they just had to find the dog. West End Primary was the only junior school in the immediate area and there Dawes played a good game of soccer (not rugby) at inside left in the winter and a poor game of cricket in the summer. The school timetable included gardening classes and Dawes can remember the embarrassment he suffered when he put the fork through his shoe and retreated out of sight to assess the damage done. Each village retained its own identity in a highly competitive way.

'I think the feature of my childhood was the way you identified yourself with your own village,' Dawes recalls. 'This very often involved battles with the other villages – soccer, cricket and even physical battles. Throwing stones at each other was the great thing. Don't ask me why. But no one was ever hurt. I do remember the stirring battles with the Llanfach mob and the West End mob! Funnily enough, we all went to the same school. But once you left school, you had this village identity.'

The character of the village of Chapel of Ease, as far as the children were concerned, was a man called Jones. 'He used to amuse us immensely because he used to keep a Billy goat and he used to take this goat for rides on the buses,' says Dawes. 'It was unbelievable seeing this goat on the bus. He also used to get two spoons and play a tune with them. To us he was an odd character and we tended to be rather unkind and make fun of him.'

However this was not entirely a one-way exercise. The great event of the year, as far as the children were concerned, was Guy Fawkes Day on November 5. 'We used to commence building the bonfire at the end of July,' Dawes recalls. 'We were terribly well organised. We would go up the mountainside and chop down the trees. We did this quite religiously and by the time the bonfire was completed, it was easily the size of a double-decker bus.' Collecting the wood was only part of the operation, for the bonfire had to be protected against sabotage raids from other villages. But one particular year, the enemy lay within in the person of Jones. He was determined to set the Chapel of Ease bonfire alight before the children did and, much to everyone's annoyance, he succeeded in getting the conflagration going two hours before the scheduled lighting. 'The fact that he put the first match to the fire really annoyed us,' Dawes remembers. 'Most of the fireworks that night were let off outside his front door!'

Dawes has no recollection of World War II, which was being fought in his early childhood. But he does recall the VE celebrations held in the village. Another national event that left an impression was the Llandow Air Disaster. In March 1950, eighty people were killed when an Avro Tudor plane, carrying supporters back from the Ireland v Wales match in Dublin, crashed near Cardiff. Four of the dead were members of the Abercarn rugby club and Dawes remembers the long funeral procession that bore the coffins of Jack Robbins, Ray Box, Ronald Rowlands and Douglas Burnett through the village up to the Chapel of Ease cemetery high on the mountainside. Only two people survived the crash and one of these, Handel Rogers, was to manage the 1969 Welsh tour of New Zealand that Dawes was to go on two decades later.

The beautiful Chapel of Ease cemetery offers its own insight into valley life. In its ten acres of tree-filled land, there are some 5,000 graves on the steep slopes above the village. The tombstones on the immaculately kept graves show the large death roll the mining industry has claimed. The Abercarn Explosion in 1878, with its 250 victims, happened at the Prince of Wales Colliery just a few hundred yards from Abercarn itself. Today the pit is closed and the site is covered by a new industrial estate. The dangers of the pit still exist and a well-kept grave dated May 14, 1964 sadly contains the body of a 20-year-old youth who died in a mining accident at the South Celynen Colliery.

The cemetery became national news in September 1971 when the saga of the Glowing Tombstone unleashed itself on a mystified public. The polished granite stone stands near the top end of cemetery and, at night, it lights up the darkness with an eerie white glow. Black magic was the cry and, for six weeks, thousands of people clambered over the railings and graves to see the Glowing Tombstone. They even came from as far as Yorkshire. Unfortunately for the owner of the property concerned, the glow could only be seen at ground level standing by a garage just outside the cemetery gates. So through the darkness people stumbled to this garage. At first, it was thought that the glow was caused by the reflection of the moon on the granite stone. Later the mystery was solved – the street lights in the village of Llanfach and West End were being reflected on the stone. Apparently in Dawes' childhood, the stone was covered so that it didn't act as a landmark for enemy planes.

When Dawes finished his schooling at West End Primary, he could have gone to one of two grammar schools – Newbridge School just a mile-and-a-half up the valley, or Lewis School eight miles away in Pengam – provided he passed his 11-plus exam. As it was he achieved a high pass mark and this gained him a place at Lewis School. Founded in 1729, Lloyd George had described it as the 'Eton of Wales'. That first day at secondary school in 1952 was something of an awesome experience for the young Dawes. Any trip outside his own valley was an adventure and that day he was smartly decked out in his black cap with the white lion on it and his new blazer with the school motto, *Ni Ddychwel Doe* (Yesterday Never Returns), inscribed on the crest. His mother took him down to the bus stop well before eight in the morning. No one else from Chapel of Ease was on the bus as it wound its way to Blackwood station. This was the meeting point for more than a hundred other schoolboys from the surrounding districts and they changed into the two special buses which took them over the valleys to Pengam and Lewis School. 'I was overawed when I finally arrived at the school to see more than 600 other boys identically dressed,' recalls Dawes. 'I also remember how we had the luxury of single desks. At West End Primary, you always sat with other pupils.'

It was at Lewis School that Dawes played rugby for the first time. He was a small figure compared to his contemporaries and he wasn't to enjoy the game. Initially he played hooker, but he was not good enough to make the school Under 13 team. Then he switched to scrum-half and gained a regular place in the school Under 14 and Under 15 teams. It was in this position that he was selected to play in a Rhymney Valley schools trial. 'I never got anywhere at all – I was a very poor scrum-half,' he says. The master in charge of rugby at the school, Bryn Jones, thought 'he was too slow around the scrum for the position'.

A year later Dawes was playing for the school 2nd XV and it was then that he decided to play as wing forward. This proved a significant move for it was then Dawes came to regard rugby as a game to enjoy rather than merely a sport that carried tremendous prestige value. As an open-side wing forward he played for the school 1st XV for two seasons in 1957–58 and 1958–59. At that time Lewis School was fielding some outstanding sides and this was reflected later in the 1960s when the Wales team invariably included a former pupil of the school. In his early years in the school, the 1st XV included Derek Morgan, the player who scored a try in the Barbarians' memorable 6–0 victory against Avril Malan's 1960–61 Springboks.

In his two years in the 1st XV, Dawes played with some outstanding players. At prop, there was John O'Shea, who was later capped by Wales five times and went on the 1968 Lions tour to South Africa. Winger Peter Rees was to play for his country four times, and Dennis Hughes, an outstanding back-row forward, later earned six Welsh caps. Add to this Dawes' own 22 appearances and you have a school side that accumulated 37 international caps. Welsh Empire Games sprinter, JC Jones, was also in the school team at the time. But the player rated above all others by Bryn Jones, who handled the school team for over twenty years, was a gifted fly-half called Elliot Williams. In the 1960s, Williams was to guide Newbridge to the Welsh Club Championship title. He was never to get a senior Welsh trial, though, and he suffered the misfortune of being at his peak when Wales had an abundance of gifted fly-halves such as David Watkins, Barry John and Phil Bennett.

Dawes began his career as a rugby captain in his final year at school when he was eighteen. Then he led the school 1st XV with O'Shea as his vice-captain. In the previous season, the

1st XV played 18 games and won all but one of these fixtures, scoring 343 points while their opponents could score only 35. In Dawes' year as captain in 1958–59, the record was slightly less impressive – 14 wins in 18 matches with 286 points for and 51 against – and this chiefly because the backline was without Elliot Williams. Although primarily a wing forward, Dawes occasionally played among the backs, and his first outing at centre was against the old boys' team. Dawes made the switch to nullify the threat posed by a large opponent who had represented the Welsh Secondary Schools as a prop forward, and apparently marked him out of the game. Dawes never obtained a secondary schools' cap but he did have an outstanding match as a wing forward in one of the trials when he was marking fly-half Ken Jones, who later played for Wales and the British Lions.

Rugby at Lewis School was regarded with extreme reverence. 'If you were in the 1st XV at school, you were a hero,' Dawes recalls. 'If you were the captain of the school XV, you were just one step away below God! When I was captain, we had a very strong pack and so tactics were fairly easy to dictate. My task was not a difficult one as I had so many outstanding players under me.' On Monday, the 1st XV would discuss the game they had played the previous Saturday. On Tuesday, Wednesday and Thursday, they would train. On Friday, they would discuss the tactics for the game being played the following day. In the school magazine, Bryn Jones said of the team Dawes captained: 'Once again, the strength of the 1st XV lay in the big, mobile pack where speed, skill and fitness were obvious in most school matches... Our greatest shortcoming was the inability to find a replacement for Elliot Williams at outside-half. No one was able in our harder matches to create the necessary openings or set the backs in motion... The personality of the side was John Dawes, whose ability to play in any position with distinction was quite remarkable. John was most unfortunate not to win a place in the Welsh Schools' International XV. However I forecast a bright future for him in first class rugby.'

Apparently he advised Dawes to play full-back when he left school – no doubt because he was a short boy by back row standards. Thirteen years later Bryn Jones recalled: 'I thought he was too slow to play in the centre. But his timing was to improve his speed. The great thing about Dawes is that he knows his limitations. If he tried to run the ball more himself, he would be shown up. He knows his limitations and he has learned to give and take a pass quicker than anyone else in British rugby. He was always a natural leader.'

It is interesting that Bryn Jones thought that Dawes was too slow to be centre – the position he was to play throughout his first-class career. Whenever you trace the rugby progress of Dawes, people invariably mention the fact that he lacked that extra yard of pace. This is no doubt because in most Welshmen's minds Welsh backs had to be nimble, elusive and fleet-footed and capable of making the devastating break. Throughout his career, Dawes was never to be a breaking centre in the Bleddyn Williams manner. His qualities lay in other directions – his unfailing judgement and his passes were to create openings for other players. The wing three-quarter is potentially the most dangerous player on the rugby field – he is the speed merchant and theoretically the main try scorer. But the wing is totally dependent on other players, for they have to give him the ball. And, as any wing knows, he has to be passed the ball at the right time. A pass delivered a split second too late can mean an opening is lost or that he has less room to move in. Wingers always remember Dawes with affection because he was the player who gave them full opportunity to utilise their talents. But for many years Welshmen failed to appreciate Dawes' gifts as a centre because he did not fit in with the traditional Welsh conception of a Welsh three-quarter.

While Dawes was never to be a player of sheer pace, it is also true to say he was not slow. At Lewis School, he was a good athlete and won the Victor Ludorum in 1958 after winning the javelin with a throw of 161ft and finishing second behind JC Jones, the future Empire Games sprinter, in the 100yds,

220yds and 440yds races. Dawes' times were 10.2 seconds for the 100 yards, 22.7 for the 220 and 51.6 for the 440. These results showed that he did not possess sustained speed. As Mr Jones mentioned in the school magazine, speed was one of the qualities of the Lewis forwards and this was reflected in the fact that the quartet who won the Glamorgan Secondary Schools sprint relay contained three forwards – Dawes, H Morgan and O'Shea – and one back, JC Jones.

An important factor in Dawes' early rugby career was the influence of his father. Dawes senior had played rugby as a wing for Abertillery and also represented Monmouthshire at county level. Despite his son's comparative lack of interest in the game until he was into his teens, Dawes senior never tried to force his son to become more involved in the game. Although this was not an intentional example of reverse psychology, it was a sensible attitude to adopt. It was with his father that Dawes saw his first game of rugby at the Abercarn Rugby Club, a good standard junior club situated in the valley by the bank of the River Ebbw. In 1953, the Dawes family moved a little further up the valley to Newbridge to live in a council house that had facilities the previous home lacked. Dawes senior, who worked in the North Celynen Colliery, was a committee member of Newbridge Rugby Club, whose ground was five minutes' walk from the family's house. While at school, young Dawes used to go down the road to train at Newbridge.

Dawes remembers his schooldays with affection. His headmaster, the late Neville Richards, was a strict but fair disciplinarian who he remembers as an excellent headmaster. Snooker halls were forbidden territory for the boys. 'To think of any member of the school in a snooker hall was terrible to him,' Dawes recalls. 'A friend of mine was seen sheltering from the rain at the entrance to the snooker hall and he found himself in the head's study the next day.' School caps were worn all the time and not to be removed until you stepped inside the door of your home in the late afternoon. There were invariably prefects on the public buses to see that the rule was not broken. Dawes' schooldays seem devoid of drama. 'I tended to be a good boy always toeing the line,' he says. 'I can't remember ever being caned.' He was a quiet and conscientious pupil and his six 'O' level passes and three 'A' level passes (Chemistry, Physics and Pure and Applied Maths) enabled him to gain a place at the University College of Wales, Aberystwyth. At the time, Dawes wanted to become a teacher and in this decision he was influenced by his father's two sisters, who were both teachers. Rare excursions out of the valleys for the young Dawes included trips to Bristol to stay with his grandparents. It was then that he saw May and Irene Dawes teaching at schools in the city. They tried to dissuade Dawes from entering the profession because it was so badly paid but he was not to be deterred. 'I'd sit in their classes when I was young,' Dawes recalls. 'I just seemed to enjoy it – the situation, the atmosphere.'

It was during the school holidays that Dawes had his first job as a £4-a-week labourer with the Forestry Commission. This work simply involved removing the ferns and the bracken from around the newly-planted trees on the valley slopes so the 12-inch trees would not be smothered. Perhaps simply is the wrong word, for Dawes and his partners in crime found it very easy to chop down the young trees by accident as they swung their scythes. 'Our efforts to hide the trees that we accidentally chopped down were very cunning because the foreman used to come up afterwards and check,' says Dawes. 'There was one character who was absolutely superb – he almost cut down a whole row of trees on one occasion.' If it rained, the rule was that you took shelter and this meant the inevitable game of cards. 'We used to look up at the sky and pray for rain so we could have a game of cards,' Dawes recalls. 'We had such a superb foreman that you could have a lovely blue sky but about fifteen miles away, you could see a little whiff of cloud and that was enough. Threat of rain! Back to the cards.' The evidence of these escapades remains today. The trees have grown to about twenty feet in height and, along the mountainside on the way to Ebbw Vale in the Western Valley, gaps can be seen in the forest.

This was the Rock and Roll era and Dawes was an avid fan. His parents gave him an expensive record player for his fifteenth birthday and he was in the enviable position of knowing a boy whose uncle worked in a record factory. So there was a substantial price reduction on the 78s and later 45s he collected. His first records were a Frank Sinatra and Nat King Cole LP and just about very Elvis Presley record would find its way into the Dawes household.

As far as books were concerned, he restricted himself to fairly lightweight subject matter, war books such as *The Colditz Story* and *The Great Escape*. But he can quote you verbatim two pages of Shakespeare's *Henry V*. This was the play he studied at Lewis School under a vague and rather doddery English master. The entire class each had a part to read in form and when the boys were due to turn over the page, they would re-read the two pages they had already covered with different people taking the various parts to add variety. 'We spent two terms reading these two pages – it was a helluva joke at the time,' says Dawes. 'The master was just sitting up there and never noticed. I don't think anyone passed English Literature that year.'

Even in his later years at school, Dawes would seldom go out in the evenings. A quiet, somewhat unworldly youth, he didn't date girls until he was eighteen. In the evenings, he would do his homework, and on Friday evening he would religiously clean his rugby boots and get to bed by 7.30pm to get a good night's sleep before the school match the following morning. Nothing would keep him up. Many of the school matches were played in Cardiff or Newport, so in the afternoons he would watch these senior clubs playing or see Wales play at Cardiff Arms Park if an international was on.

It was in 1959, near the end of his schooling, that he met his future wife – a girl from the Rhondda Valley called Janette Morris. Dawes was going with two other pupils to a sixth form conference being held in the St Nicholas country mansion. 'I first remember seeing Janette on the bus on the way out from Cardiff going to this course,' he recalls. 'I was a very shy fellow then and after the course was about three days old, I asked her out. We just went down the pub where I had my usual glass of orange.' After this initial confrontation, they began seeing each other on a regular basis while they were both at grammar school. 'I used to see Janette three times a fortnight,' says Dawes. 'She lived at Pen-y-graig, about twenty miles away from my home in Newbridge. At first, we used to meet in Cardiff and I had to catch the last bus at ten o'clock. We would go to the cinema and see a film and that was it! Then we used to meet in Pontypridd – the same distance for me but shorter for her to travel. All you could do there was go for a walk or watch a film. But Pontypridd is such a place that after two visits you haven't any more walks left!'

They continued seeing each other intermittently while Dawes was at university and they were to marry after they had both qualified as teachers. It was then that they both moved to London and, strangely enough, the turning point of Dawes' career was to come about through his wife and not himself.

CHAPTER 3

Newbridge

*'No matter who is in the Welsh side,
every valley side always has someone who is better.'*

IN WALES, THE gap between schools and first-class rugby is
surprisingly easily bridged. The same is not so in England.
In London, for instance, senior clubs such as Richmond,
Harlequins, Rosslyn Park and Wasps, run anything from five
to a dozen teams and the schoolboy invariably finds he has to
work his way through the club sides to obtain senior player
status. It is true that provincial clubs lack the same depth of
teams but, nevertheless, it is rarely you find a senior English
club that doesn't run at least two XVs. In Wales, the situation is
entirely different with only one or two of the major clubs such
as Cardiff and Newport running two XVs – let alone five or six.
So, quite apart from the obvious devotion to the game in south
Wales, the selection network is that much more efficient. After
all, if you are only running one team, there is more incentive to
ensure the best players are available, whereas in England you
know that if a player has been overlooked he will be playing in
the club's lower sides and so should eventually come to light.

Another contrast between English and Welsh rugby is that
in Wales young players come to the forefront much more
quickly. The Welsh are never reluctant to blood someone of
ability because of their youth. This was reflected in the 1960s
when Wales successfully gave first caps to four teenagers –
Terry Price (19), Keith Jarrett (18), Gareth Edwards (19) and
John Williams (19).

In this sort of rugby climate it was no great surprise that John Dawes made his debut in senior rugby for Newbridge in the winter of 1958–59 when he was an 18-year-old schoolboy. He had trained regularly at the club where his father was a committee member. And there was a large carry-over of boys from Lewis School to Newbridge through players like Elliot Williams, Dennis Hughes, Derek Morgan and, for a period, John O'Shea. One of the masters, Roy James, who in later years was to work with Dawes in London at the North London Polytechnic, was also in the club side.

In those days, Newbridge were one of the lesser clubs on the senior Welsh rugby scene. Founded in 1888, the club had five different homes before finally moving to their present venue at the Welfare Ground in 1923. It was the late Reg Edwards, the hard man of the famous England pack in the early 1920s, who brought down a Newport XV to open the ground, which had been transformed into a presentable playing surface through the efforts of voluntary helpers. But the club was not to achieve first-class status until the early 1940s. Little rugby was played in the Western Valley during the war years and through continuing to run a team, Newbridge acquired some good standard players who would have been playing for other clubs in other circumstances. Fixtures were played against service sides and Newport and Cardiff, who were running war XVs. In this way, the Welfare Ground became something of a focal point for a sports-starved public seeking some form of escape from the anxieties of war.

When the war ended, Newbridge obtained first-class status and were included in the Welsh Club Championship for the first time and they finished runners up in the 1947–48 season. The revival saw the club producing international players for the first time – players like Ray Cale, Billy Gore and Don Hayward, who played 15 times for Wales and went on the 1950 Lions tour of New Zealand. But in the 1950s, the playing record of the club deteriorated and it wasn't until the 1960s that the pendulum swung back again when Newbridge invariably fielded a back row of Test standard in Arthur Hughes (several final trials), Dennis Hughes (six caps) and Ken Braddock (three caps) and had the inspirational fly-half Elliot Williams, who some swore was the best outside-half in Wales. It was under Williams' captaincy that the club won the Welsh Championship for the first time in the 1964–65 season with their outstanding back row scoring 55 tries between them. But the revival had not come when Dawes joined the club.

Dawes played his first game for Newbridge against Loughborough Colleges at the Welfare Ground and the club won the match 13–0. 'I remember getting a card saying I had been selected and oh, how I wanted to do well,' says Dawes. 'I don't think I would have been selected if it had been a local derby match. I was very nervous in the changing room but being a boy coming in, there were many senior players to look after me. I can't say I was nervous during the game.' He cannot recall the game itself but he did play well enough to be chosen for the next game – another home match against the nearby valley club, Cross Keys. 'I think I pleased my father in that game,' says Dawes. 'The main thing I remember him telling me was how important it was to get the ball in the hands of the winger so that he had room to move in. That was my prime function as a centre – to make sure I passed the ball as quickly as I could to the wing for him to have a go.' Newbridge won the match 20–3 and the club's left wing Don Waite scored a hat-trick of tries after Dawes had given him three well-judged passes. The schoolboy played two more games for the club that season and these were both 13–11 away wins against neighbouring Abercarn and Neath.

Dawes had made a promising start to his senior career as a rugby player and those early games gave him valuable experience. His parents recall he came home after one match with a throat so sore he could hardly speak – the result of being marked by a particularly vigorous opponent who wasn't over-fond of schoolboys. 'Always remember your knees and your elbows are your finest weapons,' was the realistic advice Dawes senior gave his son. Although Dawes always believed in a policy of non-retaliation, he knew how to look after himself. 'I don't care what they do as long as we have got the ball,' he says. 'I have never retaliated – I just take protective measures.' This may sound like an example of Chinese logic but there is a difference between the two.

During the next three years Dawes was at university and student rugby was his first priority. But he was still able to play around 20 games a season for Newbridge during the vacations. At the beginning of the 1959–60 season he went on his first rugby tour with the club to Cornwall. The team stayed at St Ives, a picturesque little fishing town that provided a haven for artists and later the original beatniks and acquired trendy status in the Swinging Sixties. In the room where Dawes was staying was Derek Morgan, the former Lewis schoolboy who was to help England win the Triple Crown that season. 'We played all sorts of pranks on people,' says Dawes. 'We didn't wreck anything – we just conveniently mislaid things.' His other main tour memory was damaging his ankle ligaments on the hard ground after he scored two tries in the club's 32–0 win against St Ives on the windswept rugby ground on the upper slopes of the town. He was out of the game for five weeks – the most severe injury he was to suffer until he dislocated his shoulder 13 years later.

Dawes was never to be a flamboyant centre with a devastating break and this no doubt dates from those early days when there were no restrictions on tight marking and you could kick the ball directly into touch from anywhere.

'I was never a Bleddyn Williams type of centre and never have been, whatever the laws,' he says. 'What changed my mind was the ease with which you could blot out a player who was perhaps better than you... you had to miss a tackle for someone to make a break. That probably made me realise it's not on, so think of something else.'

This 'something else' was to come in later years when

London Welsh were to use the quick pass and the full-back in the line to create the room for running rugby to succeed. Newbridge won only seven of the 16 games in which Dawes played for them in the 1959–60 season. The following winter he was in the club team that played Newport at Rodney Parade, in a match that was to be remembered for years afterwards. This fixture was the highlight of the season for Newbridge and victory would have been a notable David v Goliath triumph achievement for the valley club. Newport, one of the giants of Welsh rugby who became the only team to defeat the 1963–64 New Zealand touring team, were not a popular club in the valleys. They were the fashionable club and if you played with them, it was said you were three-quarters of the way towards obtaining a Welsh trial. Very often, players would leave the valley clubs to go to Rodney Parade and people – rightly or wrongly – believed that Newport officials were illegally making approaches and luring players away from the smaller clubs in what was an amateur sport in which players were strictly forbidden to receive payments for playing the game. On that particular day, little Newbridge were 6–8 behind when the referee awarded the visitors a kick in front of the home team's posts – a simple kick that would have won the game for the valley club. Keith Westwood, a good rugby player who was playing alongside Dawes in the centre that day, was entrusted with the kick but he missed the penalty. 'If you miss even a pass in the valleys, you have to live with it for about a month afterwards,' says Dawes. 'So it can be imagined what life was like for poor Westwood – the missed kick that cost Newbridge victory against Newport was remembered for years afterwards.'

The following winter in the 1961–62 season, Dawes played against London Welsh for the first time. The game was in London where Dawes had only been once before, in 1953, when his aunt took him to the city to see the decorations for the Coronation. 'Coming from the valleys, my impression of London Welsh was that they were not a strong club,' says

Dawes. 'It was a question of looking upon the Exiles as easy meat – they had considerable talent but it was never organised or disciplined. My only recollection of the game is that we won quite comfortably, and secondly the playing surface at Old Deer Park – it was a superb ground.' For the Newbridge club, the match was incidental to the trip to London. They won 11–3 and Dawes scored a try, one of 11 he scored for the valley club that season.

During the three seasons from 1959 to 1962, Dawes played most of his rugby with the university team. In his first term at Aberystwyth he played in the final trial at wing forward in the first half and centre in the second half. Afterwards Denis Horgan, the secretary of the college rugby team, asked Dawes which position he preferred. Dawes replied he did not mind where he played and, as the college team was short of centres, he played there and this was to be his position throughout the rest of his rugby career. This was fortunate for British rugby. In the early 1960s, the back row game was the vogue, and the deeds of the great South African and New Zealand forwards such as Doug Hopwood, Waka Nathan and Kel Tremain gave the loose forward position a glamour of its own. But although many rated Dawes as a wing forward, he was a small man by forward standards, weighing only 12st 4lb and standing under 5ft 10in. Although it was true small players have represented their country as wing forwards, their size hasn't helped their cause and it is doubtful Dawes would have influenced British rugby in the way he did if he had remained a forward.

Dawes' first game for Aberystwyth was against the west Wales league club, Ammanford. The team travelled by coach for a late afternoon kick-off and the opposing side looked an interesting sight when the game started. 'Fifty per cent of their players were absolutely jet black,' says Dawes. 'They had just come up from the mines. I also remember that match because it was the first time I was punched in a rugby match. I was at the bottom of what we now call a ruck and some fellow was just hitting the hell out of me! I don't know why, the ball was miles away! But this is the way they play the game in Wales – very much a physical game. Obviously punches are thrown but I think they are in the heat of the moment rather than being premeditated.'

Unlike club rugby, student rugby was very much a social occasion and students would invariably spend about four hours singing a medley of English and Welsh songs after a match was over. After that first game, Horgan revealed his tremendous drinking capacity. Each member of the team bought him a port and lemon and he was also in a ten-pint round. And he managed to remain sober enough to discuss tactics on the coach journey back home.

Singing and drinking was a large part of university life. Aberystwyth has a population of around 10,000 and something like 37 pubs, which is a high ratio by any standards. The rugby team and their friends used a pub called The Ship, where they would pack into a small room and sing and drink for hours before going to the inevitable dance. The pub used to open at half-past five but, to get in, you had to be queuing for at least 15 minutes before the doors opened. The only things not tolerated by the friendly landlady were dirty songs or bad language, but this never arose. Among students drinking around ten pints an evening, it seems astonishing that Dawes never drank any alcohol while he was at university. He didn't become a drinker until 1968 and until then he simply drank orange squash because he 'didn't like the taste of beer'. But this didn't prevent him enjoying himself and fitting in well with his colleagues. But it was a constant source of amusement to those around him and there were the inevitable comments such as 'Watch yourself now, he's on his second pint. You're in trouble!' Newbridge Rugby Club claim the credit, if that is the right word, for being the first people to get Dawes drunk. This was on a tour of Ireland. The evening was a triumph for the rougher elements in the tour party, for another non-drinker, Elliott Williams, also succumbed. Down at Newbridge, they can still tell you about the night Elliott Williams ate the chrysanthemums! Dawes' only regret about his non-drinking was on the coach journeys back from matches he would be awake while everyone else slept.

Aberystwyth fielded a good standard side although they were not on a level with first-class clubs. In Dawes' three years, the college never lost more than a few games a season; they played the four other colleges that then made up the University of Wales – Swansea, Bangor, Cardiff and the Cardiff Medical School – and the winners would go on to compete in the quarter-finals of the Universities Athletic Union Championship. Dawes remembers the large crowds: 'We'd have literally thousands watching us. It was like a mini-Twickenham for the Varsity match. The atmosphere was certainly better. You'd think you were playing in front of 40,000 and not 3,000 spectators.'

In the 1959–60 season, Aberystwyth were the losing finalists in the UAU Championship. Then, in 1961–62, when Dawes was captain in his final year at the college, they repeated the feat, this time losing to Bristol in the final. Dawes blames himself for that defeat because the college wasted good ball by kicking instead of passing out to the wing where they had sprinter John Hitchen, who was a 9.9 man. The player who most impressed Dawes at university level was the fly-half, Bev Risman, who was at Manchester University. Dawes played in the Welsh Universities side against the English Universities team for whom Risman played. Dawes remembers Risman was playing at centre and at half-time, only three points divided the two teams. But then Risman switched to fly-half and the Welsh Universities team lost the match by 20 points. 'Risman had everything,' says Dawes. 'Superb pair of hands, judgement, very quick on the break and he could kick with either foot.'

At college Dawes lived away from home for the first time and the novelty of the experience was to result in him going to jail for the first and last time. He'd arrived back from rugby in the early hours of the morning to find the front door of his digs in Terrace Road locked. It didn't occur to him to ring the bell at such an early hour and he had no front door key. Eventually he wandered down to the police station and after explaining his problem, he was allowed to spend the remainder of the night in the ladies' cell!

Dawes duly obtained his Chemistry degree with a second-class honours pass. He was advised to try to get into Oxford University to gain his teaching certificate. But he decided against this course. He knew he wanted to teach but he was unsure which subject. So he decided to try to get into Loughborough Colleges where he could spend a year studying for a PE diploma in addition to the teaching certificate. He travelled by train to the town, which is just north of Leicester, on a foggy day for the twenty-minute interview, which included a try-out in the gym. 'One of the physical tests we had to do was climbing a rope without using our legs,' he recalls. 'I was made to look much better than I was because the two chaps I was with couldn't get off the ground!'

Dawes passed his interview for Loughborough but, when he started studying there, he decided that after three years of student rugby his loyalties lay with Newbridge. So each weekend he was to travel back to Wales to play for the club. The club returned the compliment making him vice-captain for that season. In the winter of 1962–63, Newbridge finished ninth in the Welsh Championship and ended the season with a record of Played 40 Won 24 Drawn 2 Lost 14 Points for: 388 Against: 187. Dawes played in twenty-one matches and the most important victory was a 6–0 win against Cardiff in the match to mark the opening of the new clubhouse built alongside the existing stand at the Welfare Ground. As a result of the victory, the fixture was retained.

This was the season that Dawes began to get noticed at a higher level. He was chosen to play for the Possibles team that were beaten 12–0 in the first Welsh trial played at Ebbw Vale. Dawes cannot recall the game itself. But he does remember what happened in the dressing room before the kick-off. The captain of the Possibles that day was the London Welsh wing forward, Robin Davies. 'He gave us this tactical talk and I remember

39

looking across to my friends who were playing,' says Dawes. 'We thought it was a little bit of a joke. Here was this fellow with an Oxford accent as the captain of the Welsh Possibles right in the heart of the valleys.' Davies was the epitome of the homeland's image of the London Welsh club. They were anglicised Welshmen with English accents, the gentlemen of the game unaccustomed to the realities of the rugby style of the valleys.

Dawes had a surprisingly fatalistic attitude towards this trial. The thought of playing for Wales is enough to stir the blood of most Welsh rugby players but 23-year-old Dawes regarded his trial in a very matter-of-fact way. 'I thought at the time, and probably later, that this match would be the pinnacle of my career,' he says. 'I never thought of myself as an international player then. It was all over my head.' He was not picked for the second trial that season. But he was made reserve for the 'hangover match' between Ireland and Wales in Dublin – the game which was originally cancelled after the smallpox outbreak in south Wales.

Dawes obtained his diploma at Loughborough plus his teaching certificate from Nottingham University. Then he was to leave the valleys for good. While it is true he achieved fame elsewhere, the influence of the valleys should not be forgotten. The environment he lived in may have lacked sophistication, but it was a world in which you learned to look after yourself and live by a worthwhile set of values.

'I think valley people are basically very happy,' says Dawes. 'It may be a narrow life you lead but when you are living in the valleys, you are completely unaware of the rest of the world. But I don't see what is wrong with that – it's a short life anyway.

'The best thing is that it makes you aware of a community, a band of people who are prepared to be loyal to each other in friendship. If you can get that out of living in such a community, then it can't be all that bad.'

For an outsider, it is difficult to appreciate the feelings generated by the game of rugby football in south Wales.

'I would say a Welsh international player – and there are very few exceptions – could walk anywhere in south Wales and be recognised by fifty per cent of the people,' says Dawes. 'I would say another twenty-five per cent would say "Hello" and a further ten per cent would stop and talk. Any Neath player in Neath would be recognised walking in the streets.

'When I moved to Newbridge, rugby was more or less the topic of conversation any time of the day. If I met someone, we would inevitably talk about rugby. First of all who was playing for the local side, and how much better he was than the chap who was playing for Wales! You get this even now. No matter who is in the Welsh side, every valley side always has someone who is better. It's that sort of atmosphere. When I started playing for Newbridge, rugby became a very dominant part of my life. I couldn't walk down the road without someone talking to me about the game.'

Hwyl is the phrase used by the Welsh to describe that indefinable state of inspiration they can rouse themselves to when playing rugby. And Dawes was to find a great deal of *hwyl* at Newbridge. Club training sessions were comparatively simple affairs then. Newbridge ran only one team and most of the playing strength of eighteen or twenty players would turn up for both the Tuesday and Thursday training sessions. Until coaching started at the club, players would just go on the field and do what they wanted to do – a game of touch, sprint training, fitness work and so on under the rather poor floodlights. Players would also run up and down the coal tip that used to be adjacent to the Welfare Ground.

Players would change at the boys' club building before the new clubhouse was built. The after-match drinking was done at a local club before the new building came. Dawes and other players like the Hughes brothers used to train throughout the summer and spend two evenings a week doing weight training – and this undoubtedly explains why Dawes has such a superb physique. The club supplied players with jerseys and socks and paid their travelling expenses. The average crowd at the

Welfare Ground ranged from 500 to 1,000 – a high count when you consider the population of Newbridge and its surrounds is only 19,000, plus the fact there is another rugby club in the town.

Dawes played 82 times for Newbridge in five seasons, scoring 171 points through 36 tries, 15 conversions, 10 penalties and a dropped-goal. He was a useful place-kicker, who used the round-the-corner method, later to become so popular. Rugby writer Owen Hughes, who covered the club's home matches for many years, says of Dawes' years with Newbridge: 'He was a very, very good stabilising influence. He was always a rock in the centre. As a defender, he was absolutely magnificent. In attack, he had an eye for the opening. There were always high hopes that he would make the top grade, but I couldn't put it any higher than that. I always thought that if he had an extra yard of speed, he would have made it before he did.'

Dawes and Newbridge were to meet on the field many times in the future after he moved to London Welsh. Down at the Newbridge clubhouse, you can meet the men Dawes played with before he moved to London. The most colourful of this band is Arthur Hughes, the back row forward who retired with a knee injury in the 1971–72 season after making a record 414 appearances and scoring more than 120 tries for the club. The bearded Hughes strikes you as the sort of character who could have been a pirate if he had lived in the 18th century. Many people rated Dawes highly as a wing forward – the position in which Hughes played most of his rugby. I asked him if he thought Dawes could have made it in senior rugby playing as a wing forward. Hughes paused and replied with a gleam in his eyes: 'Not enough intelligence – he didn't have the brains!'

CHAPTER 4

London Welsh

Dawes was in for a further shock
when he arrived at Old Deer Park.

JOHN DAWES MOVED to London in August 1963 so that his wife would have the opportunity to try to fulfill her ambition to become a professional opera singer.

'This was the only reason I came to live in London,' says Dawes. 'If I had not come, I am quite convinced that I would never have become captain of Wales and the British Lions.'

Janette Morris had always wanted to become a singer. But her parents preferred her to take the less hazardous course of using her educational grant to qualify as a teacher. And this she did as a student at Clifton Training College. In the summer of 1963, she and Dawes were married at the Methodist chapel in her home town of Pen-y-graig in the Rhondda Valley. Then, after a brief and rainy honeymoon in Cornwall, the couple moved to London, surviving on their small savings until Dawes started teaching Chemistry at Spring Grove Grammar School in Hounslow and Janette began working as a teacher at an infants' school in nearby Hayes.

Sadly her ambition to become a professional opera singer was never fulfilled. After a while it became apparent that she was getting nowhere with her part-time course at the Guildhall School of Music and Drama. And Dawes, who had to exist on a notoriously low salary, could not afford to pay for his wife to attend a full-time course at the college.

Now that Dawes was in London, he automatically joined the London Welsh rugby club when the new season began. The Exiles, as they were known, had a long and distinguished history. Officially founded in 1885, the club had seen more than 140 Welsh internationals take the field in their colours. It was an interesting rugby club, whose history was one of inconsistency and instability intermingled with a capacity for brilliance. The twin problems that faced the club throughout most of its existence was the lack of an adequate home and constantly changing playing staff. But this did not prevent the Exiles holding sway with the best rugby clubs in Britain.

The club can proudly recall how the Welsh winger, Dr Teddy Morgan, gained immortality scoring the try for Wales that beat the famous, otherwise triumphant, 1905 New Zealanders. Three other Exiles – fellow winger Willie Llewellyn and forwards AF Harding and JF Williams – were in that side that beat New Zealand 3–0. Then again, there were also three Exiles – Vivian Jenkins, Arthur Rees and Geoffrey Rees-Jones – in the Wales side that achieved the famous 13–12 victory against the 1935 All Blacks at Cardiff Arms Park.

Many of the game's greatest figures were to play for the Exiles during their careers – people like AJ 'Monkey' Gould, Rhys Gabe, Cliff Jones, Claude Davey, Ivor Jones, Bryn Meredith and Haydn Tanner. But the problem was that many just remained briefly with the club while they were in London studying at the city's university colleges and student hospitals. Nevertheless, there were many who contributed fully to the legacy of Welsh football who spent the main part of their playing career with the Exiles – names like Teddy Morgan, Wick Powell, the scrum-half with the astonishing reverse pass who played 27 times for Wales, and Vivian Jenkins, the gifted Oxford Blue who in 1934 became the first full-back to score a try in the International Championship.

The club also had a fortunate gift for producing outstanding administrators, and among these Captain Geoffrey Crawshay is remembered with particular affection. In 1924, when the club was suffering a depressing phase of mediocrity, a cable was sent to Hong Kong asking Crawshay if he would accept the presidency of the club. He replied 'Yes' and under his imaginative guidance, there was to be a sharp revival that was only halted by the advent of World War II. There were many other outstanding administrators – men like Aneurin Jenkins, who served as the club secretary between the wars. It used to be said that if the club selection committee picked a player of whom Jenkins had a low opinion, he would simply comment: 'Never mind. They may pick the team but I'm the one who sends out the cards!'

The lack of an adequate home was one of the great problems facing the club. The Exiles led a nomadic existence before they moved to Hearne Hill Stadium in 1919. But this rather inaccessible venue was hardly suitable for a major club – the pitch was situated inside a cycle track and was often muddy, while the facilities generally were poor, lacking a bar among other things. In 1957, the problem was resolved when London Welsh signed a deed of partnership with Richmond Cricket Club and moved to Old Deer Park. Thus, at long last, the Exiles had a first-class ground with a superb playing surface situated right next to Kew Gardens and right in the centre of London's main rugby area. Less than quarter of a mile away was Richmond Athletic Ground where two other major clubs, Richmond and London Scottish, played. And just across the river was Twickenham itself.

With the advent of the John Dawes era in the 1960s, London Welsh were to experience an unprecedented period of stability and success. No longer would their countrymen back home regard them as the gentleman of the game, the Welshmen with English accents. Also players came to regard the club as somewhere desirable to remain, not just as a club to play for while studying in London.

But these were far-off days when young John Dawes arrived in Richmond to attend his first training session at Old Deer Park in 1963. Dawes still vividly recalls that August evening.

45

'Janette and I lived in a flat in Hounslow and I had caught a bus to the centre of Richmond,' he says. 'When I asked people where Old Deer Park was, no one could tell me. I was absolutely staggered.

'Go to any community in south Wales and ask where the rugby ground is and they will tell you straight away. But that evening I must have asked at least a dozen people and I'm quite sure they had not heard of the game of rugby let alone where London Welsh played. And the ground was only a few minutes' walk away.'

Dawes was in for a further shock when he arrived at Old Deer Park. Initially he was heartened to see dozens of people training – many more than you would get at Newbridge. But he failed to realise that London Welsh fielded five teams compared to the one fielded by the Welsh valley club.

'I was to find out only two of the first team were taking part in the session and the club captain was nowhere to be seen,' says Dawes. 'I was amazed. Here we were in late August with the first match less than a fortnight away and virtually the whole of the first team was not training. I was to discover this was normal practice with London Welsh. When the winter was under way, the club would train once a week at the Chelsea Barracks as there were no floodlights at Old Deer Park. But most of the first team did not attend these sessions – they just turned up each Saturday for their game of rugby. But to me, rugby wasn't simply a game where you met a few minutes before the match on Saturday, played the game and then left a few hours later after a drink in the clubhouse. I used to spend five nights a week training at Newbridge and a player who did not train would not be considered for the club team. With this sort of background, you can imagine how I felt at London Welsh in those first few months. I was even considering returning to Wales each weekend to play for Newbridge again.'

Dawes was automatically placed in the London Welsh first team, and felt very unsettled in the pre-Christmas period when the club was not doing particularly well. But in the New Year, the playing record improved considerably and Dawes started to enjoy playing for the Exiles despite their undedicated attitude towards the game.

Two games Dawes played for London Welsh during that season are worth recalling. The Exiles were to surprise many people with a convincing victory over their neighbours London Scottish, who were then the kingpins of the London club rugby scene. Dawes himself scored two tries and narrowly missed a third when he intercepted the ball and ran 85 yards upfield to be tackled just short of the Scottish line.

Dawes also had an outstanding match when London Welsh played Swansea that season in Wales. The Exiles suffered a heavy 29–6 defeat and Dawes had to leave the field after scoring a 50-yard try.

'I remember I collided with a chap on my own side and split open my left eyebrow,' he recalls. 'I went off and when I returned, I was put on the wing where I marked a lad called David Weaver, who was in contention for a Welsh cap. I remember coming off the field reasonably satisfied, as this was a wing with a chance of a Welsh cap and I had found him very easy to mark. After the game the late Vernon Davies, who was one of the London Welsh selectors at the time, came up to me and said: "Well played today, You should be there now. Maybe not against England but against Scotland." That staggered me. He was saying he thought I was going to play for Wales and I had to think for a while what he meant. That was the first time – although I had played in a Welsh trial and been a reserve for an international – that I became aware that people thought of me as an international player. I believed that the centres playing for Wales at that time were far better than I was.'

The prediction made by Vernon Davies did not materialise despite the events at Swansea. But when the Welsh selectors announced the team to play Ireland for the third championship match that season, Dawes was named as a travelling reserve for that game. He flew straight from London to join the Welsh party in Ireland and, on his arrival at Dublin Airport, he was surprised to find his colleagues congratulating him. It transpired that one of the current Welsh centres, Ken Jones, had injured his ankle playing squash at Oxford University and Dawes was to take his place in the Welsh team.

John Dawes has always been something of a fatalist. Throughout his career he displayed an utter calmness that was to give the impression that he was in total control – and it was this quality that did much to explain why other players had so much respect for the man and his judgement. This quality was evident that winter in Ireland when Dawes first played for his country. The honour of a first rugby cap is regarded with high emotionalism by most Welshmen, but Dawes viewed the event with a calmness that could be mistaken for indifference. 'I wasn't nervous or excited the night before the game,' he recalls. 'I've never experienced this feeling of being unable to sleep before a big match and, on this occasion, it was probably because it all happened so quickly. I just went on the field and it was another game of rugby for me.'

Wales won the game 15–6 and Dawes barely touched the ball during the entire game. Nevertheless, he managed to score a try on his debut for Wales. Ireland were leading 6–5 for most of the match and it was Dawes' try that put the Welsh ahead.

'We were moving the ball from right to left near halfway,' Dawes recalls. 'David Watkins, who was fly-half, passed to me and I gave the ball to my fellow centre Keith Bradshaw. He made an outside break and I backed him up on the inside to take a return pass. I literally just had to fall over to score. The only other time I touched the ball in the game I had kicked ahead but the ball just cleared the tryline and the full-back was able to touch down.'

Clive Rowlands' team was kept en bloc for the final Test against France at Cardiff Arms Park. The fact Dawes retained his place meant that Ken Jones was dropped – and this created quite a fuss in Wales, for Jones was an outstanding runner. But the philosophy of the Welsh selectors has always been to retain a winning side. Wales drew the match 11–11 and thus shared the International Championship.

Again Dawes hardly touched the ball in the match. But he has not forgotten the experience of playing his first international before the legendary Cardiff Arms Park crowd: 'I do remember standing out there in front of this vast crowd and getting the feeling – I was always to get it – that 60,000 people were singing with one voice for you. You cannot explain the feeling but, as a Welshman, you feel extremely proud. It has always been said that the crowd at the Arms Park are worth five points to the Wales team. When the crowd starts singing, it is the greatest thrill you will ever get.'

The first two internationals taught Dawes that, at international level, you could not afford to make mistakes. 'I'd always been told Test football was a yard faster than club rugby. This may be a fair description but you are not aware of this difference because you automatically play a yard faster. The essential difference I found is that in an international you cannot make a mistake because it usually means a try. I greatly admired Clive Rowlands, who captained Wales when I first played for them. Clive's team talks were different to anyone else's. He generated what we call *hwyl* – enthusiasm is probably the English equivalent of the word. He would get so worked up without planning what he was going to say. It just flowed naturally.

'His team talks were all more or less the same, revolving around emotion, never tactics. His main theme was that you were wearing the red jersey of Wales and that was the greatest thing you could ever want. And you were going out in front of 60,000 people and you were not going to let them down. He would always decry the opposition saying things like: "The English are a load of peasants – let's send them back home." He would pick on individual players among the opposition that the press had given good write-ups to, and say so-and-so was rubbish. He would tell the person marking him: "I want you to eat him – he's nothing." This was very much psychology to

49

make the chap feel good. He would always make sure the other fourteen players were on the same wavelength as himself.'

In the summer of 1964, Dawes went to South Africa with the Wales team. This short tour was the first time the Welsh national team had toured abroad and they faced a formidable task in the one Test on the trip, for Wales had never beaten South Africa and now the Springboks were to have home advantage for the first time.

Dawes was in the Wales team for the Test at Durban and remembers the outdated training methods used by the tourists. 'We concentrated solely on fitness work. I cannot remember any ball work in those training sessions. We were so fanatical that the assistant manager had us doing two physical fitness sessions on the day before the Test when we should have been resting. They each lasted a couple of hours – it was absolutely ridiculous.'

The Test itself was ultimately a disaster for the Welsh – they were beaten 24–3 and it was the biggest defeat they had suffered for 40 years. But in Dawes' view, the Welsh might even have won the match but for a crucial wasted chance after Ken Jones, who was playing on the wing, had rounded his opposite number Dirksen, and raced towards the corner. The winger's 50-yard run ended just short of the tryline. But the Welsh forwards won the loose maul and the ball was moved to the backs. But fly-half David Watkins attempted an unsuccessful drop-kick and this was a terrible piece of misjudgement, for outside him lay his centres Dawes and Bradshaw, and winger Dewi Bebb, faced by a solitary defender.

This opportunity, if taken, would have put Wales ahead. As it was, the scores were level at 3–3 until well into the second half before the Springboks, inspired by a long dropped-goal by full-back Lionel Wilson, cut loose scoring three tries in the final quarter. Dawes himself was marking John Gainsford, who was considered the best centre in the world at the time. 'Up until those final minutes, I had given him no opportunity to do anything,' he recalls. 'Marking is very much a positional art. If you lie slightly inside your opposite number, he has the difficult task of passing you on the outside. This means to succeed he has to be five or six yards faster than you over 20 yards. So if you take a direct line, he won't beat you no matter how good his sidestep is. But towards the end of that Test, my alignment was slightly out and Gainsford beat me with a sidestep running through my outstretched arm and this led to a try. They tried a lot of back row moves and I also remember having to tackle their No. 8, Doug Hopwood, time and time again.'

The four match tour was a failure – not so much because the Welsh lost two games, winning the other two, but because of the way they played their rugby. A new law had just come in ruling that backs had to be 10 yards away from lineouts and also that they had to be beyond the rear end of set scrums. This was aimed at giving backs more room to move, but the Welsh played unimaginative rugby on the tour, failing to exploit the new law. And it isn't unfair to assume the Welsh captain, Clive Rowlands, who was renowned for his kicking, was to blame for the Welsh approach.

'Clive was a superb kicker,' says Dawes. 'He dominated the domestic scene. Many people thought of him merely as a kicker to touch. But he was also a superb attacking kicker – he put up the ball so accurately that you had a good chance of arriving underneath it. This paid dividends in Britain but it didn't work on tour. His kicking kept us in the game in the Test against South Africa until those last twenty minutes. But whilst he made sure we didn't go backwards, he equally made sure we didn't score. We should have tried to move the ball out to Ken Jones more often because he was our matchwinner. Another factor which didn't help was that David Watkins wasn't a three-quarters fly-half. He was really an outstanding individual player but he didn't link well with the backs outside him. But to be fair he was playing when the three-quarters in Wales were not that strong.'

Dawes was twenty-four when he went to South Africa in 1964. 'I do remember at the time how much I regretted that

I would be too old to go on the New Zealand tour we had arranged to make in 1969!'

After the tourists returned home, Dawes was to play for Wales throughout the 1964–65 season. This was the winter Wales won the Triple Crown for the first time in thirteen years after beating England 14–3, Scotland 14–12 and Ireland 14–8. It was in the Ireland match that Dawes was knocked out and this was the only time he suffered this experience in his long rugby career. 'The ball went loose and I fell on it,' he says. 'From then on, I don't remember anything. I was told later I had been kicked on the temple while I was on the ground. I was off the field for twenty minutes. And I remember looking out of the changing room window and trying to focus on the cricket scoreboard next to the rugby ground – but I couldn't see it.'

Wales were already assured of winning the championship when they went to Paris to play France in their final match of the season. The Tricolours created a sensation by taking a 22–0 lead in this match – an experience that no Welsh international side had suffered before.

'We seemed to spend our time behind our own lines,' says Dawes. 'I do remember Alun Pask shouting away, trying to restore our morale. Then we started to fight back. One incident I vividly recall was when we broke from our own line. There were three of us outside David Watkins, and we only had one Frenchman to beat. It should have been a certain try but David Watkins kicked to touch. It just showed you the ideas of players in those days – you just didn't contemplate running the ball from your own line. I don't think that chance would be wasted today.'

The Welsh were to score three tries through Dawes, Stuart Watkins and Dewi Bebb and the final score was 22–13. But Dawes believed Wales could have won the match if a Welsh forward had not dropped a crucial pass near the tryline. This match was the last Clive Rowlands played for Wales. Although he much admired Rowlands, Dawes did not agree with the view held by many rugby men that the Pontypool player was a great reader of the game. 'A great tactician must have the ability to change his tactics when they are not working,' says Dawes. 'Clive was inflexible. But what he could do was play the type of game he wanted and extremely well.'

As far as London Welsh were concerned, the winter of 1964–65 was something of a disaster. The club lost two out of every three matches, ending the season with a playing record that read: Played 36 Won 12 Lost 24 Points for: 437 Against: 515. It was a new experience for Dawes to play in a team with such a terrible record. But strangely enough, Dawes enjoyed that season and it was to produce an important change in his attitude towards the game.

The reason for this apparent paradox can be summed up in two words – Haydn Davies. A former Cambridge Blue, Davies won two Welsh caps and captained the club from full-back that season.

'Because I am prejudiced towards the man, I remember only the good things about Haydn's year as captain of the club,' says Dawes. 'Some of the things he did would not be accepted these days but I remember this as a very enjoyable season and I can only put this down to Haydn. He was responsible for a major change in my philosophy towards the game. I always played rugby to win and still do. But I used to play to win, full-stop. Through Haydn I learned that the most important thing was to enjoy your rugby. I mellowed somewhat.

'He was one of the most gifted players I have ever come across but he never realised his true potential as he never trained and was totally casual in his approach to the game. I used to tell John Williams that he was the second best full-back I have ever seen – behind Haydn Davies. John would get annoyed about this! Haydn was the first person who showed me the value of the attacking full-back. He was a big man – 6ft 1in and 14 stone – but he came into the line so well from anywhere. The man was so casual – he never thought of safety first, although he was a good defender. I saw him fall flat on his face because he had the wrong studs in his boots! But he would just get up and laugh, although we would all be cursing him. I remember how as a captain he would use terribly English expressions like "Gird up your loins" when he shouted at the pack. No one knew what he was talking about. But he'd just smile and say: "Well, you've got to say something, haven't you?"

'I've known Haydn Davies to arrive at Old Deer Park three minutes before the game started when we were all changed and ready to go on the field. "Sorry chaps, I'll quickly get changed," he would say. Even if we had played the most terrible game, he would come off the field with a smile and crack some silly remark like "Oh, we were great today". And we had been appalling. He was unique and, under his captaincy, defeat was not the depressing experience it can be.'

By now, Dawes was realising there were compensations for the apparent lack of devotion to the game of rugby in London. 'I came to find it a blessing to be up here. When you left Old Deer Park that was the end of rugby. No one knew you and it was great. But in Wales, you could never get away from rugby.'

CHAPTER 5

The Robin Hoods of Rugby

'People would literally be sick
and crawling on the ground unable to move.'

THE ACHIEVEMENTS OF John Dawes as one of rugby's greatest leaders had their origins back in the winter of 1965–66 when Dawes was first appointed captain of London Welsh rugby club. This seemingly unimportant event was to have far-reaching repercussions that no one could have possibly foreseen at the that time.

A true test of a person's qualities is provided by adversity and when Dawes took over the captaincy of the Exiles, he faced an unenviable task. The club had just gone though a terrible season during which they had lost two out of every three matches. In plain terms, they were a mediocre club where most first-team players didn't even bother to turn up to training sessions. And the main rugby clubs in Britain regarded their fixtures with the Exiles as an easy win.

But Dawes always believed that London Welsh had the players to achieve much – it was just that they were not fulfilling their true potential. And in a record six years as captain, he was to remedy this situation with a vengeance.

Ronnie Boon, who served as the club secretary for more than a decade, was the person who approached Dawes on the steps of the Central Polytechnic near Oxford Circus after the club's annual meeting and asked him if he would captain the club. 'We were going through a difficult period,' recalls Boon. 'John Dawes was one of those players who gave the side a sense of stability, which was exactly what we needed at the time. He was influential, yet he never pushed himself forward. Anyone could see he had this unobtrusive leadership quality.'

Dawes had two main objectives when he became captain. 'Firstly, I thought organised training twice a week at Old Deer Park was essential instead of the once-a-week sessions we were having at Chelsea Barracks. Secondly, I wanted only footballers in my side – it may have been that people playing for the first team were the best available but they were not my type of player. The accepted thing was that forwards had to be big players. But I maintained that the ability to handle the ball and be at the right place at the right time were more important than sheer physical bulk.'

Floodlights were erected at Old Deer Park and Dawes and his vice-captain Roger Michaelson, a back row forward who had earned a high reputation as captain of the successful 1962–63 Cambridge University team, started getting down to training in earnest. The sessions held by these two men were to become legendary for their ferocity, and they formed a devastating contrast to the sedate, badly-attended sessions held in the past.

Fitness, sheer fitness, was the theme of these training sessions in Dawes' first season as captain. The Tuesday and Thursday sessions lasted up to two hours and were taken alternatively by Dawes and Michaelson.

'If Roger took a session, it was very, very hard indeed,' says Dawes. 'I tried to make it as hard but I wasn't the driver he was. He relied on verbal bullying done in a superb way and I don't think he ever encouraged anyone. He was a very hard taskmaster, but he did it in a way that made you fight on and not resent it. There are very few people who can do this.

'We used to stand on the goal line, run to halfway and then come back to the 25 sprinting all the time. Then we'd run back to the halfway line and return to the goal line. This sprint was about 140 yards, all told, and we would do a minimum of ten.

'Then we used to go on longer sprints interspersed with exercises such as press-ups and trunk curls. Then we would end the session with a minimum of six 400-yard sprints.

'After these long sprints, people would literally be sick and crawling on the ground unable to move. This is what we judged the standard of the session by – how many people were being sick or lying on the ground. It might sound rather sadistic but it was the making of the club, for instead of not turning up to training because the sessions were too hard, everyone started attending these sessions.' The response to Dawes' new training policy was staggering. For the first time in the history of the club virtually all the first team were training twice a week throughout the season. At the start of the season around 80 players were attending and throughout the winter the average was around the 50 mark.

Interlinked with the training programme was Dawes' other policy decision that he would only pick footballers for the club's senior XV. This was a courageous decision, for it meant that among the forwards he was ignoring bulk and placing ability as the prime requirement.

At that time London Welsh had no really large forwards with the footballing ability Dawes was looking for, and this meant he fielded a very small pack of forwards by everyone else's standards. In the second row, traditionally the stamping ground for the biggest men in the game, the regular London Welsh combination that season was George Patterson and DB Evans – and these two men both weighed under 14 stone and were only 6ft 1in tall. But they had the qualities of spirit and skill Dawes wanted.

The result of Dawes' policy was that on the field of play, the Exiles' small set of forwards were dominated by most teams in the set scrums and lineouts. But what they lacked in size, they made up for in courage, fitness and skill. They were lighter and quicker than their opponents and so, invariably, were the first to reach a breakdown in play. And because they were footballers, they knew what to do with the ball once it was in their hands. The club had the ideal back row for this type of game in Tony Gray, David Richards and Roger Michaelson. Gray was an exceptionally fast flanker, who scored a prodigious amount of tries for the Exiles. Richards was the physical contact type of wing forward, constantly involved in everything. And Michaelson at No. 8 was a combination of attacking flair and solid defence. Out of this trio, Gray was the only forward over 6ft in height.

New Zealander Brian Cooke, who hooked for the club in those days, recalls: 'London Welsh at that time had a fantastic club spirit. The rugby was a joy to play and they had the will to win, more so than in New Zealand even. The forwards were real terriers. We must have had the lightest pack in Britain. We knew we couldn't win the ball from set pieces so we concentrated on getting to the ball first in the loose. The emphasis was on fitness. I think we put down only one scrum in training the whole time I was there.'

Dawes remembers: 'What we did was play a poaching game. Knowing we couldn't win the ball from the set pieces, we knocked the opposition down when they won the ball and, because we were much fitter, we got the ball away from the loose.'

After a poor start to the season, Dawes' faith in his own rugby philosophy was to more than justify itself and London Welsh ended the winter of 1965–66 with their best playing record (Played 38 Won 24 Drawn 4 Lost 10 For: 389 Against: 211) since the war.

The game that symbolised the qualities of London Welsh that season was the 9–3 victory against Bristol at Old Deer Park. The West Country forwards dominated the set pieces – the scrums were won by the monstrous margin of 11–2 strikes against the head while David Watt, the future England lock forward, ruled the lineouts. Now the laws of rugby logic decree that no team should win a rugby match under such a handicap. Yet win it they did after Dawes had given the Exiles the lead with an early dropped-goal.

The revival continued under Dawes and Michaelson the following winter when the Exiles had an almost identical playing record (Played 39 Won 23 Drawn 4 Lost 12 For: 471 Against: 279). But significantly in this season, the Exiles won their first trophy when they headed the Clubs in England table organised by *The Sunday Telegraph*. Also this same season the new London Welsh style began to emerge with its emphasis on total attack, quick passing and continual support for the man with the ball. Again it was the match against Bristol that highlighted London Welsh's exciting philosophy that it was possible to run the ball from anywhere with decisive results. For most clubs, there were certain positions on the rugby field where you always put the ball into touch and played safe. But not with the Welsh.

In this particular match at the Memorial Ground, the Exiles assured themselves of victory with a sensational try when Bristol kicked ahead and Colin Gibbons, the speed merchant in the London Welsh team who was playing full-back that day, fielded the ball 10 yards from his own line.

'Most people would have kicked to touch,' says Dawes. 'But Colin ran with the ball right through the middle of the field with his devastating sidestep, beating three or four players. He gave the ball to Tony Gray and Tony passed to me. I ran 20 yards and literally walked the last 10 yards to the tryline.

'Why I remember this try is because when I looked around over my shoulder, the nearest nine people to me were London Welsh players. That made me feel very proud. It was one of the greatest tries we as a club have scored and the Bristol crowd gave us a standing ovation.'

Those were exciting days for the London Welsh club. In many games, they seemed to be proving the unlikely theory that you can still win matches even if you barely see the ball. This David v Goliath atmosphere, allied with the imaginative way the Exiles played their rugby, caught the imagination of the press and public. But the consistent success of the team caused a certain amount of resentment back in Wales where the strong Welsh clubs regarded the Exiles as a 'soft' side unable to hold court with the tough teams from the valleys. Many tried to undermine Dawes' 'footballers only' philosophy.

'They said we were going to come unstuck against sides who played tight rugby if we didn't pick big men,' recalls Dawes. 'And this was true. The way to beat us was to keep the game tight and we had no answer to this.'

But the answer was coming from large forwards with footballing ability who were now joining the club. By the end of the 1966–67 season, the Exiles had Geoff Evans and Ian Jones in their second row. A graduate from Bangor University, Evans was a massive man, 6ft 4in tall and weighing 16st 7lb, who was to play for Wales and go on the 1971 Lions tour of New Zealand. Ian Jones, an Oxford Blue, was also a large man and he too was capped by Wales. With these two in the pack, the Exiles were no longer dominated in the lineouts.

Another new arrival in the 1966–67 season was John Taylor, the future Wales and British Isles flank forward, known as 'Basil Brush', whose outstanding qualities as a running forward compensated for his lack of size. Taylor's rise to fame was one of those remarkable success stories that occurred at London Welsh during the John Dawes era. He came to the club from Loughborough Colleges, where he wasn't rated good enough to merit a first-team place. At London Welsh he was also unable to win a place in the club's first team. But when London Welsh toured Wales at Christmas, he took the place of the unavailable Tony Gray and the Welsh selectors were so impressed with Taylor's performance against Swansea that he was selected for the Welsh trials and later played for Wales in their four championship matches that season. The bizarre feature of this remarkable affair was that London Welsh still did not think Taylor was good enough to play in their first team, even though he was playing for Wales.

'We thought our two best flankers were Tony Gray and

David Richards,' says Dawes. 'But we have this policy that if someone plays for Wales, he must play for our first team. We thought Tony Gray was near an international cap, so we dropped Richards, which was grossly unfair to the player. Even to this day, I am not sure it was the right decision to make that particular season.'

Another significant arrival was Billy Raybould, a brilliant attacking centre who was to play 11 times for Wales and also go on the 1968 Lions tour of South Africa. Together Dawes and Raybould were to form a brilliant centre partnership for the Exiles.

At international level Dawes was dropped from the Welsh national team and only played one match – against the 1967 Australians – for his country in his first two seasons as captain of London Welsh. Dawes scored a try against Australia but neither he, nor his team, played well and the tourists surprised everyone by winning the Test 14–11. The Australians impressed Dawes, for they fulfilled at international level his philosophy of 'Let the ball do the work'.

'I believed in the quick-passing game and they did it at the highest level,' says Dawes. 'They revolutionised the game by the scrum-half getting the ball away as quickly as possible and the fly-half doing the same with the full-back coming into the line to make the extra man. This is what we were doing at London Welsh and the Australians confirmed my belief that this type of game could succeed at the highest level.'

Dawes, of course, was a masterful distributor of the ball – the ideal player for the quick passing game. But the Welsh selectors dropped him after the Australian Test and continued their search for a more flamboyant type of centre.

'No matter how good you are, if you are a centre you will not beat your opposite number from set piece play if he takes the right defensive alignment,' insists Dawes. 'In my view, the centre is a linkman with the wing three-quarters. But you look at the type of player wanted in the centre and it has always been the flashy individual. Even after the Australian tour when the

61

value of the swift passing game was shown, the Welsh selectors still went for this type of centre. It wasn't until three years later, when Arthur Lewis and myself were in the Welsh team, that the sands of time seemed to have finally changed. As a London Welsh selector told me, they would never have selected Arthur and myself a decade earlier – the thought would have horrified them. It just shows the change in thinking that was to take place in Wales.'

But the disappointment of being away from international rugby was compensated by the success of the Exiles. At London Welsh Dawes was creating a style of play that was capturing the imagination of the public. 'It was a terribly exciting period,' says Ronnie Boon. 'We often had to start attacking from behind our own line and we used to score many tries by sweeping the field. And at that time, we were the greatest Robin Hoods in the business.'

CHAPTER 6

A Time to Remember

'Another Welsh club captain used
to describe us as "a bunch of fairies".'

THE LONDON WELSH team coached by and led by John Dawes was to become recognised as a great club side in the winters of 1967–68 and 1968–69. It was during those two seasons the Exiles became the most talked about club in Britain. It was true that Dawes' team was by no means unbeatable, and it was also true that other clubs could boast equally impressive playing records in those seasons. But what made London Welsh different from any other club was their style of play and their ability to positively tear apart the best club sides in the land.

The great irony of these years was the attitude of the Welshman back home in Wales, for they viewed the success of the Exiles with a mixture of cynicism and envy. Indeed, a strange situation.

'We were more determined to beat the Welsh clubs than any of our other opponents because we wanted to be recognised in Wales,' says Dawes. 'We were very aware and proud of being Welsh but we were not accepted by our own people. Perhaps bitterness is the wrong word but we were very disappointed about this attitude towards us. We seemed to be resented because we had left our homeland to live in London. I will always remember the way Brian Thomas of Neath shouted at John Taylor: "Go back to England, you Englishman." This happened all the time during matches and Thomas really meant it. Taylor would just laugh, but this epitomised the feeling there was against us.

'I also remember how another Welsh club captain used to describe us as "a bunch of fairies". This again reflected the attitude back in Wales. They looked upon us as a soft team who loved running the ball. My view was it didn't matter what the opposition did to us as long as we won the ball. We wouldn't necessarily forget about illegalities but they would not be allowed to interfere with the reason we were on the field of play. This was one of our strengths but, in Welsh eyes, it was a weakness.'

The London Welsh record at the end of the memorable 1967–68 season was Played 35 Won 24 Drawn 3 Lost 8 For: 524 Against: 290. Despite the demands on their leading players by international, county and other representative calls, the Exiles won two *Sunday Telegraph* pennants – one for being the best club in England and the other for heading the English/Welsh club table organised by the paper. Only one match was lost at Old Deer Park throughout the winter, and the club climaxed the season by winning the Middlesex Sevens tournament at Twickenham.

But statistics cannot really convey the impact of Dawes' side that season. In a winter of many highlights, three games in particular stood out. On January 20, 1968, London Welsh played Cardiff at Old Deer Park on the morning of the England v Wales international at Twickenham. Cardiff had not lost at this venue for a decade, but that morning they finally fell and the final score of 14–6 gives no indication of the manner in which they were defeated.

Rupert Cherry in his report for *The Daily Telegraph* captured the mood of the morning vividly when he wrote: 'Away with your modern jumble of jargon: I was among 8,000 enthusiasts who saw an age-old principle dazzlingly re-established by the inspired London Welsh in their first triumph over Cardiff for ten years. Many decades ago, the simple fact became obvious that if sufficient players supported the man with the ball, no power on earth could stop them. The All Blacks rediscovered this for us, and with it these exiled Welshmen have shattered the greatest club sides of the moment in the land. Three tries the Londoners scored; and the last one was due entirely to this simple principle of backing up. Almost the whole London Welsh team swept abreast in line for 60 yards or more until Dai Davies dived over the line. This was rugby for the Gods. Would that it had been in a larger arena, for many hundreds of the 8,000 who were on the ground could not see the play, and scores more climbed trees, goalposts, scaffolding and a cricket sightscreen. It was a game worthy of Twickenham crammed full.'

The brilliant London Welsh team then beat London Scottish 35–9 at the Richmond Athletic Ground the following Saturday. The Scots were having an outstanding season and just before half-time, only four points divided the sides. But then the Welsh cut loose, scoring four tries in the space of 16 minutes. The game was a memorable example of the style of attacking rugby created by Dawes in full flow. And a significant feature of the afternoon was the way Gareth James, an outstanding utility player, showed the value of the attacking full-back game.

The rugby critics were quick to appreciate that they had witnessed something out of the ordinary. Victor Swain in *The Sunday Telegraph* wrote: 'London Welsh touched the heights with a classic performance which bewildered, broke and finally destroyed the Scottish exiles. Scottish, good and gritty enough with an outstanding record this season, ran themselves exhausted against a brilliant display of passing and support for the man with the ball. The Welsh have bought this fundamental to such perfection that it is difficult to see how any defence can cope with it.'

Geoffrey Nicholson, *The Observer* critic, was in no doubt that he had seen one of the great club sides at its best: 'The

Welsh are wonderfully entertaining,' he wrote. 'But that is only the start. Any side can be entertaining by playing recklessly. The Welsh do it by running cleverly with the ball and backing their handling against all comers... Dawes trains his side until the usually perilous odds of a breakdown have lengthened to infinity. To the bewildered energy of their approach, the cumulative ways of attack, the Welsh add the remarkable combined talents of Dawes and Raybould. Dawes may be the creative talent behind so many moves, but today it was Raybould who stood out. Three times he breasted his way through when the Scottish three-quarters thought they had all the possible gaps sewn up.'

SCOTS SUNK IN DELUGE

The Observer

London Scottish 9 London Welsh 35
January 27, 1968, Richmond Athletic Park

London Scottish – S Wilson* (P); AJW Hinshelwood* (T), GR Greig, JAP Shackleton*, CG Hodson (Captain); IR Robertson (D-G), A Ramsey; TK Macdonald, IR Walker, A Corstorphine; AJ Beattie, BJ Morrison; JP Fisher*, AWH Boyle*, MA Walsh.

London Welsh – G James (3P, 4C); A Morgan (2T),
WH Raybould*, SJ Dawes* (Captain), C Gibbons (2T);
C Yorath, RJ Davies; D Bowen, BI Rees* (T), F Williams;
IC Jones, G Evans; J Taylor* (T), G Patterson, D Richards

*International

A month later, Neath, the Welsh club champions, came to Old Deer Park and a capacity crowd was there to see the clash between two contrasting rugby styles.

The Neath players had a reputation as the hard men of Welsh rugby – a fact reflected in the reputation of their captain, Wales forward Brian Thomas, who once played the second half of a club match in his bare feet. Theoretically they were the ideal side to prevent the Exiles playing their free-flowing style of rugby.

What happened that memorable afternoon was the club rugby equivalent of the sinking of the *Titanic* for Neath were defeated 45–3. As in the London Scottish match, John Dawes' men had showed their flair for humiliating the very best opposition. Such was the supremacy of the Exiles that in the final half hour of the match, they scored 29 points. Their forwards enjoyed a field day smuggling the ball from hand to hand like card players and the two London Welsh flankers, John Taylor (2) and Tony Gray (4), scored six of their side's ten tries. It was true that two Neath players were injured in the game but this could not excuse the devastating margin of the defeat.

'A time comes when superlatives are not up to the task,' wrote rugby critic Robert Oxby. 'Perhaps once in a lifetime one sees a performance of sheer perfection. London Welsh produced such a one over Neath. To catch its true quality is to attempt to describe the indescribable.'

The standard of teamwork and search for perfection that were part of the team Dawes built were reflected at one point in the game when the Exiles scored one of their ten tries. 'While the conversion was being taken, I went up and talked to our forwards,' says Dawes. 'You could see their heads nodding. They knew they were taking it easy.'

The Neath defeat staggered a Welsh rugby public who were reluctant to give Dawes and his team the credit they deserved.

'After the Neath defeat you could detect a different attitude towards us,' says Dawes. 'The Neath team were very, very shattered. From then on, we became a side to beat. We had beaten three big Welsh sides easily (Cardiff 14–6, Newbridge 19–3 and Neath 45–3) and we were now accepted as a force in Wales and no longer had to sell ourselves.'

WONDERFUL WELSH LEAVE NEATH GASPING
Daily Telegraph

London Welsh 45 Neath 3
February 24, 1968, Old Deer Park

London Welsh – GW James (5C); A Morgan (2T), SJ Dawes *
(Captain), W Raybould*, N Thomas; C Yorath (T, D-G),
J Davies; F Williams, B Rees*, D Bowen; I Jones, G Evans;
J Taylor* (2T), G Patterson, A Gray* (4T)

Neath – G Hodgson*, H Rees, G Ball (T), R Thomas,
H Williams; K Evans, D Parker; A Hughes, N Rees,
W William; B Thomas* (Captain); W Lauder, D Morris*,
M Truman

*International

Such was the impact of John Dawes and his team at the time
that people were suggesting that Dawes should lead the British
Lions when they toured South Africa in the summer of 1968.
This was a wonderful tribute to Dawes' ability as a captain
for at that time he wasn't even playing for Wales. This wasn't
merely clubhouse gossip – many people were advocating it in
print.

Christopher Ford wrote in *The Guardian*: 'If anyone is
starting a kitty to get John Dawes on the Lions tour, a famously
thrifty British wing is supposed to have remarked that his
will be the first contribution. Many leading players, shrewdly
guarded in their tributes, go still further and vote Dawes as
captain. Yet so far this season, he has not even added to his
eight Welsh caps. His reputation orbits with London Welsh,
the team to whom he has given so much and who have repaid
him so buoyantly. For Dawes and most of the side, one feels
London Welsh is a concept, a way of life.'

It was the Neath victory that finally persuaded the Welsh
national selectors to make Dawes captain of Wales against

Ireland in Dublin. What followed was perhaps the saddest episode of his career.

'I was really thrilled but I was also very apprehensive,' recalls Dawes. 'It was very much like the old days when you assembled out of the blue on a Friday to play an international the following day. That would have been okay because with this method, I could have dictated how I wanted the game to be played. But when I came in, coaching had just started under David Nash. I was never sure of my role as captain when Nash was there as coach. It was all very well for people to say I was captain and I should play the game I wanted. But I had not played Test rugby for two years and, coming in from the cold, you are not sure how players will react to you, you are not sure what to say, you are not sure of many things. I was lacking in confidence. I was on trial – they had picked me because of my reputation. They expected me to play the London Welsh game overnight. But I knew you didn't get this game overnight by talking in the dressing room. It had to be practised, it had to be believed in.

'The Welsh team was quite prepared to play this type of game until we went on the field of play and things started to go badly. I felt I had no control over the set-piece moves. We intended to play the London Welsh overlap game. In the practice sessions before the Test, I took the backs and we had the Swansea full-back Doug Rees coming into the backline all the time. We really concentrated on this but in the game itself, he never came up at all. Any balls that went over our heads, Rees kicked to touch. As it happened that day, Ireland were winning all the lineout ball and kicking to touch was the worst possible thing we could do. But although I kept telling Rees "Come on, we're with you, let's run," he just kicked to touch and therefore we lost the game.

'Undoubtedly it was my fault – I should have insisted that he ran with the ball. But I was never that sort of captain – I never used the verbal assault to inspire players. My feeling was the Welsh selectors needed a driving force at that time.

Unfortunately David Nash was a similar type to me. The whole trouble was I was put in a position of authority without the authority.'

Dawes was essentially a captain who ruled by suggestion rather than outright command. He didn't need to shout at players because they respected his judgement. But this type of situation never existed when Wales played Ireland that winter. The Irish won the game 9–6 and when the Welsh selectors announced their next side, Gareth Edwards was made captain and Dawes was dropped from the team. Unrealistically the Welsh selectors had expected Dawes to transform Wales into a replica of London Welsh overnight. And when this didn't happen, they cast him aside and time was to show the stupidity of this decision. As it turned out Dawes did play against France, taking the place of the injured Gerald Davies, and the Welsh team was beaten 14–9.

At the end of the 1967–68 winter, it seemed that Dawes' international career was over. He was 28, he had captained his country and been judged a failure and he wasn't included in the Lions team to tour South Africa.

It is ironical that JGB Thomas, the influential Welsh critic, wrote at that time: 'With a few extra yards of pace, Dawes could have been a world-class centre. It was a lack of a yard or two of extra speed for the outside gap that prevented him making the Lions tour and from holding his place in the Wales XV.'

There was a sad postscript to the Welsh captaincy saga. Dawes was appointed captain of the Wales 'B' team for a tour to the Argentine in September 1968. Dawes looked forward to the tour for he was originally put in sole charge of the playing side and this meant he had a real chance to put into practice the London Welsh concept of the game at representative level. But then at the last minute, the selectors decided to appoint Clive Rowlands as tour coach.

'I knew our game was right and I was determined to run things along London Welsh lines,' says Dawes. 'But control was taken out of my hands. The pre-tour training programme I had planned was very much geared to fitness as the players had been out of action during the summer. Clive Rowlands agreed in theory, but in reality his ideas of fitness were completely different to mine. He was not a fitness fanatic and one of the reasons we failed on tour was because we were never truly fit.'

In their six matches, the Welsh won three games, drew two and lost one. They were beaten 9–5 in the first unofficial Test against the Argentine side, the Pumas, and they drew their second match against the host country 9–9. On the field, the Welsh had to contend with notoriously poor refereeing and off the field the tour was equally unsatisfactory. The party spent the entire tour at the Hurlingham Club, a lavish country club for English exiles situated just outside Buenos Aires.

'If you tour New Zealand or South Africa, you are treated like kings and these were the stories that filter back to the youngsters and perhaps add to their ambition to make a rugby tour,' says Dawes. 'But by the end of this tour, they were really glad to get home. The lads very much wanted to meet members of the opposite sex and see what developed from there! But it simply wasn't on. Only one chap had contact with a woman throughout the trip – I don't know quite how he achieved this, but he was the envy of everyone. The only entertainment available at Hurlingham was golf – but clubs were hard to find and golf balls cost 50p each.'

It was on the Argentine tour Dawes started drinking gin for the first time. 'I became a gin man. Gin is a very large drink out there and I thought I'd try it. I enjoyed the first one and after I'd had about eight, I was feeling rather merry. But there was nothing to do. They even closed the bar before ten. Everything I say about the Argentine tour may seem on the bad side. But it was!'

But while Dawes was suffering a series of disappointments at representative level, London Welsh continued their triumphal progress. The winter of 1968–69 was to prove another memorable winter for Dawes' team and the Exiles ended the season with a record of Played 34 Won 25 Drawn 1 Lost 8 For: 649 Against: 321.

If one match above all others highlighted the greatness of the team that Dawes built, it was the match that London Welsh played against Newport at Old Deer Park that season.

'The significant feature of this match was not our playing record up to that time but Newport's,' says Dawes. 'They were striding out well ahead of the Welsh Club Championship table and had lost only one out of the 18 matches they had played. They came to us fully confident of seeing us off – not over confident, but confident.'

Newport were a shattered side by the time the game was twenty minutes old. In that time, London Welsh had scored three tries and dropped a goal. The final score was 31–5 and Dawes' conviction that rugby players should be ball handlers first and foremost received its ultimate vindication when veteran prop forward Freddie Williams, who had given the scoring pass for the first try, crossed the line himself for the sixth and final Exiles' try.

The rugby writers paid due homage. Terry O'Connor wrote in the *Daily Mail*: 'Combining the best of the French and Welsh games, London Welsh produced the finest display by a club team I can remember. At times, this bubbling game was more like a seven-a-side match. The flexible Welsh switched attacks with such speed and handling skill that Newport were continually forced to fall back disorganised.'

John Reason in *The Daily Telegraph* said: 'Newport were put to the sword by one of the most brilliant exhibitions of club football it has been my privilege to see.' And Rex Alston in *The Sunday Telegraph* wrote: 'All the tries were the result of speedy support work which kept the movement forever going forward... Dawes, as usual, was the brains behind it all.'

The game could not be interpreted as just an off day for Newport. Their outstanding form continued throughout the season and they ended the winter as Welsh Club Champions losing only four out of 45 games.

'Thirty-one points to five was an accurate reflection of the game – we really ran all over them,' says Dawes. 'They were really upset. The atmosphere in their changing room after the game was like a graveyard and in Wales they just could not believe that Newport had been beaten 31–5. I remember my father saying he was down in the Newbridge clubhouse when the result came through on the television and no one could believe it. Everyone rushed out to get the papers.'

Two comparatively unknown players in the London Welsh side against Newport were John Williams and Mervyn Davies. Williams, an 18-year-old full-back, had proved to be the star of the Argentine tour and was now in London studying at St Mary's Hospital. At that time Dawes was convinced Williams would be Wales' next full-back, and so it proved to be.

The rise of Mervyn Davies was the most sensational success story Dawes encountered in his rugby career. Like Williams, Davies was a newcomer to the London Welsh first team that season.

'We were rather concerned about our lineout play,' Dawes recalls. 'Our second-team captain, Glan Richards, told us: "There's a boy in the seconds. I wouldn't recommend him for the firsts – but he will win the ball at the back of the lineout." So we played him.' Mervyn Davies, a 21-year-old teacher from Swansea, made his debut for London Welsh against Moseley on November 2, 1968. On February 1, 1969, he made his debut for Wales against Scotland at Murrayfield. In other words, Davies had risen from the obscurity of second-team rugby to play for his country in a mere three months!

NEWPORT CRUSHED BY BRILLIANT LONDON WELSH
The Daily Telegraph

London Welsh 31 Newport 5
November 28, 1968

London Welsh – JPR Williams (2C); AK Morgan (T),

73

WH Raybould*(T), SJ Dawes (capt)* (T), CT Gibbons (2T);
GW James (3D-G), RJ Davies; FT Williams (T), AG Griffiths,
D Langley; TG Evans, G Johnson; J Taylor*,
M Davies, DA Evans

Newport – G Britton, SJ Watkins*(T), K Jarrett*, I Taylor,
PM Rees*; M Parry, G Treharne; M Webber, V Perrins,
B Llewellyn; B Price (capt)*, W Morris*; D Haines,
P Watson, K Poole (C)

*International

The Newport victory was just one of many outstanding performances by London Welsh in the 1968–69 season. Aberavon were beaten 52–8 on their own ground and in a normal season, the 34–11 win against Pontypool at Pontypool Park would be regarded as a memorable win. Then there was an epic struggle late in the season in atrocious conditions at Ebbw Vale when the Exiles took the Welsh club's unbeaten home record with a narrow 6–3 win. The game is worth recalling because that day conditions were so bad that London Welsh could not hope to play their normal running game. But the Exiles won the match because by then they had an outstanding pack. Their forwards against the valley side were Bowen, Rees, Freddie Williams, Geoff Evans, Roberts, Taylor, Mervyn Davies and Gray and ultimately six of this pack played for Wales. When the 1968–69 season came to a close, no English club had won at Old Deer Park for two years.

The only regrettable aspect of the success of London Welsh was that the Welsh selectors failed to fully realise the significance of what Dawes had done. He had not only shown he was an outstanding captain, he had also showed his supreme ability as a reader of the game by creating a style of play that was ultimately to change the destiny of British rugby. By this time, training at London Welsh had progressed from pure fitness sessions; outside assistance included some valuable help from Dr Hugh Burry, the former All Black now working in London. Dawes himself was the club coach in all but name and he made sure that his men perfected the basics that are so often neglected. Swift passing, for instance, was an art constantly practised in training. Players would run across the field trying to beat the ball as it was passed down a line of six players. 'They would never beat the ball,' says Dawes, who didn't care how the ball was passed as long as it was effective.

On the field, the Dawes dictum of 'Let the ball do the work' was put into practice. Unlike the traditional Welsh fly-half, the outside half at London Welsh was picked for his ability to touch and give the ball – in other words, his ability to get the backline moving quickly. This contrasted with most teams where the fly-half was often the fulcrum of play, the man who dictated play. The passing ability of the Exiles meant that the wings were brought fully into play. And in using the full-back as an attacking force, Dawes was years ahead of others in adding this new dimension to the game. Add to these factors the Exiles' superb work and their flair for the counterattack and you have the main ingredients of the free-flowing style of play that captured the imagination of the rugby public. But it was another two years before Dawes was given the opportunity to show that the London Welsh game could succeed at the highest level.

At the end of the 1968–69 season, Dawes was recalled to the Wales team for the final match of the season at Cardiff. Throughout the winter, Dawes had been a member of the national squad trained by Clive Rowlands. When Dawes was picked for the England match, the famous former Welsh international centre, Bleddyn Williams, wrote in *The People* newspaper that Dawes was too old and not good enough to play for his country. But Dawes justified his place in the side that won a massive 30–9 victory against the old enemy. Winger Maurice Richards scored four tries that afternoon and Dawes' passing ability and the interventions of full-back John Williams into the line played an important role in the success of the gifted Richards.

The evening after the game, the Welsh tour party was announced for the short tour to New Zealand in the summer of 1969. There were four London Welshmen in the party – John Williams, Mervyn Davies, John Taylor and John Dawes.

CHAPTER 7

The Suicide Mission

*'There must have been close to
10,000 people there just to welcome us.'*

THE YEAR 1969 was one of the most important in the history of Welsh rugby. For the first time, Wales were leaving their homeland to tour New Zealand and the visit included two Test matches against the All Blacks.

Tradition had seen a very special rivalry between these two great rugby nations. New Zealand had toured Britain six times and suffered only seven defeats in a total of 158 games played on these tours – an extraordinary record. And six of these defeats had taken place in Wales. Instant immortality was the reward Welshmen conferred on her teams who defeated the New Zealanders and, on three occasions, the Welsh national team had performed the feat. The two countries played each other for the first time in 1905 when Wales won a memorable 3–0 victory at Cardiff over the First All Blacks, who won all their other 31 tour matches. For decades afterwards the two countries were to argue about the controversy of that game – the disallowed Deans try that would have drawn or more probably won the match for the tourists if the referee had ruled that the New Zealand centre, Bob Deans, had crossed the Welsh tryline. New Zealand gained their revenge beating Wales 19–0 at Swansea in 1924. But the Welsh beat the tourists 13–12 in 1935 and 13–8 in 1953. Then the All Blacks levelled the series three-all, with their wins at Cardiff in 1963 (6–0) and 1967 (13–6). Now the New Zealanders were to have home advantage for the first time.

Wales left Britain in the summer of 1969 as European champions after their Triple Crown success and their draw with France. Critics said great things about this Welsh team and it was even said it was the greatest side Wales had produced. The players did not put themselves on this high cloud, but they did think they could beat New Zealand in the Test series. They faced an unenviable task. The All Blacks dominated world rugby in the 1960s and could justifiably call themselves the unofficial world champions. Brian Lochore's team was undefeated on its 1967 tour of Britain and the only serious rivals to the All Blacks' supremacy were the South Africans. But they lost the Test series 1–3 on their 1965 tour of New Zealand.

John Dawes looked forward to the tour. 'I think everyone was thrilled to go to New Zealand, then Australia and finally Fiji just to play rugby,' he recalls. But by the time the tour was over, the affinity between the Welsh and the New Zealanders had been scarred by controversy and the trip came to be called The Suicide Mission because of the ridiculously tough fixture list that had been compiled.

The tour party flew straight from Britain to Auckland, covering 12,000 miles without a stop. After arriving in Auckland Airport on Friday May 23, they travelled to New Plymouth and came out onto the balcony of the Criterion Hotel to acknowledge the crowd. 'There must have been close to 10,000 people there just to welcome us,' says Dawes. 'The main street was absolutely jam-packed with people – there was no traffic at all. It was unbelievable coming all that way and getting this fantastic welcome.' The next day, people came in their thousands to watch the team training. 'There must have been more people to watch us train than a first-class club in Britain draws to see a match,' says Dawes. 'It was absolutely incredible. They couldn't have been impressed with our training though, as we were far too tired.'

On their fourth day in New Zealand, the Welsh played their first match, drawing 9–9 against a strong Taranaki side. Then, the following Saturday – their eighth day in the country – they played New Zealand in the mud at Lancaster Park, Christchurch. They lost the game 0–19, conceding four tries, and the prime movers in the All Blacks' win were the magnificent New Zealand forwards, who ran rampant despite the conditions. Welsh coach Clive Rowlands called those New Zealand forwards the greatest pack he had ever seen. 'When we made mistakes, we didn't lose six yards as we did at home – we lost 80 yards,' he said reverently. The other feature of the match was the punch thrown by the great New Zealand second row forward Colin Meads, which broke the jaw of the Welsh hooker, Jeff Young. The Welshman had been jersey pulling as the New Zealanders burst through a lineout. Although the tour officials remained silent about the incident, the reaction of the players was less calm. 'We were very bitter and it would be silly to say we were not,' says Dawes. 'Young pulled a front row forward's jersey. But instead of the New Zealander concerned doing something about it, Meads threw a punch and broke his jaw. Meads had nothing to do with the incident. It was the sort of unwritten law that you sort out your own battles and this question of jersey pulling was the front row forward's business. It wasn't Meads' fight and we were bitter he hit Jeff Young when he was unprepared.'

So the Welsh had played two games, including a Test match, in the space of eight days after making a non-stop 52-hour plane flight across the world. It was an insane playing schedule. And if the tour proved nothing else, it should have showed the problem of jet lag must be allowed for. As Dawes says: 'The metabolism of your body just doesn't adjust after such a long journey and we were not aware of this. I'd say it is suicidal for any team to go to New Zealand in a straight journey as we did and then play two games, including a Test, in eight days. You need at least a week to acclimatise. No matter how much you sleep – and most of us were going to bed at nine o'clock in that first week – you find yourself waking up at about four or five in the morning and feeling really alert. Then in the afternoon at about four or five, when it is night time in Britain, you feel really tired. Your mind knows you have crossed the world but your body just doesn't adjust.'

After such a decisive defeat in the first Test, many people regarded the Welsh team as a write-off. But they came back with two fine victories against Otago, 27–9, and Wellington, 14–6, the provincial sides who had beaten so many British touring teams. Winger Maurice Richards set everyone talking with his three tries against Otago. 'I remember the try he scored from near the halfway line,' says Dawes. 'We broke down the blindside and Maurice had about 50 yards to go with one player in front of him and another covering from the side. They were both about to pounce when he did this superb sidestep off his left foot and went between them. They collided and you could hear the crowd gasp. Richards was very, very quick, as fast as Gerald Davies. He also had footballing ability. What I liked about him was that off the field he never drank, he never smoked and he was the most religious man I have ever met. But was he stroppy on the field! You've never met anyone like him – he would have a go at anyone!'

Dawes played in the Otago match and then led the Welsh to victory against Wellington, the Ranfurly Shield holders who had beaten the 1965 Springboks 23–6 and the 1966 Lions 20–6. Absent from the first Test team, Dawes was picked for the second Test. The side was altered, with Gerald Davies switching from centre to replace Stuart Watkins on the wing. This was to prove a significant move, for Davies was to develop into a great winger and there is no doubt his devastating talents as a runner were wasted in the centre. Before the second Test, Dawes made one of the few bad mistakes of his career. Talking to a leading rugby writer, he had said: 'You give us forty per cent of the ball and we will beat New Zealand by 30 points.' This comment made headline news. Even allowing for Dawes' proviso that his side had to obtain a worthwhile share of the ball against the giant New Zealand forwards, it was an extraordinary statement to make. How could anyone delude themselves into thinking that the All Blacks could be beaten by 30 points? But Dawes always believed that British backs had the ability to tear apart the New Zealanders provided they got enough good ball. In the next few years, Dawes was to lead two great rugby teams, the 1971 Lions and the 1973 Barbarians, who were to show that his belief was not wholly unrealistic. 'I had no doubt in my mind that it was true,' says Dawes. 'I said all along that if you could match the All Blacks up front, you would beat them behind. But I had no right to say it and the 30-point statement caused a certain amount of embarrassment among some of our players.'

After their two wins against two of the strongest provincial sides in New Zealand, the Welsh believed they could win the second Test despite the power of the home forwards. They started the game well, taking a 6–3 lead after centre Keith Jarrett kicked a penalty and Richards scored a magnificent try after a 30-yard run to the corner. But Jarrett later missed three straightforward penalties and, against the All Blacks, chances such as these just had to be taken. When the final whistle went, the scoreboard read New Zealand 33 Wales 12. The 55,000 crowd at Eden Park, Auckland, had seen Wales humiliated. The New Zealand full-back Fergie McCormick scored a record 24 points with his kicking, while his team scored three tries to the two scored by the tourists. In the view of the Welsh there was only one reason for this huge defeat and this was the refereeing of Mr Pat Murphy. The allegiance of Mr Murphy had clearly been shown when he jumped in the air with joy when McCormick landed a drop-goal.

'It was very sad for a referee to allow that sort of emotion to be displayed,' says Dawes. 'We suffered as a result of sheer bad refereeing. Our morale simply disintegrated because of this and the fact we had not taken out chances. There was no doubt New Zealand were the better side – they had such a magnificent pack. But what annoyed us was the margin – they were never 21 points better than us and this is what hurt.'

Others in the tour party expressed themselves more strongly than Dawes on the refereeing of Murphy. 'Whenever we started to go, Mr Murphy stopped us,' said the Welsh captain Brian Price. Tour manager Handel Rogers observed drily that Mr Murphy had performed his duties to 'the best of his ability' and the Welsh fly-half Barry John entered full moan mode saying that he never wanted to tour New Zealand again. 'This was the sheer bitterness felt after that Test,' says Dawes. 'Barry wasn't reacting to either the New Zealand hospitality or the play of the All Blacks. There were two mistakes. One was the way the press interpreted the remark and the biggest mistake was making the comment in the first place. And I think Barry would agree with that.'

The New Zealand attitude to the 1969 Welsh side was vividly summed up by their most perceptive of rugby writers, Terry McLean. In his book on the tour, *Red Dragons of Rugby* (AH & AW Reed, 1969), he wrote: 'One of the principal troubles with the Welsh was they could not and would not believe there was anything seriously wrong with their ideas on rugby. In the words of one of the jauntier Gilbert and Sullivan songs, they were 'Up In The Air, Sky High, Sky High' about themselves. On the night of their match with Fiji, the last on the tour, they behaved as if they had won the world championship. They thought their defeat of Wellington was one of the finer acts of modern rugby and were embittered when New Zealanders, not forgetting, so they said, Gray, the Wellington captain, spoke critically of Wellington rather than in praise of the Welsh. Reactions like this, which tended to be characteristic, stressed that the Welsh were good at explaining things, not least to themselves. Thus the loss of the first Test with the All Blacks was travel fatigue (fair enough, no reasonable man would quarrel with this). But the defeat at Auckland was Mr Murphy, always Mr Murphy. No one else? God save us, Mr Murphy undoubtedly did make mistakes; but if he had penalised the Welsh forwards for all their offside play, there might scarcely have been a match; and if he had taken action against the worst Welsh whingers, there mightn't have been many players for the All Blacks to play ("It was embarrassing," some of the All Blacks said. "The Welsh moaning was the worst we have ever encountered").'

Later McLean was to get to the essence of the Welsh failure. 'In the two Tests against the All Blacks, the Welsh forwards were cowed,' he wrote. 'In so many words, they were not the Welshmen Welsh forwards used to be. It was the most staggering aspect of the tour.' Was McLean right? Well his view was confirmed by a respected Welsh critic who commented on his return home that he was ashamed of that Welsh pack. In his view – and it wasn't put in print – the Welsh eight were scared of the New Zealand pack. But this was not a view shared by Dawes – and he was a member of the team.

After the New Zealand trip, Wales played Australia, winning their Test match against the Wallabies 19–16, with Gerald Davies scoring a superb try in his new position on the wing. There was an unusual incident five minutes from the end of the match after the Australian full-back McGill scored a corner try, which he converted himself. Richards had argued with the referee's decision, the ultimate verbal behavioural crime on a rugby field, and Craig Ferguson quite justifiably awarded Australia a penalty from the kick-off position. Fortunately for the Welsh, the long kick had to be taken in the mud-heap in the centre of the field and the penalty attempt fell well short.

Finally Wales played Fiji and won this match 31–11 with Dawes' old friend, Dennis Hughes, performing the rare feat of scoring three tries playing in the pack.

From the Welsh point of view, the highlights of the tour were the heroic play of full-back John Williams and the outstanding running of the wings, Richards and Davies. Scrum-half Gareth Edwards and fly-half Barry John did not live up to their pre-tour press reports and the forwards were a severe disappointment. And Dawes was Dawes. 'A strong ready player, especially gifted in his timing and delivering of a pass,' said McLean, the doyen of rugby writers.

Despite the successes in Australia and Fiji and the victories over Otago and Wellington, nothing could eradicate the memory of the failure in the two Tests. New Zealanders, brought up on stories of the legendary prowess of Welsh rugby, were to see the death of a legend. It is true that if the Welsh had been able to avoid the ridiculous itinerary and the refereeing of Mr Murphy, they would have returned home defeated rather than humiliated. But it is also true that the Welsh seemed obsessed with making excuses to cover their own deficiencies whilst forgetting the merits of the New Zealand team with its great set of forwards. This did much to ruin the special relationship that had existed between the two countries for 64 years. Had not Clive Rowlands said: 'The greatest thing a Welsh rugby man can do is to play against the All Blacks'?

If you try hard enough, you can usually find an excuse for everything and the Welsh undoubtedly have a flair for casuistry that even the Jesuits would find hard to match. But there are two sides to the equation. The massed choirs at Cardiff Arms Park singing the battle hymns of their ancestors to inspire their heroes testify that rugby is more than a game to the Welsh. It is in their blood and they have this unshakeable belief in their ability. As one New Zealand international once said: 'You don't beat Wales, you just score more points than they do.' Any other nation of rugby players would have left New Zealand with a giant inferiority complex. But not the Welsh. They found logical reasons to explain the inexplicable and if they had not, possibly the 1971 Lions would never have achieved their historic victory. Dawes and eight other members of the 1969 Welsh tour party were to tour New Zealand with the Lions and the image of Welsh rugby was to be restored in new glories.

CHAPTER 8

Out of the Wilderness

'Gareth and Barry John looked upon themselves
as kingpins and we lost the game as a result.'

THE QUALITIES OF people are often reflected in the achievements of others. It is probably no coincidence Maurice Richards' rise to fame coincided with John Dawes' return to international rugby.

By the time the 1969 Welsh short tour was over, Richards was regarded as the best winger in the world. He had begun a prolific spate of scoring with his four tries in the game against England at Cardiff and this was the match that saw the recall of Dawes to the Wales team. In New Zealand, Richards scored three tries against Otago, one against Wellington and one against the All Blacks in the second Test. Then he ended the tour with two against Fiji. Thus he had scored 11 tries for Wales in five games and on each occasion Dawes was the centre immediately inside him. It is interesting to conjecture how Richards would have fared if Dawes had not been alongside him. Rugby history is filled with examples of great wingers whose potential has been wasted through the inadequacies of those alongside them. So often one sees potential scoring opportunities wasted because players have been unable to deliver the right type of pass at the right time. This is not a fault one can attribute to John Dawes – the hallmark of his game is his magnificent pass.

Former Welsh international winger Stuart Watkins once said of Dawes: 'It was easy to play with John for he always gave you the ball at the right time.' No doubt Maurice Richards would say the same of Dawes.

The London Welshman had established himself as a regular in the Wales team on the 1969 short tour and he was to play for his country in all five Tests during the 1969–70 season. That winter both Richards and Jarrett had turned professional, playing rugby league, and winger Gerald Davies had given up international football for a season to concentrate on his studies at Cambridge University. Thus the Welsh back division was severely depleted. Wales opened the season with their match against the South African tourists. Wales had never beaten South Africa and they were extremely fortunate to salvage a 6–6 draw in terrible conditions at Cardiff after a mud-covered Gareth Edwards scored a blindside try in injury time.

Wales opened their International Championship programme with an 18–9 win over Scotland in Cardiff. Dawes scored one of the four Welsh tries but the side's backline lacked rhythm, with scrum-half Gareth Edwards attempting too much on his own and fly-half Barry John over-kicking. Next Wales won a memorable encounter with England at Twickenham. Edwards left the field injured twenty minutes from the close with Wales trailing 6–13. But, inspired by his replacement, Chico Hopkins, Wales staged a tremendous rally to eventually win the game 17–13. 'I would say England threw the game away,' says Dawes. 'They were firmly in control until Gareth went off but then they made the mistake of relaxing their grip on the game.' Dawes showed his value as a defender when he covered across to bring David Duckham down a few yards from the tryline when the English centre was in full flight. Then Wales departed to Dublin to attempt to win the Triple Crown but, to everyone's astonishment, lost 14–0. Amid the severe Welsh disappointment, doubts were expressed about the Welsh tactics and the way Gareth Edwards was captaining the side.

'Gareth was a player who inspired by example but not by his tactical appreciation of a game,' says Dawes. 'I don't think in his position with his type of play he had time to think of the wider issues. In the centre where I was you're a little bit away from the forwards and you are in a far better position to know what is going on. Gareth by his very nature – he's such a fierce competitor – looks at the game very much from his own point of view. But he is still young and this is something I am sure will come. There is no doubt we lost the game tactically against Ireland. This match needed a great deal of planning because the Irish, with all their talent, are essentially spoilers. And we played the type of game that fell right into their hands. Gareth and Barry John looked upon themselves as kingpins, the match winners, and we lost the game as a result. Instead of stretching them with the flowing game, it was Gareth's kicking and breaks and Barry's kicking we relied on and, against the Irish, this was the wrong thing to do.'

Dawes' view was confirmed by the match highlight – the brilliant try by the Irish No. 8, Ken Goodall. Wales were awarded a short penalty by their own 25 and Barry John kicked ahead. Goodall caught the ball on the burst and tore straight through the Welsh defence into open field. He then kicked ahead and showed his speed by winning the race to the touchdown.

'When the penalty was awarded, we all lined up expecting the ball to be passed down the backline,' Dawes recalls. 'But Barry John, for reasons known only to himself, and he occasionally did it in later years, decided to kick ahead. If he had released the ball straight away, we would not have been in any trouble!'

In none of the Tests that season did Wales use what Dawes called 'the flowing game' used by London Welsh, and the qualities of John Williams as an attacking full-back were wasted.

'There were people who thought Wales couldn't play the overlap game,' says Dawes. 'It all depends though on who you have at full-back. We started it at London Welsh because of

Haydn Davies and then continued it with Gareth James and John Williams. It was no secret as far as we were concerned. We were playing it and playing it well, but in most Welshmen's eyes we were just fairies who liked the running game! Now Wales and the Lions have fully exploited the attacking full-back game and everyone wants to do it. But it is still the game we were playing six or seven years ago.

'I have thought for a long time that against a good side you won't make a break from set pieces – certainly not in midfield. Therefore there had to be a way around this. The New Zealanders found a way with centre Ian MacRae taking the tackle and setting up the ruck. Then there was the second option – the overlapping full-back.'

Both these methods were to be used successfully by Wales later under Dawes' captaincy. But in the 1969–70 winter, Wales did not seem prepared to trust their backline with the ball. 'I'm sure there wasn't a great deal of confidence in our three-quarter line for the usual type of Welsh game – the flashing centre, that type of thing,' says Dawes. 'Bill Raybould and myself wanted very much to play the London Welsh type of game that season when we played for Wales. But it didn't materialise. It could well have been that Barry John at fly-half had no confidence in the backline and I'm not saying that he was wrong. I remember him saying years later, during the Lions tour of New Zealand how great it was playing with people like Mike Gibson, Gerald Davies and John Williams outside him because he knew he could let go of the ball and it wouldn't get mishandled. He said he never had the same confidence in Welsh rugby or always felt that if he let the ball go a mistake would be made, that is why he adopted his kicking tactic.'

At that time, Barry John was primarily a kicking fly-half and it wasn't until he played under Dawes' captaincy that he played the running game for Wales and the British Lions. He forsook what was little more than ten-man rugby, and then came the public adulation.

After the Ireland defeat, John Williams' father, Dr Peter

Williams, told Dawes that he thought there would be a change of captain and the London Welshman would once more take Edwards' place as leader of Wales. They bet a couple of gins on this and, sure enough, the Welsh selectors made Dawes captain for the final international of the season against France at Cardiff Arms Park. Ironically, Dawes decided on tactics that were the opposite of the London Welsh style of play. 'I went completely the other way,' he recalls. 'Basically when you play the French, you have got to make no mistakes and put a lot of pressure on them. I have an expression "getting amongst them" and when you do this, the French will panic and eventually make mistakes. I decided that every time Phil Bennett, who played fly-half as Barry was injured, got the ball, I wanted him to kick high and everyone was to go after the ball. In defence, I wanted to see us all up and making sure we were among the French players. I used these tactics not because I doubted the ability of our three-quarter line but because we were playing the French.'

The game went exactly as Dawes planned and Wales won the match 11–6 and so shared the championship title with France, who had come to Cardiff with three successive victories behind them. The one Welsh try came directly as a result of Dawes' 'getting amongst them' ploy. Dawes himself grabbed hold of the French fly-half, Pariès, and swung him around. The Frenchman then threw the ball back and the Welsh flank forward Dai Morris intercepted the intended pass and ran 30 yards to the posts. It was in this game that Arthur Lewis made his debut for Wales in the centre and so began his successful partnership with Dawes. A determined, competitive player with a very good tackle, he lived only a few hundred yards away from the house where Dawes' parents lived in Newbridge.

Dawes derived much satisfaction from the French match. It eradicated the unhappy memory of the first time he had captained Wales against Ireland in 1968. Dawes was now a regular in the national side and the players responded to his leadership. He never looked back.

CHAPTER 9

The Grand Slam

'Every time the phone went, I felt nervous.'

JOHN DAWES SUFFERED much from the misjudgements of others during his long rugby career. But when the London Welsh captain was finally given the opportunity to achieve rugby immortality, the chance was not wasted.

In a remarkable 18-month period, Dawes was to lead London Welsh through their best ever season, captain Wales to the Grand Slam and finally guide the British Lions to their historic victory against the All Blacks in New Zealand.

This remarkable sequence of events began in the winter of 1970–71. This season was orientated around the Lions tour of New Zealand taking place in the summer of 1971. Every major match played was regarded as a guideline for the selection of the tour party and, if early events are to be taken at their face value, Dawes' chance of making the New Zealand tour was indeed remote.

He was not included in the England & Wales team which met Scotland & Ireland on October 3. 'I think I was about tenth reserve for that game,' he recalls with some humour. Neither was he in the Barbarians team which was beaten 29–9 by the Fijians at Gosforth on October 24. More surprisingly, London Counties did not want Dawes for their match against the Fijians.

Martin Turner, the London Counties' team secretary, phoned Dawes and told him: 'There's a lot of feeling that you are too old and they want to play a younger man.' He added that he was willing to fight on Dawes' behalf, but the 30-year-old Welshman replied that it did not matter. An injury meant that Dawes did play in the counties side that beat the Fijians 22–0, but the fact remained that the London Counties regarded Dawes as a spent force. But Dawes took it all philosophically.

'If I had listened to all the people who said I was too old to play the game, I would have retired years before I did,' he says.

Although Dawes appeared to be getting ignored on many influential fronts, he had the opportunity to convince those in doubt of his qualities when the Welsh selectors retained him as captain of the Wales XV. Wales opened their international campaign that winter at Cardiff Arms Park with a decisive 22–6 victory against an England side containing seven new caps. It was a commanding victory and the fluency of the Welsh play was illustrated by the fact their wings, Gerald Davies and 19-year-old newcomer John Bevan, scored the three Welsh tries.

The two tries by Gerald Davies are worth recalling for they give an indication of the value of the Welsh squad training sessions run by Dawes and coach Clive Rowlands. Both these tries were beautifully executed moves that had been rehearsed in training. The first came when the strongly built centre Arthur Lewis crashed straight into the England backs to set up the ruck in the New Zealand manner. The Welsh forwards won the ball and it was swiftly passed down the Welsh backline which full-back John Williams had joined. Dawes, noticing that the England wing, Duckham, had made the error of moving slightly infield towards him, then gave Gerald Davies a perfectly judged pass 30 yards out and the winger's electrifying speed did the rest.

'Gerald had only the cover to beat,' Dawes recalls. 'I say only the cover but if you give Gerald the ball with no one in front of him, he will score ninety-nine times out of a hundred.'

The third try was another rehearsed move. The call went

down the backline that scrum-half Gareth Edwards was hoisting a high up-and-under to the English posts from a lineout 35 yards out. As arranged, Arthur Lewis lay back deep when the ball was thrown in. By the time the ball was won in the lineout, he was level with fly-half Barry John and still the legal 10 yards away from the forwards. And, by the time Edwards hoisted his perfect kick, Lewis was level with the scrum-half and going flat out. The idea was that Lewis should tackle the English full-back, Rossborough, as he tried to field the ball. Then Dawes, who had not come up so quickly, was to gather the loose ball and pass it to Gerald Davies. The only thing that didn't go to plan was Rossborough dropped the ball. So Lewis fed Dawes the ball and the Welsh captain, who could have scored himself, unselfishly passed the ball to the unmarked Gerald Davies. It was a perfectly executed move – in fact, it was so well done that many people incorrectly thought Lewis was offside as he swiftly followed up the Edwards kick.

Next Wales played Scotland at Murrayfield in a match that was to rank as one of the most exciting internationals in rugby history. The lead changed hands five times in the match and the game entered its nerve-wracking climax with Wales leading 14–12.

This is how Dawes described those memorable final minutes: 'Scotland again took the lead when Peter Brown added his fourth penalty. Then John Bevan had a clearance kick charged down. John Williams fell on the ball and I went to gather it. But for some reason, it popped up into the hands of centre Chris Rea, who was fractionally outside me. I held onto his jersey for two or three yards but he really was accelerating and I had no hope of stopping him as he broke clear to score by the posts. That made it 18–14 to Scotland. I didn't think the game was over but I knew it would be terribly difficult to score twice to regain the lead. I was aware the clock showed it was quarter-past four and there were no more than five minutes to go. Then Brown took the conversion from virtually point blank range and it hit the post. I knew then we would win.

'We started to throw the ball around. Ian Hall in the centre made a half-break and kicked ahead, but the ball bounced awkwardly for Gerald Davies. From the ensuing lineout, we again quickly moved the ball across the field. Hall made another half-break and we won the ruck. Barry John went left and I knew we would score if we could get the ball out quickly to John Bevan. But, unfortunately, Barry threw out a pass more or less on my shoulder and it went behind me as I tried to quickly pass it on. Barry swept around behind me and put the ball in touch near the Scottish line. It was Scotland's throw but Delme Thomas won the ball with a magnificent leap and again we moved the ball quickly down the backline. We missed out Ian Hall in the centre and John Williams entered the line to create the overlap, and when Gerald Davies received the ball he was a yard or two outside his wing. Very few full-backs would have stopped Gerald in this situation and Ian Smith had no chance. But Gerald couldn't get around to the posts. We were now 17–18 behind and all depended on the difficult conversion kick from about 10 yards in from touch. I gave the ball to John Taylor without thinking. He was a good pressure kicker and the right hand side of the field was the correct side for his around-the-corner method as he was left footed.'

Amid acute tension, the London Welsh forward sent the ball high between the uprights to give Wales a 19–18 victory. The game was something of a triumph for Dawes' captaincy. The interesting feature of the game was the way the brilliant Welsh found a way through the Scottish defence. That final Gerald Davies try was not the result of a desperate team throwing everything into a disorganised attempt to achieve an unlikely victory. The Welsh side moved with conviction to victory and Dawes' instinctive feeling that his side would win seemed reflected in the play of his colleagues.

Now only Ireland stood in the way of Wales and the Triple Crown. Backed by a marvellous crowd at Cardiff Arms Park, Wales, with their forwards scrummaging superbly, won a handsome 23–9 victory with Gareth Edwards and Gerald

Davies each scoring two tries apiece. The crowd stormed the pitch after the match to carry their heroes off and it was the third time Dawes had been in a Triple Crown team. The margin of victory was especially satisfying. Matches between Wales and Ireland were invariably close-fought struggles and, on this occasion, Dawes' team had won a conclusive victory after trailing 0–6 when Mike Gibson had landed two penalties.

The Lions team was selected on the Sunday after the Irish game. And still there were those who doubted Dawes should go on the tour. His age and lack of true pace were still regarded as major arguments against his selection and many believed that he was not good enough to make the British Test team which, in fact, was the main argument put against him when the selectors discussed the team. Dawes was not optimistic about his chances of making the tour party and his hopes were not increased when he was asked to captain the Barbarians to an unconvincing 18–14 win against the East Midlands on March 4. Both Carwyn James and Doug Smith saw this match and before the game, the Barbarians dressing room was crowded with the administrative VIPs of British rugby. This had one meaning to Dawes – he was on trial.

'The East Midlands should have thrashed us,' he says. 'I knew before the game I should never have accepted the invitation to captain the Barbarians. If they wanted a captain of the Lions, they had seen enough of me with Wales to make a judgement. I believe that Barbarians match was a game in which the doubting Thomases wanted to see me play so they could knock me down rather than pick me up.'

Another aspect of the Lions captaincy problem was the fact that Dawes was a Welshman. Only once before had a Welshman led the Lions and this was no mere quirk of fate. The Welsh were regarded as insular and moody and basically unsuited to make the best use of a touring party made up of four different nationalities. Thus, in 1966, the selectors had picked the unfortunate Scotsman Campbell-Lamerton to lead the Lions and passed over the obvious choice, Welsh forward

Alun Pask. Five years later, Doug Smith and Carwyn James both wanted Dawes to lead the Lions. But James did not have a vote on the tour selection committee and so it was left to Smith to use his powers of persuasion to see that Dawes got the post.

Dawes spent an anxious Sunday at his home in Sunbury-on-Thames waiting hopefully for the telephone call telling him he was on the tour. But it did not come.

'It was the most agonising day I have ever had,' says Dawes. 'Every time the phone went, I felt nervous. The later it became, the worse it was because everyone started phoning me to find out whether I was captain of the Lions. The phone was ringing literally every five minutes. I went to bed convinced I had not been chosen. But, early in the morning, the phone rang again. It was a journalist from the Press Association asking if I knew I had been selected as captain of the Lions. I had an immense feeling of relief and joy.'

Later Dawes found out that thirteen Welshmen had been picked for the 30-strong tour party and six of these were London Welshmen – John Williams, Gerald Davies, John Taylor, Mervyn Davies, Mike Roberts and Dawes. During the tour, Geoff Evans was flown out as a replacement to bring the total of London Welsh Lions to a remarkable seven. Surprisingly, the achievement was not unique, for the Newport club had contributed the same number of players to the 1910 British team that visited South Africa, although one of their number, the Lions captain, Dr Tom Smyth, was an Irishman.

After the selection of the Lions team, Wales played their final international of the season against France in Paris to decide the outcome of the International Championship. Victory for Dawes' team meant they would win the coveted Grand Slam through four wins in four games – a feat last achieved by the Welsh back in 1952. Defeat meant that they would have to share the championship with France, who had beaten Scotland 13–8 and drawn with both England 14–14 and Ireland 9–9. After winning the toss, Dawes decided to play into the wind, knowing that if the Welsh could hold the unpredictable French in the first half, they would win the game in the second half.

The game developed into a titanic struggle and with the wind behind them, the Tricolours threatened to run the Welsh off their feet with a succession of brilliant handling movements. They opened the scoring with a try by No. 8, Benoît Dauga, which was converted by full-back Pierre Villepreux. But somehow the Welsh defence prevented the French from scoring again.

'For the first half and periods of the second half, the French played to the best of their ability,' says Dawes. 'And when France play to the best of their ability, it takes a helluva good side to keep them out. But our defence was magnificent. Two tackles I remember in particular. The first was a perfect example of a head-on tackle by John Williams, who sent the French winger Bourgarel yards back. The second was a try-saving tackle by John Bevan, who appeared from nowhere to jump on a French back just a few yards from our line. The one moment of anxiety I had was when Barry John left the field for a short time with a bleeding nose. Many people said Barry had injured himself tackling the massive Dauga, but I still think he couldn't get away from the French forward quickly enough!'

The Welsh were quite content to be just 0–5 down as the interval drew near. But then came the sensation of the match. The French were once again on the attack with the powerful Roger Bourgarel running into the Welsh 25. He cut infield and John Williams, realising the French winger was covered by a defender and about to pass the ball, went for the interception. It was a superb piece of judgement and Williams caught the ball and ran 60 yards upfield. Inside the French half, Williams cut inside to try and beat the cover defence. Then suddenly, out of nowhere, the Welsh scrum-half Gareth Edwards appeared on the left touchline, took a pass from Williams and sprinted 30 yards to the corner to reduce the deficit to 3–5. This was the killer try as far as the French were concerned and the record 60,000 crowd was equally stunned.

Wales were to win the match 9–5 in the second half after

Barry John landed a simple penalty and ghosted through the French defence for an amazing try. The build-up to the John penalty was an indication of the tactical depth of this Welsh side. From a scrum near the French posts, Edwards flew past Barry John and did a scissors with Arthur Lewis. A ruck followed, Wales won the ball and this time Edwards dummied past two players before doing a scissors with Dawes, who burst through the gap to be halted just five yards from the French line. It was from the subsequent loose maul that the French were penalised.

'The quality of the rugby in that French game was way above anything else in our other three Tests that season,' says Dawes. 'You had a side attacking well and a side defending well at the same time. I think this was a great Welsh team because we had the ability to win the ball and also the ability to use it.'

Dawes was not alone in rating the 1970–71 Wales team as a great side. Vivian Jenkins, the former Welsh international, wrote in *The Sunday Times:* 'Whether this is the greatest Welsh team of all time is difficult to say. But certainly no Welsh team of comparatively modern times has surpassed this one on collective will-to-win and capacity to keep going to the end of the most testing game.'

Rarely has a national side boasted so many world-class players among its backs. Scrum-half Gareth Edwards scored the remarkable tally of four tries for Wales that season, while Barry John ended the championship with 31 points (2T, 3D-G, 4P, 2C). Then on the wings, Gerald Davies (5) and John Bevan (1) scored six tries between them. In the centre, Dawes and Lewis provided the ideal link between the halves and the wings. And behind this backline was John Williams, the attacking full-back *in excelsis*. In four Tests, the Welsh side scored 13 tries and fulfilled Dawes' belief that the free-flowing game he developed at London Welsh could be successfully adapted at international level.

While Wales dominated the European rugby scene, London Welsh had their best season ever in Dawes' record sixth and final season as captain of the club. The Exiles final record was Played 36 Won 28 Drawn 3 Lost 5 Points for: 646 Against: 280 – a staggering achievement when you consider the club fielded below strength sides while their leading players were playing representative rugby. Five London Welshmen played in Wales' matches while six were in the Surrey side that won the County Championship. All told, London Welsh first team contained 14 internationals, 11 Barbarians and four former university captains.

For the first time in the Dawes era, the club won every match they played on their tours of Wales at Christmas and Easter. The sequence of five wins began on Boxing Day before a 12,000 crowd at Stradey Park where London Welsh beat Llanelli 5–3 after John Williams sent over a touchline conversion with the last kick of the match. Then London Welsh took Swansea's ground record with a 14–6 victory before a 10,000 crowd. Then at Easter, the Exiles beat Aberavon 17–11, Newport 15–14 and Pontypool 17–0.

There was also the memorable weekend when London Welsh beat Neath 14–9 at the Gnoll and then Béziers, the French champions, 12–8 in Paris the next day. The club's ability to devastate the best British clubs still remained and in the final home match of the season, a capacity crowd gathered at Old Deer Park to see John Dawes and the five other London Welsh Lions make their last London appearance before the tour. They were not to be disappointed. Swansea, who had only lost ten of their 40 matches that season, were humiliated 41–6.

Vivian Jenkins in his match report in *The Sunday Times* said: 'One had thought, in advance, that the Welsh might not have things altogether their own way. Instead, we saw them run in eight tries by bewilderingly intricate passing movements, with forwards and backs coming up in waves to back one another up and make the final man over. No one did better in this respect that John Dawes himself, who played as well as ever I have seen him, while the man who benefited the most was one of only five non-internationals in the side, Commonwealth

Games sprinter Terry Davies on the left wing. He got four sparkling tries, one of them a turf-scorching run of 80 yards, and it made one wonder why one had not heard of him.

'The more London Welsh go on producing these amazing performances, the more one asks oneself how they can do it. Undoubtedly the captaincy of Dawes in these six halcyon years has been mainly responsible. Even now, he turns up twice a week for training and expects every other member of his team to do so. Splendid facilities, including the new £100,000 clubhouse, have also played a big part in attracting players as well as the faithful following of supporters that averages 4,000 a match.'

A few weeks later, London Welsh won the Middlesex Sevens at Twickenham with their six British Lions watching the tournament from the stands.

International Championship 1970-71

	Played	Won	Drawn	Lost	For	Against	Points
Wales	4	4	0	0	73	38	8
France	4	1	2	1	41	40	4
England	4	1	1	2	44	58	3
Ireland	4	1	1	2	41	46	3
Scotland	4	1	0	3	47	64	2

Wales 22 England 6
January 16, 1971, Cardiff Arms Park

Wales – JPR Williams (L Welsh) (P); TGR Davies (L Welsh) (2T), SJ Dawes (L Welsh) (Captain), A Lewis (Ebbw Vale), JC Bevan (Cardiff) (T); B John (Cardiff) (2D-G), GO Edwards (Cardiff); DB Llewelyn (Llanelli), J Young (Harrogate) D Williams (Ebbw Vale); WD Thomas (Llanelli), MG Roberts (L Welsh); WD Morris (Neath), TM Davies (L Welsh), J Taylor (L Welsh) (2C)

England – PA Rossborough (Coventry) (P); JP Janion (Bedford) CS Wardlow (Northampton) JS Spencer (Headingley) D Duckham (Coventry); I Wright (Northampton) JJ Page (Bedford); DL Powell (Northampton) JV Pullin (Bristol), KE Fairbrother (Coventry); PJ Larter (Northampton), BF Ninnes (Coventry); AL Bucknall (Richmond) (Captain), RC Hannaford (Bristol)) (T), A Neary (Broughton Park)

Referee – DP d'Arcy (Ireland)

Scotland 18 Wales 19

February 6, 1971, Murrayfield

Scotland - ISG Smith (L Scottish); WCC Steele (Bedford), JNM Frame (Gala), CWW Rea (West of Scotland) (T), AG Biggar (L Scottish); JWC Turner (Gala) DS Paterson (Gala); J McLauchlan (Jordanhill College), FAL Laidlaw (Melrose), AB Carmichael (West of Scotland) (T); GL Brown (West of Scotland), AF McHarg (L Scottish); RJ Arneil (Leicester), PC Brown (Gala) (Captain) (4P), NA MacEwan (Gala)

Wales – JPR Williams (L Welsh) (P); TGR Davies (L Welsh) (T), SJ Dawes (L Welsh) (Captain), I Hall (Aberavon), JC Bevan (Cardiff) (T); B John (Cardiff) (T,P,C), GO Edwards (Cardiff) (T); DB Llewelyn (Llanelli), J Young (Harrogate) D Williams (Ebbw Vale); WD Thomas (Llanelli), MG Roberts (L Welsh); WD Morris (Neath), TM Davies (L Welsh), J Taylor (L Welsh) (T,C)

Referee – M Titcomb (England)

Wales 23 Ireland 9

March 13, 1971, Cardiff Arms Park

Wales – JPR Williams (L Welsh) ; TGR Davies (L Welsh) (2T), SJ Dawes (L Welsh) (Captain), A Lewis (Ebbw Vale), JC Bevan (Cardiff) (T); B John (Cardiff (2P, C, D-G), GO Edwards (Cardiff) (2T); DB Llewelyn (Llanelli), J Young (Harrogate), D Williams (Ebbw Vale); WD Thomas (Llanelli), MG Roberts (L Welsh); WD Morris (Neath), M Davies (L Welsh), J Taylor (L Welsh) (T,C)

Ireland – BJ O'Driscoll (Manchester); ATA Duggan (Lansdowne), FPK Bresnihan ((L Irish), CMH Gibson (NIFC) (Captain) (3P), FL Grant (CIYMS); BJ McGann (Cork Constitution), RM Young (Collegians); JF Lynch (St Mary's College), KW Kennedy (L Irish), RJ McLoughlin (Blackrock College); MG Molloy (L Irish), WJ McBride (Ballymena); JF Slattery (University College Dublin), DJ Hickie (St Mary's College), ML Hipwell (Terenure College)

Referee – RF Johnson (England)

France 5 Wales 9

March 27, 1971, Stade Colombes

France – P Villepreux (Toulouse) (C) ; R Bourgarel (Toulouse) R Bertranne (St Bagnères), JP Lux (Tyrosse), J Cantoni (Béziers); JL Bérot (Toulouse), M Barrau (Beamont); M Lasserre (Agen), R Benesis (Narbonne), J Iracabal (Bayonne); W Spanghero (Narbonne), C Spanghero (Narbonne); JP Biémouret (Agen), B Dauga (Mont-de-Marsan) (T), C Carrere (Toulon) (Captain)

Wales – JPR Williams (L Welsh) (P); TGR Davies (L Welsh), SJ Dawes (L Welsh) (Captain), A Lewis (Ebbw Vale), JC Bevan (Cardiff); B John (Cardiff (P,T), GO Edwards

(Cardiff) (T) ; DB Llewelyn (Llanelli), J Young (Harrogate), D Williams (Ebbw Vale); WD Thomas (Llanelli), MG Roberts (L Welsh); WD Morris (Neath), TM Davies (L Welsh), J Taylor (L Welsh)

Referee – J Young

London Welsh 1970–71
Played 36   Won 28   Drawn 3   Lost 5   For: 646   Against: 280

Penryn	away	W 12–6	Swansea	away	W 14–6
Camborne	away	W 39–14	Bath	away	W 14–6
Cardiff	away	L 3–8	L Scottish	home	W 17–11
Wasps	away	W 25–6	Saracens	home	W 9–3
Abertillery	home	W 35–6	Bedford	home	W 29–3
Richmond	away	W 17–3	Newbridge	away	W 19–6
Bridgend	away	L 30–12	RAF	home	W 36–3
Llanelli	home	D 6–6	Neath	away	W 14–9
Neath	home	W 25–21	Béziers	away	W 12–8
Harlequins	away	W 14–5	Coventry	away	L 6–11
Moseley	home	W 30–9	Blackheath	home	D 11–11
Pontypool	home	W 19–3	Rosslyn Park	home	W 17–8
Bristol	away	D 8–8	Harlequins	home	W 19–13
Newport	home	W 14–0	Swansea	home	W 41–6
Aberavon	home	W 41–5	Aberavon	away	W 17–11
London Irish	home	L 10–14	Newport	away	W 15–14
Met Police	home	W 37–3	Pontypool	away	W 17–0
Llanelli	away	W 5–3	L Irish	away	L 6–19

CHAPTER 10

The Fall
of the All Blacks

*'He would easily smoke forty a day but as soon
as he stepped on the paddock for a training session,
there wasn't a cigarette to be seen.'*

SPORT IS NO stranger to the unexpected, but few people thought
that the 1971 British Lions had even the remotest chance of
winning a Test series against New Zealand.

History was steeped against the 1971 Lions. The game
originated in Britain but after the arrival of the 20th century,
the world rugby scene was dominated by the two giants of
the game, New Zealand and South Africa. Confrontations
between these two countries came to be regarded as battles for
the mythical world rugby championship, while British rugby
struggled to maintain some sort of parity with these two great
rugby nations. Since 1903, Britain had sent 13 teams to New
Zealand and South Africa and never managed to win a Test
series. Then, when our teams had the home advantage, a long
succession of New Zealand and South African touring teams
came to Britain and suffered only rare defeats.

History left British rugby with an inferiority complex. Her
teams took to the field against these two great rugby nations
not as equals, but as the underdogs trying to raise their game
to produce the unexpected. Rare victories were regarded as
epic triumphs. Then there was the frustration of knowing that

British rugby was consistently producing outstanding backs – but what could they achieve while the forwards in front of them were being dominated? Critics came to wonder aloud whether Britain was capable of producing forwards with the physique, ability and dedication to match the All Blacks and Springboks. Then, suddenly, the South African dominance came to an end when the Springboks made a catastrophic short tour to Ireland and Scotland in 1965 and an equally disastrous long tour to Britain in 1969–70 that was constantly interrupted by anti-apartheid demonstrations. But still the legendary reputation of the New Zealanders remained intact.

There seemed no reason why New Zealand should not continue to be a graveyard for British teams. No British touring team had ever won a Test series in that country, and the Lions had managed to win only two out of sixteen Tests during their tours in 1930, 1950, 1959 and 1966. The All Blacks had dominated the world rugby scene throughout most of the 1960s. And the 1966 Lions had been whitewashed in their Test series against the All Blacks losing the internationals 3–20, 12–16, 6–19 and 11–24. All told, Campbell-Lamerton's team had won only 15 of their 25 tour matches, losing eight and drawing two in New Zealand. In 1969, Wales had suffered two massive Test defeats, 0–19 and 12–33, when they made a short tour to New Zealand. In between these two tours, Brian Lochore's 1967 All Blacks – christened The Unsmiling Giants – toured Britain undefeated, winning all their matches aside from a 3–3 draw with East Wales. It was true that the New Zealanders' decade of dominance had been halted on their 1970 South African tour when they surprisingly lost the Test series. But this was due to the Springboks' strength and their crucial home advantage, rather than weaknesses among the New Zealand forwards.

It was against this background that the 1971 Lions set off for New Zealand. It was obvious that they had a tremendously talented backline, but Britain had always been sending outstanding backs abroad. It was among the forwards that the crux of the forthcoming struggle lay and it didn't seem that this particular team were any better or worse than their predecessors in this respect. Many believed that the back-row forwards selected would prove to be too small to withstand the massive New Zealand loose forwards.

But the 1971 Lions were to achieve greatness in the months to come and one of the principal reasons for this was, at long last, a British Lions team making full use of its potential. The people responsible for this were the triumvirate who headed the tour party – manager Dr Doug Smith, coach Carwyn James and the captain John Dawes. They ensured the Lions were the best prepared team – in the mental, physical and tactical sense – that Britain had ever produced.

Doug Smith and Carwyn James were appointed virtually a year before the tour took place and so had a whole season to assess players and prepare for the trip. James was a quietly-spoken bachelor, who had played twice for Wales in the late 1950s. He was coach of the powerful Llanelli side, and the squad system he used with the club he applied directly to the Lions tour so that the strongest combination of players would take the field in key matches, which he labelled 'peaks'. James showed outstanding qualities as a coach in the week-long training session at Eastbourne prior to the departure from Britain.

'We trained in a way that was completely enjoyable and this set the pattern for the tour,' says Dawes. 'Officially no player was allowed to leave Britain unless he was one hundred per cent fit. But Carwyn told Mike Hipwell and Chris Rea, who were both injured, not to push themselves to the limit trying to prove they were fit. This was the first of his many trump cards. Hipwell told me that because of this attitude he was immediately prepared to do almost anything for Carwyn. I found that Carwyn was extremely quiet, very sincere and interested in many things apart from rugby, such as the arts. Rugby was just part of his life but a very serious part. He was also a very heavy smoker. He would easily smoke forty a day but as soon as he stepped on the paddock for a training session, there wasn't a cigarette to be seen.'

Dawes and James were to immediately strike up an understanding and they both had this quality of quiet authority. Doug Smith, by contrast, was an extrovert. A 1950 Lion, he had won eight caps as a winger for Scotland and was a General Practitioner from the small Essex village of Orsett. 'Doug was a man of great character and very popular,' says Dawes. 'His bark was worse than his bite but he had this capacity to be very firm when the need arose. One of the things you are inundated with on a major tour is invitations to attend functions here, there and everywhere. Here Doug was very good, for he protected us from what we called "the heavies". Having been a colonel in the army, he was a stickler for punctuality and if you were late, he would always say "Merry Christmas". If disciplinary action looked as if it needed to be taken – and it never had to be taken – he would threaten mountains would fall on you. He was a pleasant extrovert and he didn't make you feel you wanted to get out of his company. Anyone could make fun of him and he'd laugh along with it. Chico Hopkins used to call him "The Big Bagpipe". We used to listen intently to his speeches to pick up his stories but we could never remember them as he told a different one after all the twenty-four matches in New Zealand!'

Allied to the intensive thought that went into the tour was the party's belief that New Zealand could be beaten. Doug Smith created a sensation when he predicted the Lions would win the Test series 2–1 with the other Test being drawn, and this caused an even greater sensation when his prediction came true. The point was the Lions did not place themselves under a handicap through not believing in themselves.

The attitude of John Dawes was remarkable. 'I'm on film saying I thought we would go through the New Zealand tour unbeaten – even in Test matches,' he says. 'I based my assumption on the fact that we certainly had the class behind the scrum to beat the All Blacks. I knew with Wales we had played the strongest provincial sides and while we had not beaten them easily, we had beaten them.'

Dawes was initially unsure of the quality of his forwards, but his doubts were removed before the tour started. 'The management were very wise here,' he says. 'In the week we trained at Eastbourne, they arranged for me to share a room with the Irish prop forward Ray McLoughlin. Ray is probably the greatest thinker and practical man, as far as set scrummaging is concerned, I have ever met. He is an extremely clever man reputed to have an IQ of 160 or 170 – in other words genius level. He is extremely methodical, very technical and very realistic. He broke everything down in ABC fashion and said if we did this, the rest would fall in...

'Ray wasn't satisfied with the standard of our scrummaging. It wasn't entirely a one-man show though. McBride, for example, had this great thing about binding. When you pack down around another forward, you were to grip him as tight as you could – not this casual hanging on you tend to get. This may sound a minor technical detail but it was important for it meant your eight forwards were an absolutely solid unit when they shoved against their opponents. After being a week with Ray McLoughlin, I simply had a belief that we were going to do well up front and I had no qualms about behind the scrum with our class of players.'

When the tour was under way, the New Zealand rugby public was staggered to see their best provincial packs being shoved back yards in the set scrums and their front row forwards being lifted right out of the scrum – the ultimate humiliation. Even the New Zealand Test pack was to be out-shoved, which was an unprecedented state of affairs as far as the British were concerned. The technical expertise of the scrummaging of the Lions was symbolised by the fact that the small Scottish prop, Ian McLauchlan, who was nicknamed 'Mighty Mouse', was able to get the better of the giant New Zealand front row forward Jas Muller. McLauchlan was only 5ft 9in tall and weighed only 14st 6lb, while Muller was a massive 17 stone forward.

'At London Welsh, we had pushed Newport and other sides back in the set scrums but this happened only occasionally,' Dawes says. 'But in New Zealand, this was something happening throughout the tour and it was something I had never experienced. It was a joy to be in the three-quarters because this put you one, possibly two, up on your opposite number. It was quite a revelation.'

Another vital factor was that the Lions forwards adopted a policy of 'When in Rome, do as the Romans do' where the lineouts were concerned. So we purposely practised illegalities to counter the notorious tactics used by the New Zealanders.

'They moved across the lineout for a start, which is not allowed,' says Dawes. 'But I think it would wrong for us to pass comment about it now. But if you analyse lineout play in New Zealand, you just have to look at a rugby film and it is there for all to see. We learned from the experience of people like McLoughlin and McBride on the 1966 Lions tour. We decided we were not going to be messed around and this attitude was to make a significant impact during the tour. The lineout laws are such a shambles at the moment that you can get away with illegalities. Everyone knows this and it is about time something was done to change the laws.'

The tour opened with two matches in Australia and the Lions lost the very first match they played 11–15 against Queensland. Here was the team that was to win a Test series in New Zealand losing to a state side which had never previously beaten a Lions side. It was an inauspicious start and in their second match the Lions won a narrow 14–12 victory against the strongest Australian state, New South Wales. The play of the Lions in Australia moved Des Connor, the well-known coach who had played Test rugby for both the Wallabies and the All Blacks, to comment that Dawes' side was the worst international team he had ever seen. But Dawes was unperturbed. In his view, the poor start was simply due to the same acclimatisation problem the Welsh had suffered in 1969. 'We played that Queensland game 36 hours after arriving in Australia,' he says. 'We were very much aware of the fact that we were not ready to play that game. If you see a film of it, you can see we should have been at least a dozen points up in the first twenty minutes of the match.'

When the Lions arrived in New Zealand, they settled down to success after success and gradually the realisation dawned that this was an exceptional rugby team. The 22–9 win in the second match of the New Zealand tour against King Country and Wanganui was an important psychological victory. This was the side which had beaten the 1966 Lions and it was led by the great Colin Meads, who many would argue is the greatest forward rugby has produced. He symbolised the might of New Zealand rugby and, in this match, the Lions got the better of Meads whose ribs were damaged in a tackle, and the forwards he led.

The first major peak of the tour was against Wellington, one of the strongest provincial sides. The Lions shattered the New Zealanders by demolishing the provincial side by the humiliating score of 47–9. 'It absolutely staggered the New Zealanders,' says Dawes. 'This was some of the finest rugby ever seen at Athletic Park, but the crowd was so disappointed that people were leaving before the end of the game. I wasn't surprised by the score. As far as I was concerned, we were only fulfilling our potential.' Graham Williams, the Wellington captain, said after the match: 'We might be criticised for not tackling – but we couldn't catch them, let alone tackle them.'

This was one of the greatest performances of all time by a British team and it set the tour alight. The brilliance of the Lions was highlighted when full-back John Williams fielded a kick-ahead near his own line, slipped a tackle and passed to centre Mike Gibson about 15 yards from the British line. The 28-year-old Irishman then jinked off his left foot past three defenders and ran to the halfway line where he passed the ball to John Bevan. The young Welsh wing, whose fearsome running was one of the early highlights of the tour, then ran the rest of the length of the field to score a sensational try.

It is interesting that Dawes rated Gibson as the greatest of the Lions backs on the tour. 'I put Mike's display against Wellington above anything I have seen from any other back at any time during my career,' says Dawes. 'Everything he did that day was superb – his running, his kicking, his passing and his tackling. It was as near perfect a display as you could possibly get. If Mike had a weakness, it was one of attitude. Playing in a relatively weak back division with Ireland for years, he didn't have the confidence to attempt the things he attempted in this game.'

Originally Gibson had been selected for the tour as a fly-half. But the Wellington match established the outstanding midfield partnership of Barry John at fly-half with Gibson and Dawes in the centre.

Wellington 9 British Isles 47
June 5, 1971 Athletic Park, Wellington

Wellington – J Gregg (2P); BM Koopu, GA Batty, M Cull; RS Cleland, JP Dougan (D-G); IN Stevens; TK McDonald, P Barrett, GA Head; AEK Keown, DM Waller; JWH Kirkby, AR Leslie, GC Williams (Captain)

Lions – JPR Williams (C); JC Bevan (4T), SJ Dawes (Captain), M Gibson (2T, C), D Duckham; B John (T, 5C, 2P), G Edwards; R McLoughlin, J Pullin, S Carmichael (T), WJ McBride, D Thomas; F Slattery, TM Davies, J Taylor (T)

Referee – WJ Adlam (Wanganui)

The Lions were to further enhance their reputation during the next fortnight with their wins against Otago, 21–9, and Canterbury, 14–3. 'Otago were the supreme rucking side in New Zealand and we were delighted to win the game and even more delighted we had measured up to their rucking standards,' says Dawes.

The Canterbury game was played in front of a 53,000 crowd – a record gathering for a provincial match in New Zealand. Canterbury were the Ranfurly Shield champions and they took to the field with the intention of punching and kicking the Lions off the park. The aftermath of this notorious match was the tourists' two first-choice prop forwards, Sandy Carmichael (five fractures on his cheekbone) and Ray McLoughlin (broken left thumb) were to take no further part in the tour.

'We knew what to expect and we selected what was to be our best team,' Dawes recalls. 'However Barry John dropped out, which we were grateful for afterwards. Mike Gibson took his place at fly-half and it was just as well he did as he was strong enough to take a great physical hammering. What annoyed us was that after the first lineout, I was knocked over nowhere near the ball. But it was that sort of match. Among the backs, it was mainly obstruction and jersey pulling. In the forwards, there was a lot of punching and kicking. It was a pity really because I honestly thought Canterbury were a good side and if they had played football, they might have won. But they lost the aim of the game and the result was that they not only suffered defeat but also a tremendous amount of bad publicity after the match. The thing that gave us most pleasure was John Bevan's try. There were two men in front of him and one coming from the side and he just ran straight through them and they literally bounced off him. All the backs were very proud of our forwards that day – they not only stood up to Canterbury but gave a bit back.'

The atmosphere at the reception after the match was naturally rather bitter. Manager Doug Smith, handing a plaque over to the opposition, said: 'Let us hope this reminds us of the day the British Lions beat Canterbury at Christchurch.' Dawes spoke only for a few seconds, saying that he was glad the referee was a doctor. The referee, Dr Humphrey Rainey, had much to answer for. At one stage during the game, he had called the two captains together and, to Dawes' astonishment, said that from that point on he was going to watch the ball, so the players could sort themselves out.

The extraordinary sequel to the match came when the chairman of the New Zealand selectors, Ivan Vodanovich, who was nicknamed 'Ivan the Terrible', said that the first Test could become another Passchendaele if the Lions continued to ruin 'a delightful part of New Zealand rugby' by lying on the balls in the rucks. The Lions looked upon this as an absurd allegation – if they were lying on the ball, why had their injuries not occurred in the rucks? 'We were not going to let statements like that affect us,' was Dawes' attitude.

The Lions were unbeaten in New Zealand with ten consecutive wins when the time came to play the first crucial Test against the All Blacks. This was the match the Lions had to win and the 45,000 crowd at Dunedin were to see the tourists produce an epic rearguard action. 'The All Blacks started with such a sustained stampede that they looked as if they were going to sweep the Lions off the end of the ground and into the sea two miles away,' wrote John Reason, *The Daily Telegraph* writer. This set the pattern for the match and somehow the Lions were to survive a massive series of assaults by the giant New Zealand forwards led by Colin Meads. And incredible to relate, the scoreboard read British Isles 9 New Zealand 3 at the end of the match.

'This was a great psychological victory,' says Dawes. 'New Zealand deserved to score in that first half and it was more through good fortune than good defence that we survived. In the second half the pressure was fantastic. They just kept throwing wave after wave of forward attacks against us. But this time, I thought it was more due to good defence than luck that we survived.'

The Lions points came through two penalty goals from Barry John and a try by the small prop forward Ian McLauchlan. 'He seemed almost offside all the time,' said Carwyn James of the Scotsman after the match. McLauchlan's try was a tribute to his remarkable speed around the field for he was the player who charged down a clearance kick and fell on the rebound for the only try of the match.

The other significant feature of the match was the scrummaging of the Lions forwards and the tactical kicking of Barry John, who was gaining 40 to 50 yards along the touchline with his clearance kicks. These two factors enabled the tourists to get some relief from the barrage of attacks launched from the lineout and loose by the New Zealand forwards. And full-back Fergie McCormick, one of the villains of the Canterbury match, was to be crucified by John's tantalising kicks. 'I heard that Carwyn told Barry before the game "I want you to get rid of McCormick",' says Dawes. 'This is exactly what happened. The crowd was embarrassed for him and even the New Zealand players were shouting at him. The selectors dropped him after this Test. Barry's kicking that day was the best display of tactical kicking I have ever seen at such a high level.'

Dawes also believed New Zealand made a tactical error by playing their talented wing, Bryan Williams, who was christened 'The conscience of New Zealand rugby', in the centre. 'I've said all along it's easy to blot out players in midfield,' says Dawes. 'Mike Gibson and I knew Williams was a dangerous runner going off his left foot. So we really concentrated on our alignment, forcing him across the field so that he had to beat us on the outside – and of course, he didn't.'

A fortnight later, after three more provincial match victories, the Lions played New Zealand in the second Test before 57,501 spectators at Christchurch and the All Blacks won the match 22–12. For British viewers watching the televised broadcast of the match back home, it seemed reality was now upon us and New Zealand rugby was showing its true strength. In both Tests the initiative remained with the New Zealand forwards, but at Christchurch the superiority was translated into points. The power of the All Blacks was symbolised when their great wing forward, Ian Kirkpatrick, emerged from a loose maul and showed his tremendous strength and speed by scoring a 70-yard solo try. What hope had the Lions against forwards of this calibre?

But, strangely, John Dawes was even more confident that the Lions could win the Test series after the second Test than he had been after the first Test victory. The reason for this apparent paradox lay in the two tries scored in the match by right wing Gerald Davies. 'These two scores came so easily

Colorsport

The Great Enabler, John Dawes, with his strong physique honed in the hard school of valleys rugby, showing his skill as the master passer of the ball. On duty here for London Welsh, the club he transformed. "The wonderful thing about John Dawes was he inspired people," said the much-admired former Welsh fly-half and BBC broadcaster Cliff Morgan. "He brought a sense of adventure and wonder to the game. You had to win with a certain style and that is what London Welsh means to me. It was a place where you had such fun."

LONDON WELSH
CYMRY LLUNDAIN

The Best of Times at Old Deer Park

In October 1971 *Evening Standard* sports editor JL Manning watched rugby at Old Deer Park. "All in all the best time I have spent since VE Day, " he wrote. "It was a bit like it too… John Dawes, the British Lions' captain, sold me a couple of miles of raffle tickets to buy Kew Gardens for miners' allotments… Funny thing that splendid £100,000 clubhouse. The grandstand cost £7,000 and accommodates fewer people… London Welsh is unique in sport. Not because, with the help of Carwyn James, it beat the All Blacks. It is a vibrant organization of the community for recreation. It has done all that is good for as many as want to feel good."

The ultimate tribute paid to the team Dawes built – the seven London Welsh players selected for the 1971 British & Irish Lions tour of New Zealand, led by the Exiles captain. Standing L–R: No. 8 Mervyn Davies, full-back JPR Williams, lock Mike Roberts and fellow second row Geoff Evans, who joined the tour party as a replacement. Sitting L–R: wing Gerald Davies, tour captain centre John Dawes and flanker John Taylor, the tour choirmaster. A third of the Lions Test team were Exiles; they proved key players in the historic 2–1 series victory.

January 15, 1972. The clubhouse scene when a record 8,000 crowd (unofficially 10,000) watched the Cardiff match.

Western Mail

Exiles captain John Dawes introducing the Prince of Wales to Mervyn Davies when the new £100,000 clubhouse opened in October 1969.

Colorsport

Scrum-half Edwards the Great (aka Gareth Edwards) sending that famous long pass to Barry John in the second Test.

Getty Images

Edwards heading for the tryline creating the Peter Dixon try in the fourth Test.

Getty Images

Fly-half and rugby magician Barry John christened 'The King' on the 1971 Lions tour, showing his immense talent as a kicker for the tourists.

Colorsport

Left wing, Englishman David Duckham showing why he was rechristened 'Dai Duckham' in Wales after the famous 1973 Barbarians win. In the 1971 Test series, he played a vital defensive role in the final drawn Auckland Test.

Colorsport

The multi-talented Irish centre Mike Gibson playing for his country. Free of the burden of playing for average Ireland sides, he was one of the major stars on the 1971 Lions tour.

Getty Images

Centre and Lions captain John Dawes – normally the creator rather than finisher – here scoring one of his four tour tries in the 21–9 defeat of Otago, who had in 1950, 1959 and 1966 beaten the Lions.

John Reason

The incomparable right wing Gerald Davies leaving two Hawke's Bay players grounded. The late John Reason, *Daily Telegraph* rugby correspondent, took the photograph during the Welshman's virtuoso four-try performance against the province.

John Bevan, the 20-year-old hard-running Welsh wing who scored a record equalling 17 tour tries in New Zealand, played in the first Test before being replaced by Duckham.

Fearless full-back JPR Williams. Equally great defender and attacker who symbolized the Dawes vision of attacking rugby created at London Welsh.

The Lions Trinity who created history: Captain John Dawes (far left), manager Doug Smith and coach Carwyn James with New Zealand captain, Colin Meads (centre), and lock Gordon Brown (far right) in Auckland after the series was won.

Colorsport

Master coach Carwyn James, who guided the 1971 Lions to their historic series victory. "Complex Carwyn brought simplicity to rugby: weapon of choice – the brain," said broadcaster Eddie Butler.

John Dawes, in front of England forward Bill Beaumont, in a reflective mood during his unhappy return to New Zealand as Lions coach in 1977 on the Bad News Tour. "Events quickly overtook him leaving him a sad figure, " Beaumont later recalled. "He seemed to have lost his sense of purpose and direction."

Colorsport

Thuggery on the 1971 Lions tour. All Blacks prop Jas Muller demonstrating his kicking skills in the Auckland Test.

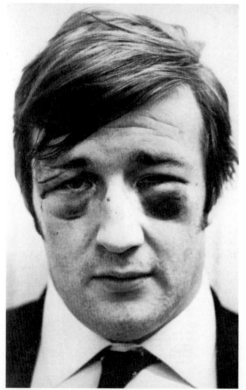

Lions prop Sandy Carmichael's face photographed by *Daily Telegraph* writer John Reason after the notorious Canterbury match. Thankfully the ten-minute sin bin and sophisticated camera coverage have eliminated the extreme violence found in the game's amateur era.

Colorsport

John Dawes, followed by the England & Lions hooker John Pullin, leads out the Barbarians for his final triumph on the international stage against Ian Kirkpatrick's Seventh All Blacks at Cardiff Arms Park on January 27, 1973. Disappointingly none of the Home Countries had managed to beat the tourists, but Dawes, reunited with eleven of his '71 Lions colleagues, won a famous 23–11 victory.

Colorsport

Few photographers captured the action of THE TRY in the 1973 Barbarians match, as the move began so early in the match. But the roles of John Dawes and Tommy David were pictured. Dawes sends a trademark perfect pass to David while Edwards in the background second right tracks the action.

Colorsport

David sends a less than perfect one-handed pass to fellow forward Derek Quinnell who had to stretch full tilt to gather the ball.

Salute Dawes and his lionhearts—this was the greatest

PHIL BENNETT decided to have a go ... John Pullin passed instead of kicking within three minutes ... and the result was the most fantastic try Cardiff Arms Park has seen.

More important, the breath-

Barbarians 23 New Zealand 11 : By TERRY O'CONNOR

lenge to play a key role in this great match.

The 1971 Lions produced some magnificent performances, but they never played the All Blacks with the majesty and daring with which Barbarians set up a 17—0 half-time lead.

always there to change direction of attack.

Finally Mike Gibson, elated the fervent Welsh support squeezed through two All Black and a try was on.

The fiercely competitive Joh Williams, was up for the fin

Sound the trumpets—They did it!

.... 3 pts
.... 9 pts

tight-head side. But an did not end there, en the Lions crossed he try that broke the d. It also gave the game.

the All Blacks foll under pressure to his nd, 10 yards from his attempted to kick for the "Monne" up in raw, charge down the rebound, behind the sked-back from the imeti, as the referee then raced back to enraptured Lions could a prop-forward 2" since more Tar e he was born, and club, where he also location, can well be was always the first

stic was not yet over ry John missed the , just as he had a s, and when McCor- 25-yard penalty just was nothing in it ly for a man who 4 points for the All Auckland two years used with a "sitter" ard in line with the

missed another one, e second half, and from das—not that t week's Lions match

missed goal-kicks, ted all through by tg hook-kicking he saved the Lions tame tame- of up to 10 teemed to make the he touchline, only a armuck's grasp. John

got the two penalty goals which sealed the All Blacks' doom. One was from 35 yards, in the 14th minute of the second half, the other from 40 yards three minutes from the end; and they were both beautifully struck from considerable angles. Until that second penalty, the second half had seemed the fiddest I have ever known.

The All Blacks forwards were still pounding away. For 20 minutes they kept the Lions pinned in their own quarter. The New Zealanders were winning the line-outs handsomely. At the end the count in their favour was 26-12, thanks largely to Kirkpatrick's palming back at the end of the line. They also won the rucks 15-7, but here the Lions fought back to the end, with McBride a giant in this as in other phases of play.

But the most wonderful part of the Lions performance in that endless second half was the heroic tackling by Gibson and Dawes in the centre and the covering work by the three

❝ I hope I never have to live through such a tense match again. If ever there was a wet rag walking, it was your correspondent as he tottered out at the end. ❞

loose forwards, Dixon, Mervyn Davies and Taylor. Then there was Jonn Williams at fullback, playing the game of his life, catching towering up-and-unders, taking fearsome punishment from the All Black forwards and always coming up for more.

"It was spirit that did it," said Dawes afterwards, and so, for all to see, it was. The All Black backs had endless ball, but they had neither the skill nor the pace to round the tigerish Lions defence in midfield.

Whenever a try threatened there were two or three Lions there to seal off the gap, and always John and his kicking.

I have not mentioned Gerald Davies and Bevan on the wings; "Chico" Hopkins, who substituted for Gareth Edwards at scrumhalf after 10 minutes, or Delme Thomas in the pack. But believe me, they all earned

A Union Jack is waved, the All Blacks are beaten and John Dawes calls for a handclap for the vanquished

Those British Lions roar again !

Barbarians 23,
New Zealanders 11

By
BARRY NEWCOMBE

THE BRITISH Lions lived again at Cardiff today as the Barbarians, led by the 1971 Lions captain John Dawes, rammed in four tries to beat the seventh All Blacks in the

glitter in their attack, they showed grit as well in defence.

After 31 minutes, Wyllie was penalised for punching Edwards and Bennett kicked an easy goal. Five minutes later, from a New Zealand heel, Slattery took the ball and barged through for a try. Bennett converted.

Three minutes later, with the All Blacks rocking, Bevan took a loose ball to shoulder past

BRYAN WILLIAMS, New Zealand wing, speeds away following a scrum in the thriller against the Barbarians at Cardi

aroud more points than any of the 25 sides the All Blacks had played before today. They were confident, urgent and organised.

After 44 minutes Karam

Kirkpatrick dropped the ball over the line and Karam missed a penalty from the 40 yards.

Dawes and ran on to score. Karam failed to convert—and the tourists were still trailing by six points.

Wonder Lions go from strength to strength

Wellington

THE BELLS are ringing out loud and clear for the Lions here. They gave a fabulous display in beating, nay thrashing, Wellington by seven goals, two penalty goals and two tries to two penalty goals and a dropped goal, and a crowd of 45,000 who had come to cheer on their own heroes were moved instead to round after round after round of applause for the tourists.

It was a just tribute to the wonderful rugby served up by John Dawes and his men, even though the home team were engulfed. This time the Lions really clicked. In the previous four matches, though they were well won, the Lions' backs had never quite cashed in on the fine work of the forwards. This time, all 15 men in the team really came into their own, with backs and forwards combining in one dazzling movement after another, until the tough Wellingtonians were run to a standstill. John Bevan, on the left wing, got four more marvellous tries to add to the six he had scored in three matches. Barry John, a conjuror and kind of wilo'-the-wisp at fly-half, had another 19 points on top of his previous 47 (excluding Australia). He seems hardly able to put a foot wrong.

Yesterday, his contribution was made up of five conversions, two penalty goals and a try, and his seven successful kicks came out of only nine attempts. Several of the kicks too came from between two

THE SUNDAY TIMES, JULY 11 1971

John Bevan (British Lions) scoring one of his four tries against Wellington.

Lions storm back to draw—and win series

A CLASH OF GIANTS as Whiting (centre) and Muller of New Zealand clash in the early stages of the final Test.

AUCKLAND, Saturday. — The magnificent British Lions entered rugby union history here today, as they held the mighty All Blacks to a 14—14 draw in the final Test—to win the series 2—1.

It was the first victory by a British Isles team in New Zealand and the first time the All Blacks had lost a home series since they were beaten by South Africa in 1937.

With fly-half Barry John kicking eight points plus penalties and a conversion and further points coming from Peter Dixon (try) and J. P. R. Williams (dropped goal) the Lions fought back from trailing 8—4 after only 12 minutes to draw the match.

New Zealand's points came from tries by Wayne Cottrell and Tom Lister and two penalties and a conversion by Laurie Mains.

Struggling

The turning point in the match came in the three minutes before half-time. Playing into the wind and sun, the Lions were struggling to make up the eight points total plus penalties Blacks, putting them ahead in the fourth minute with a well-taken try, which Mains converted.

New Zealand went further ahead in the 12th minute when Lions hooker John Pullin was caught offside, and Mains made the target with his penalty attempt. Then came the Lions' rally in the dying minutes of the half and with the scores level at the interval, the British Isles looked set for victory with the wind advantage in their favour.

Burly All-Black prop Brian Muller received a warning for rough play after two minutes of the second half and from the resulting penalty John kicked his second penalty to put the Lions...

Beaten! But it's not All Black

BRITISH LIONS
VIVIAN JENKINS REPORTS

New Zealand .... 22 pts
British Isles .... 12 pts

Christchurch

LONG is the way, and hard, that out of Hell leads up to light! That, or some variant of it, was told at school, and there are no halfpenny this time. Instead, muffled drums and the Dead March might be more in keeping with the mood.

But that, in spite of the Lions' defeat by two goals, a penalty goal and three tries to a penalty goal, a dropped goal and two tries in the Second Test at Christchurch would be a rather too sombre a conclusion.

The Lions' unbeaten record in New Zealand, it is true, has now gone. Also the series, it is so much harder to win than if it had been 2-0 with two to go. But there are at least some consolations. This was a truly great game of rugby between two...

Turning point in the second Test: Lions trail 3-4 and Gerald Davies obstructs Bryan Williams to concede a penalty try.

Super Lions send All-Blacks packing

Bad Rugby!

AS John Dawes said afterwards: "This was British Rugby at its best," but New Zealand manager Ernie Todd did not agree. "The Barbarians played a type of Rugby that we have not met before on the tour," he said. "A lot of it was bad Rugby."

So now we know!

JOHN DAWES'S glorious British Lions came to life again in the guise of the Barbarians at Cardiff and showed the All-Blacks—not the most popular of sides to visit us—how Rugby should be played. It was the British game at its most brilliant best.

To be fair to Ian Kirkpatrick's men they did attempt to run the ball—not their normal game—but they could never hope to equal the breathtaking poetry of the flowing Baa-Baas.

And so they ended the 26-match tour of these islands with the worst record any team from New Zealand has ever had here. It read:—

Won: 16. Lost: 4. Drawn: 3. For: 580. Against 318.

But, barring two, three and dream one of those fine draws one of their young, immature side can still return home as successful tourists.

by JOHN REED

Barbarians 23 All-Blacks 11

magic of the Barbarians' play did not cease. New Zealand's tackling, one of their strongest points, just melted before the Baa-Baas' continuous support play.

There were only three tries—Lions in the British side but all played a vital part. Llanelli hooker, Tom David, one superb in attack and defence and scored a try. Welsh cap scrum half Gareth Edwards and Bob Williams was also strong in the cover play. Its half-Phil Bennett showed vastly improved kicking skill.

But it was the Lions who mainly captured the crowd's imagination. We had magnificent running from Duckham...

Lions maul All Black sheep

Duckham leads them a dance

CLEM THOMAS

Barbarians .....23 pts   All Blacks 11

OF ALL the previous teams of Barbarians some have been a greater force, for the cause of rugby than these can through the minds of those who saw them, but all their talents could not compare to the performance given yesterday at the Arms Park as they beat the Barbarians, or the best of British Isles rugby, at their glorious best.

The exhilarating beauty and break-taking skill of this match was seen at its best when the Barbarians, with dazzling power and verve, made the All Blacks look ordinary. But from the kick-off, with Barry John slinging high up-and-under, and the cheers of the people, came Wales' great Bennett, electrifying the crowd, and he started to jink and swerve past player after player. Soon he reached the half-way line where he passed to John Dawes, his captain, and two following players, Tom David and J. P. R. Williams, who carried on with this dazzling movement of power and...

Ron Urlich gets possession as Sid Going while Carmichael and Quinnell look on.

Salute Dawes and his lionhearts—this was the greatest

Barbarians 23 New Zealand 11 : By TERRY O'CONNOR

ALL BACK Grant Batty is too late to stop John Williams scoring the Barbarians' last try.

PHIL BENNETT decided to have a go . . . John Pullin passed instead of kicking within three minutes . . . and the result was the most fantastic try Cardiff Arms Park has seen.

More important, the breath-taking 100-yard movement of sheer magic which ended with Gareth Edwards stealing a try-scoring pass meant for John Bevan, set the pattern for the finest Rugby game in the lease to play a key role in this great match.

The 1971 Lions produced some magnificent performances, but they never played the All Blacks with the majesty and daring with which Barbarians set up a 17—0 half-time lead.

Former Lions captain Dawes urged this team to go on for 20 points. It is the cause British Rugby needs, he told them.

But it was the character of the New Zealanders that excelled in the early part of the second half always there to change direction of attack.

Finally Mike Gibson elated by the fervent Welsh support, squeezed through two All Blacks and a try was on.

The fiercely competitive John Williams, was up for the final push.

All Blacks captain Ian Kirkpatrick, justly elected afterwards to the Barbarians club, admitted that final try shattered his team.

'It was an incredible game and the first time he have played a...

JOHN DAWES, inspiration of London Welsh's magnificent display on Saturday, in full flight for the Newport line.

TERRY O'CONNOR DESCRIBES

Finest club display I have seen

FREDDIE WILLIAMS, a chunky 15st. prop-forward, illustrated perfectly why London Welsh shattered Newport 31—5 by providing the pass for the first try and bounding in to score the last of six himself.

Rugby Union

CARWYN JAMES PLOTS MEMORABLE BARBARIANS WIN

By JOHN REASON

Barbarians ...23pts   New Zealanders ... 11

CARWYN JAMES talked to the Barbaraians for 20 minutes and in that time he convinced them that they could go out at Cardiff Arms Park and play just as they had when they were Lions in New Zealand.

He convinced them that they could beat the All Blacks in the last match of the tour, despite their crippling lack of match practice, and he convinced them

they could do it with no compromises to their own supreme brand of 15-man football.

Bennett kicked a penalty goal, when Wyllie tangled with Edwards at the back of a ruck, and he converted a try by Slattery, who whirled over the line after Edwards had hustled Going after

All Blacks are given a lesson to take home

Lions pick up threads in Barbarian shirts

By DAVID FROST : Barbarians 23, New Zealand 11

Over the past 25 years, the Barbarians have regularly provided touring teams from overseas with their last opposition in the British Isles, and the series has produced some great games. But Saturday's match at Cardiff Arms Park, in which All Blacks by two goals, two tries, and a penalty goal to two tries and a penalty goal, before a singing capacity crowd of 51,000 was probably the best of the lot.

The occasion of a touring team's final appearance is itself bound to stimulate all concerned. The tourists want to be remembered by a worthy performance. The spectators, especially the emotional Cardiff crowd, want to see memorable rugby from the players to whom they have the privilege of bidding farewell.

On Saturday, in addition, there was a special situation created by

Barbarians of many of the Lions who had won the Test series in New Zealand in 1971. There was John Dawes, the Lions captain, coming out of semi-retirement to lead on yet another big day at the Arms Park. And there was the question : Could the Lions rediscover their teamwork after 18 months of separation?

In the event the Lions and the Barbarians found more than teamwork, they straight away found their old identity and, in an upsurge of strong character and personality, they displayed some wonderful rugby. They began with a breath-taking try, in which audacity and high skill swept the ball from hand to hand and from one end of the field to the other. And their richly experienced forwards, most of whom had learned to ruck in New Zealand, then hounded the All Blacks in a way few New Zealand packs have been subjected to in the loose.

In terms of initial possession the Barbarians were well beaten at the line-out but, with Quinnell

middle and Pullin coming round from the front of the line, the Barbarians were sometimes able to spoil Going. They could him, too, at serious where their power and expertise on All Blacks put-ins won them a try all this Tom David, a late replacement for Mervyn Davies, played a full and telling part. What an enviable stock of loose forward Wales possess at the moment.

Behind a pack in such a mood Edwards wasted nothing. He was at his instinctive best, mentally sharp and agile, making a startling and decisive intervention into the multi-passing movement of that first great try, of which he was also the scorer. Bennett, who initiated this move with some deft dodging in his own "25," never tried to do too much and the basic soundness of Dawes who played one of his most constructive games, and of Gibson created the opportunities for the flair of Duckham, Bevan and John Williams to flourish.

Duckham was at his most

Tom David resists an All Black tackle to make his pass and start the move which led to Gareth Edwards scoring Barbarians' first try

Colorsport

John Dawes making his crucial break out of the Barbarians 25 versus the All Blacks at Cardiff Arms Park in January 1973. The move ended with Gareth Edwards scoring what has been hailed as 'the greatest try ever'.

Western Mail

Dawes carried aloft by supporters after the Barbarians match in 1973. Twelve of his great 1971 Lions side were in the memorable 23–11 triumph in his last match against the men in black.

that we were sure we could take the All Blacks apart behind the scrum in the last two Test matches,' says Dawes. The first try was a remarkable combined move that swept almost the whole length of the field. Full-back John Williams caught a kick-ahead near his own posts and then started running. He linked with Mike Gibson, who gave Gerald Davies the ball near the halfway line. The London Welsh winger's electrifying speed enabled him to outrun the cover defence to score in the corner. The second try came from a set scrum when a missed move plus Williams' intervention in the backline created that extra yard of room to enable Gerald Davies to sprint to the corner for another beautifully executed try.

The Lions continued their winning ways in the provincial matches they played in the next three weeks and, at the same time, began their preparations for the vital third Test. The Lions back-row trio had been criticised for weak tackling in the second Test but Dawes' view was that the pack had stayed down, pushing for too long in the set scrums. This seemed confirmed by an incident in the match when the Lions forwards were shoving the New Zealand eight yards back, yet scrum-half Sid Going was still able to gather the ball and break down the blindside, despite the fact his forwards were on the retreat.

'We decided to play open- and blind-side wing forwards in the third Test, instead of left and right, because of what happened in the second Test,' says Dawes. 'We realised if we could stop Going breaking near the scrum, they would be struggling attacking-wise. By playing open- and blind-side wing forwards, we had the same man looking after Going's blind-side breaks all the time. We had the ideal man for this in Derek Quinnell. He hadn't then been capped by Wales but he was a big forward, a really hard aggressive man. His job was to mark Going on the blind-side. Gareth Edwards watched him on the open side – and he really did look after him. Originally we chose Fergus Slattery for the open-side flanker position to get in amongst their backs as he was the fastest forward we had. This back-row problem took about four hours to decide, it was the only time we had a long selection meeting. But Slattery had tonsillitis and dropped out. So John Taylor took his place and he really played superbly – his tackling was quite unbelievable.'

Another forward change was the selection of Scotsman Gordon Brown in the second row as the number five jumper. The rapidly improving Brown totally justified his selection and Brian Lochore, the great No. 8 recalled rather unwisely to play in the second row, had a poor match against him. 'Quinnell also helped here,' says Dawes. 'His job was to act as a blocker in the lineouts and he made sure no one touched Gordon.'

But most important of all was the attitude of the Lions as they went into the third Test. 'We were determined to take the initiative,' Dawes recalls. 'We were going to run it at them from the word go instead of waiting from them to come at us as perhaps we had done in the first and second Tests. So when I won the toss, we played with the wind instead of against it in the first half as we had done in the two previous internationals.'

The Lions 13–3 win against New Zealand in the third Test before a capacity 50,000 crowd at Athletic Park, Wellington, was one of the greatest victories in British rugby history. The policy of Dawes' men to take the initiative from the outset was devastatingly effective. The Lions took a 3–0 lead after the game was only three minutes old, after they had run the ball from their own 25 in a situation where other teams would have kicked to touch. 'There was a lineout on the left hand side of the field on our 25,' Dawes recalls. 'We won the ball and Barry spun the ball out. It went along our three-quarter line, with John Williams joining the backs and Gerald Davies running outside his wing to the halfway line. When he kicked ahead, the New Zealand wing Hunter was covering the kick but, by the nature of his line of run, he had to run into open field and John Taylor caught him. Mervyn Davies won the ruck and Mike Gibson fed Barry, who dropped a goal. And that was really early on.'

After eight minutes play, the Lions were 8–0 ahead. Gareth

Edwards fed Gerald Davies on the blind side and the London Welsh winger went through a cluster of defenders to score in the corner when he appeared to have no room to make the tryline. John's superb conversion kick went over via an upright. Then another Lions try came after Gareth Edwards revealed his power as runner. The move started when Taylor tapped the ball into no-man's-land from a lineout on the New Zealand 25. Edwards came through to gather the ball on the burst and then sent the New Zealand fly-half Bob Burgess yards back with a jolting hand-off before passing to Barry John who simply had to cross the line. John added the conversion and, after 17 minutes of the match, the Lions were leading New Zealand 13–0.

At that moment it seemed the Lions were on the verge of tearing the All Blacks apart and the stunned crowd was prepared for a massacre. Could Dawes' conviction that given enough ball, British backs were capable of beating New Zealand by 30 points become a reality? 'I felt that if we scored another try, we would really murder them,' says Dawes. 'But we never did and they came back into the game. In the second half we really had to defend well and they were unlucky not to score more than one try. Although we were 2–1 ahead and could not lose the Test series, I still felt some disappointment after the match. We played so well in those opening 20 minutes but didn't keep it up. But we started off at such a tremendous pace it was terribly difficult to maintain.'

The Lions forwards had played a crucial role in this great victory. One critic worked out that the Lions won the lineouts 37–15, which was a remarkable margin of superiority against the All Blacks. While the New Zealand forwards had the better of the loose rucks, the initiative remained with the British pack. As Terry McLean wrote: 'It was many a year since an All Black team had so sadly and badly suffered in the contest for the ball of a Test match.'

New Zealand 3 British Isles 13
July 31, 1971, Athletic Park Wellington

New Zealand – LW Mains (Otago) (T); KR Carrington (Auckland), HJ Joseph (Canterbury), BA Hunter (Otago); WD Cottrell (Canterbury), RE Burgess (Manawatu); SM Going (North Auckland); A Guy (North Auckland), RT Norton (Canterbury), BL Muller (Taranaki); CE Meads (King Country) (Captain), BJ Lochore (Wairarapa Bush); AM McNaughton (Bay of Plenty), AJ Wyllie (Canterbury), IA Kirkpatrick (Poverty Bay)

*MG Duncan (Hawke's Bay) replaced Burgess after 66 minutes

British Isles – JPR Williams (Wales); D Duckham (England), SJ Dawes (Wales) (Captain), CMH Gibson (Ireland), TGR Davies (Wales) (T); B John (Wales) (D-G, T, 2C), G Edwards (Wales); I McLauchlan (Scotland), J Pullin (England), S Lynch (Ireland); G Brown (Scotland), WJ McBride (Ireland); D Quinnell (Wales), TM Davies (Wales), J Taylor (Wales)

Referee –JPG Pring (Auckland)

After the third Test win, the British press party provided a champagne celebration for the tourists. And the celebrations continued until the Sunday evening at the Grand Hotel in Palmerston North. That evening was labelled 'the wild night' of the tour. 'It was the one time I was absolutely paralytic,' says Dawes. 'We just took over the bar. I was just drinking gin and tonics quietly with Geoff Evans and I left Geoff for a brief talk with Carwyn James and JBG Thomas, the *Western Mail* rugby writer. When I got back to Geoff, I said: "It's your round." My glass was empty and his was still full. So he downed his drink in one and fled to the bar and returned in about ten seconds with one empty glass and one full glass and told me it was my round!' And the vicious circle continued and the two London Welsh players drunk about eight gins in the space of an hour. The rest of the tour party were also well into the swing of things by this time, and the drinking continued until three in the morning. 'The bill was quite colossal,' says Dawes. 'That night worked out at something like £10 a head!'

Three more victories before the fourth and final Test meant that the Lions had won every provincial match they played in

New Zealand – a feat no other British team had come anywhere near achieving. The 11–5 victory against North Auckland provided the crowd with the unusual sight of fly-half Barry John being penalised for dirty play. Nicknamed 'The King' by his tour colleagues, he played his rugby with a casualness that was most deceptive but, in this particular match, he lost his temper for once. 'He was so annoyed with one of their players that he kicked him,' Dawes recalls with some amusement. 'But the kick was such a feeble effort – it was just like something out of a *Tom and Jerry* cartoon. Then Barry just ran like hell! We almost said if you are going to kick him, why don't you really kick him!'

The fourth Test, played before a 56,000 crowd at Eden Park, Auckland, was not a classic match but what it lacked in quality, it made up for in terms of sheer excitement.

'The tension for this game was far greater than anything else I have experienced,' says Dawes. 'The game started off like an explosion and the man who really calmed everything down was the New Zealand captain Colin Meads.'

The Lions were criticised after this Test for their lack of adventure in the match, but when New Zealand took an 8–0 lead after only twelve minutes' play, Dawes saw the match and the series slipping away. 'I remember saying "All right, let's cut it out. No more mistakes." We had played a somewhat adventurous game until then with the limited ball we had won and they had a strong breeze behind them. I was aware if they scored another converted try and went 13–0 ahead, the match would have been lost.'

Dawes' change of policy had the desired effect, for the All Blacks did not increase their lead in the first half. In fact, the scores were level at 8–8 at half-time after two quick scores in injury time in that half. First Barry John, who had earlier missed a penalty less than 20 yards from the posts, landed a 32-yard penalty. Then he converted a try scored by the English wing forward Peter Dixon, who went over from a loose maul after Gareth Edwards had broken from a lineout. Then, early in the second half, John added a superb 48-yard penalty and the Lions were leading 11–8 having scored 11 points in only eight minutes.

The drama heightened as the All Blacks took control once more and levelled the scores 11–11 with a try by flank forward Tom Lister. Once more, the Lions had to survive some severe pressure and left wing David Duckham made some memorable match-saving tackles. It was an extraordinary dropped-goal from 50 yards out by John Williams that put the Lions into a 14–11 lead and throughout the remaining twenty minutes of the match, the initiative remained with the Lions although Mains finally levelled the scores at 14–14 with a penalty six minutes from time.

The 14–14 draw in the fourth Test meant that the Lions had won the Test series 2–1. They were the first British team to win a Test series in New Zealand and joined company with the only other rugby team to defeat the All Blacks in a series on their own soil – the legendary 1937 Springboks. Altogether, the 1971 Lions played 24 matches in New Zealand and won 22, suffering only one defeat. Their 555 points total included 92 tries and both Barry John (180 points) and the England full-back Bob Hiller (102 points) had beaten the points' record set by the South African full-back, Gerry Brand, in 1937.

For John Dawes, the tour was a great personal triumph. Not only had his team made history but his own rugby philosophy had been realised at the highest level. The 1971 British Lions were playing the London Welsh game where the emphasis was on swift passing, use of the wings, the attacking full-back and the sudden counterattack from defensive positions. Half the Lions tries were scored by the party's four wingers, Davies, Duckham, Bevan and Biggar. In John Williams, the Lions had the attacking full-back par excellence and he was invariably in the backline during set piece moves. And the Lions willingness to counterattack from defensive positions was symbolised by the brilliant try in the Hawke's Bay match, when Williams caught the ball after an attempted drop-kick had struck the posts, and started running. By the time Gerald Davies touched the ball down for a try, the movement had covered almost the whole length of the field.

How great were the 1971 Lions? Some said they were the greatest touring team of them all. Certainly it is difficult to think of any international side that possessed such a backline as the Lions fielded in the Test series with Edwards and John as the halves, Dawes and Gibson in the centre, Davies and Duckham on the wings and Williams at full-back. It was true that the 1971 New Zealand forwards lacked the stature of the great packs fielded by the All Blacks in the 1960s. But the All Blacks still had outstanding forwards and it needed a supreme defensive effort from the Lions to hold the assaults launched by Meads and his forwards in the Test series. You could argue that the 1971 Lions faced a more difficult task than the 1937 Springboks, for the South Africans played only three Test matches and New Zealand still had not overcome the problem forced upon her when the International Board made her famous 2–3–2 scrummage formation illegal.

Unquestionably the 1971 Lions established John Dawes as one of the game's greatest figures. New Zealand's celebrated rugby writer Terry McLean, in his book on the tour, *Lions Rampant*, produced as shrewd an analysis of a rugby player as has surfaced in print when he wrote:

> It was truly staggering to consider that anyone else might have been appointed as captain. As a player he was deceiving. It was even seriously suggested, both in the British Isles and New Zealand, that he might not be good enough to win a place in the Test matches. The very supposition was the most arrant poppycock. Dawes concealed his great skills as a player and his high virtues as a leader by the quietness of his methods. He instinctively adjusted his play to suit his partners. As a leader, he had the maturity to understand each of his players intimately and to bring the best out of them. Thus, in the first Test, he talked not at all to John, even during the heat of play, about rugby. He understood what John wanted, above all, distractions. So they

chatted amiably to each other about ships and shoes and sealing wax and cabbages and kings. At half-time in the third Test, Dawes cracked jokes as his players stood about him. Anything to disperse the tension. Anything to establish peace of mind. Only a profoundly gifted man could see this need.

The astute Mclean detected little fault in 'Dawes, The Quiet One', who 'preferred to be part of the tapestry'. But while praising his fine feeling for words, McLean did find his 'constant use' of the remark 'and that's what it is all about' in reference to rugby, maddening. Oddly, in the many hours I spent talking to Dawes about his career, I can never remember him using this remark.

Even though everyone makes mistakes, McLean found it hard to fault Dawes either as a general or as a player:

> One stared disbelievingly in the Canterbury game when, with Duckham lined up alongside, he cut back infield at the cost of a probable try. If he had a weakness as a captain, it was that he too much, perhaps even too often, allowed John to do the tactical dictating at the cost of the explosive attacks the Lions' backline could mount.
>
> There were times when the Lions' backs, especially in the second Test, misunderstood the percentages of four men to three or three men to two and plumped instead for the safe kick to touch. If these were flaws in Dawes, no one – the record again is the criterion – could safely say that very great harm resulted.

McLean was unreserved in his praise of Dawes the rugby player:

> He was superbly built, strong of torso and thigh; he had instant perception; he was so sound a support player that you scarcely noticed he was there – but he always was – and when the whim took him, which was not often because he modestly refrained from taking starring roles, he had a lick of his own, he had developed a low-slung sidestep, difficult to check and extremely elusive when he built up speed.
>
> His whole game, as an attacking player, was based upon his

appreciation of the well-timed pass that gave his support a fraction more time and space than might otherwise have been possible. It was Dawes who first exploited a kind of pass I had never seen in an international, even with the French. As he ball came to him, high, in a situation where everyone was rushing and time was supremely the essence, he made no attempt to catch and then pass the ball. He simply reached out his hands and as these made contact gave a twist and a flick of the wrists and sent the ball on, uncaught, to the wing… You can put it most simply by saying that he was absolutely essential to the best functioning of the Lions' backline.

If more people had possessed the astute judgement of Terry McLean, Sydney John Dawes would not have had to wait until he reached the age of 30 for the chance to fulfil his potential as a great leader and player at the highest level in the game of rugby union.

The 1971 British Lions

Played 26 Won 23 Drawn 1 Lost 2 For: 580 Against: 231

In Australia

Played 2 Won 1 Lost 1 For: 25 Against: 27
Queensland L 11–15 New South Wales W 14–12

In New Zealand

Played 24 Won 22 Drawn 1 Lost 1 For: 555 Against: 204

Thames Valley Counties	W 25–3	Taranaki	W 14–9
King Country-Wanganui	W 22–9	New Zealand Universities	W 27–6
Waikato	W 35–14	NEW ZEALAND	L 12–22
New Zealand Maoris	W 23–12	Wairarapa-Bush	W 27–6
Wellington	W 47–9	Hawke's Bay	W 25–6
South Canterbury-Mid		East Coast-Poverty Bay	W 18–12
Canterbury-North Otago	W 25–6	Auckland	W 19–12
Otago	W 21–9	NEW ZEALAND	W 13–3
West Coast-Buller	W 39–6	Manawatu-Horonwhenua	W 39–6
Canterbury	W 14–3	North Auckland	W 11–5
Marlborough & Nelson Bays	W 31–12	Bay of Plenty	W 20–14
NEW ZEALAND	W 9–3	NEW ZEALAND	D 14–14
Southland	W 25–3		

Tour Party

	Age	Height	Weight	Caps
R B Hiller (England)	28	6 2	14 4	17
JPR Williams (Wales)	22	6 1	13 12	16
DJ Duckham (England)	24	6 1	14 0	15
AG Biggar (Scotland)	24	6 1	14 3	10
TGR Davies (Wales)	26	5 9	11 8	17
JC Bevan (Wales)	20	6 0	13 0	4
SJ Dawes (Wales) (Captain)	30	5 10	12 12	21
A Lewis (Wales)	29	5 11	13 7	4
JS Spencer (England)	23	6 1	14 5	14
CWW Rea (Scotland)	27	5 9	12 0	13
CMH Gibson (Ireland)	28	5 11	12 10	34
B John (Wales)	26	5 9	11 6	21
GO Edwards (Wales)	23	5 8	12 10	22
R Hopkins (Wales)	24	5 8	12 8	1
AB Carmichael (Scotland)	27	6 2	15 7	22
RJ McLauchlan (Scotland)	29	5 9	14 6	9
J F Lynch (Ireland)	28	6 0	15 7	4
RJ McLoughlin (Ireland)	31	5 10	15 8	21
CB Stevens (England)	29	5 11	15 4	5
JV Pullin (England)	28	5 11	14 7	20
FAL Laidlaw (Scotland)	29	5 10	13 7	32
WD Thomas (Wales)	28	6 3	16 4	16
WJ McBride (Ireland)	30	6 3	16 8	45
M Roberts (Wales)	25	6 4	16 9	4
GL Brown (Scotland)	23	6 5	16 4	11
TG Evans (Wales)	28	6 4	16 7	4
TM Davies (Wales)	24	6 4	14 12	16
PJ Dixon (England)	27	6 3	15 2	1
J Taylor (Wales)	25	5 11	13 9	18
JF Slattery (Ireland)	21	6 1	14 0	9
D Quinnell (Llanelli)	21	6 3	15 12	–
RJ Arneil (Scotland)	26	6 4	14 8	18

Individual scorers
In Australia

	Matches	T	C	P	D-G	Total
Hiller	1		1	2		8
John	1		1	2		8
Dawes	2	1				3
Bevan	1	1				3
Spencer	1	1				3

In New Zealand

	Matches	T	C	P	D-G	Total
John	16	6	30	26	8	180
Hiller	10	2	24	14	2	102
Bevan	13	17				51
Duckham	15	11				33
TGR Davies	10	10				30
Biggar	9	9				27
Gibson	15	5	1	1	1	23
Williams	14	2	2	1	1	16
Dawes	17	4			1	15
Taylor	14	4				12
Spencer	9	3				9
Edwards	15	3				9
TM Davies	13	3				9
Rea	10	3				9
Dixon	14	2				6
Lewis	9	2				6
McLauchlan	16	1				3
Hopkins	10	1				3
Quinnell	9	1				3
Evans	6	1				3
Carmichael	5	1				3
McLoughlin	4	1				3
		92	**57**	**42**	**13**	**555**

CHAPTER 11

Aftermath

*'An airport official said it was the
biggest welcome he had seen since the Beatles.'*

THE EFFECT OF the 1971 Lions tour was to create an unprecedented level of interest in the game of rugby union in Britain.

In Wales, the audience figures were obviously high for the television and radio coverage. Many Welshmen were worried about the increasing interest being shown in soccer in the Principality to the detriment of rugby and this had been reflected for a number of years. But now, after the victory over New Zealand, a new generation of Welsh schoolboys had new idols to worship such as Barry John, who was to get the full superstar treatment from the media when he arrived back in Britain. In England, where rugby takes a distant second place to soccer, the BBC found the public were taking a tremendous interest in their early morning radio broadcasts of the Test matches and, because of this, they decided to increase their television coverage of the tour.

But the Lions were not aware of the level of interest in their progress back in Britain. They left Auckland on the Sunday following the fourth Test for the forty-hour flight back via America. The high planning standards of the tour were to do a disappearing act on the flight home. 'Our first stop was Fiji,' says Dawes. 'We had carefully planned when we were going to sleep and when we were going to drink. But in the end, we just had one helluva party. It started in Fiji and then we were drinking and singing on the plane. We genuinely planned to sleep before we arrived in New York. But on the six-hour stop in San Francisco, we decided we couldn't miss the sights, so we saw the bridge, Chinatown, Alcatraz and so on. Then when we got on the plane again, a small group of us were at the front having a nightcap when Arthur Lewis joined us and we started singing quietly. And we continued singing and drinking and all of a sudden we were in New York. It was a shambles of an organisation because there was no breakfast for us. By the time we arrived in London, all our plans had gone astray and we just managed to get about half-an-hour's sleep. We had sobered up quite well by the time we landed at London Airport and we were more tired than drunk. We tried to look smart for the small reception we were going to have at the hotel opposite the airport.

'Then we were absolutely staggered by the welcome we received. There were at least 2,000 to 3,000 people there to welcome us. One figure put the figure as high as 5,000. Only hints had come through to us of the following we had back home. I remember when I left the hotel, you could see the coaches from Swansea. An airport official said it was the biggest welcome he had seen since the Beatles. I was amazed.'

The tour party faced a formidable programme of social engagements in their honour in the months following their return. The most hectic two days started when Dawes and another dozen Lions went to open a dry-cleaning shop in Battersea, South London, of all things. 'It was a delightful occasion,' says Dawes. 'We just wandered in and had a few drinks and then cut the tape. It was a nice little formal ceremony but there was no one there at all! People walking past didn't have a clue what was going on.' The party were then taken to lunch by the owner. After this they had to hurry back to central London to check in at the Russell Hotel before their tour of the Gordon's Gin plant in the East End. 'They ginned us up superbly,' says Dawes. There was also a brief tour of the distillery and the party managed to get stuck in the lift, and so had to commence a clambering operation to get out of the lift shaft. Then it was back to the hotel and off again to the special dinner in their honour given by the National Sporting Club at the Café Royal. There they were joined by the rest of the Lions and more than seven hundred guests.

After returning to the hotel in the early hours of the morning and continuing with their own party, the Lions rose the next day to attend a lunch in their honour given by the British Sportsmen's Club at the Savoy Hotel. This in itself was an unusual occasion because the club always entertained incoming tourists such as the Australian cricketers or the All Blacks and this was the first time their familiar practice had been broken. Then, in the evening, the party went to their fifth engagement in two days – a champagne reception given by the Prime Minister, Edward Heath, at No. 10 Downing Street.

There were many other engagements both in London and back in Wales for the tourists. The Sportsmen's Club in London named the third Test victory as the outstanding sporting achievement of July 1971. The entire party was also hosted by the Anglo-American Boxing Club at the Hilton Hotel in Park Lane and both the Sportswriters' Association and the BBC elected the Lions as the sports team of 1971. Dawes was also present at the luncheon given by the Lord Mayor of London for outstanding British sportsmen. During the meal he sat next to Princess Anne. 'She was very pleasant and very natural,' he recalls. 'She was very keen to get in the Olympic equestrian team but she knew all the talk about her making the team was just paper talk. She was embarrassed as you would expect any top-class sportsman to be.'

Both Dawes and Doug Smith were awarded the OBE in the New Year Honours List. Undoubtedly Carwyn James would also have been honoured but for his adherence to the Welsh Nationalist cause. 'I knew very well it was because of what the team achieved that I received the OBE,' says Dawes modestly. 'I thought it was a pity there was no way of dividing it 33 ways. The Queen Mother presented me with the medal at Buckingham Palace. There were around 120 people there and I thought it was great that she knew just what we had achieved when she spoke to me.'

Dawes estimates Doug Smith received some 3,000 letters in the months following his return congratulating him on the Lions achievement. 'What impressed me more than anything else was that he always replied to every letter. He also wrote a letter to every member of the tour party thanking them, which was very nice. He didn't receive many back in reply and I think this upset him. But then rugby players are not that type – they don't write down their gratitude. They take it for granted that it comes in a handshake or a word.' Dawes himself was getting six letters a day at one stage and attending an average of four functions a week in the months preceding Christmas.

The aura of the Lions' achievement was reflected in the fact that Dawes and his wife Janette were guests in the Royal Box at Wimbledon in the summer of 1972. Racing driver Jackie Stewart and the former heavyweight boxing champion Henry Cooper were also there with their wives. 'Henry was very funny,' recalls Dawes. 'He kept using this expression "bleeding" all the time!' They saw the young American Jimmy Connors in action, accompanied by the constant shouting of his notorious mother. 'Every time Connors did something, we were looking to see the reaction of his mother and Henry said: "I'm more interested in his bleeding Mum than the tennis".'

Dawes decided to retire from international rugby after the Lions tour simply because he wanted to spend more time with his wife and their two children, Michael, aged three, and Catherine, who was then a year old. The family lived in Sunbury-on-Thames, some six miles away from the London Welsh ground at Richmond. Their home is a two-storey house, which was newly built when Dawes bought it for £6,000 in 1968. On his decision to retire from international rugby, Dawes says: 'The demands on a representative player these days are really immense. I had been there or thereabouts for eight years. If you are a Welsh international, it virtually means spending every weekend away from home between Christmas and Easter. I decided to call it a day on these grounds.' His wife, a soprano who sings regularly in amateur and semi-professional operatic productions, is tolerant of the demands the game has placed on her husband. 'I resent it sometimes,' she says. 'But as long as I can do the things I want to do, such as singing, I'm happy. I'm rather selfish really. I nearly always watch every home match John plays and I know enough not to cheer in the wrong places. I never think of John getting hurt on the field. If something is going to happen to him, my worrying is not going to prevent it.' Dawes also gave up teaching on his return from New Zealand and took on a new appointment as a £3,000 a year lecturer at the Polytechnic of North London with special responsibilities for the recreational and management course being run at the polytechnic.

Most of the Lions took a rest from rugby following their return home and missed the opening months of the 1971–72 season. This should have been a handicap to London Welsh, with their seven British Lions absent, but to everyone's astonishment they started the season with an incredible sequence of massive wins. Dawes had retired as captain of the club after six years because he would miss the early months of the season because of the Lions tour, and flanker Tony Gray succeeded him. This was the season the value of the try was raised from three to four points and in their opening five matches, the Exiles amassed 261 points, including a record 72–6 victory against Wasps. But these early matches were not against the strongest opposition and their winning sequence was halted in a remarkable match at Old Deer Park when the Metropolitan Police, down 0–16 after an hour's play, came back to win the match 18–16. But although the under-strength Exiles could not sustain their remarkable start, they continued to achieve some notable victories, including a 26–14 defeat of Neath at the Gnoll and a massive 48–6 victory against Harlequins at Twickenham. 'Only sadists or Welshmen, and there seemed to be 10,000 present, could have relished the slaughter of the Saxons,' wrote Christopher Wordsworth in *The Observer*.

Dawes and the other Lions returned to the team after playing matches in the club's lower sides. In late November, Westminster Hospital played the Dragons, the London Welsh third team, and took to the field to find Dawes at fly-half and John Williams and Gerald Davies in the centre! Not surprisingly, the Hospital lost by 40 points and, at one point during the game, Gerald Davies was in full flight with young winger Rhodri Ellis screaming at him for the ball. 'Here you had Gerald Davies, the world's No. 1 wing at full tilt and this youngster telling him to give him the ball!' recalls Dawes. 'Gerald duly passed and this youngster went off his left foot and sprinted 50 yards to the posts. I found out afterwards he was a sprinter from Borough Road College – a 9.9 man himself!'

The Exiles lost their first match of the New Year, going down 6–13 against Northampton when nine of their players were away on Welsh trial duty. But with all the Lions back in the side, the club went on to win all their remaining matches of the season to end with a record of Played 42 Won 32 Drawn 1 Lost 8 For: 966 Against: 391. This consistency of performance gave them the prize that had always eluded them – the Welsh Club Championship run by the *Western Mail* newspaper. They clinched the title on April 12 with a 27–0 victory against the powerful Coventry club at Old Deer Park. A few weeks later, a 50,000 crowd saw the captain of the 1971 Lions leading his club to a 22–18 victory against Public School Wanderers in the final of the Middlesex Sevens at Twickenham.

CHAPTER 12

The Return of the Quiet Welshman

'England needed a Dawes among the backs.'

BRITISH RUGBY FACED its first major test of strength after the 1971 Lions tour when Ian Kirkpatrick's Seventh All Blacks came to Britain in the winter of 1972–73. The hope that the achievement of the Lions would herald a new era for British rugby seemed confirmed when a lowly rated England side had toured South Africa in the summer of 1972 and sensationally beat the Springboks 18–9 in a Test match at Ellis Park. Now the All Blacks were coming, and the public waited expectantly hoping that this New Zealand team was not going to be allowed to ride roughshod over the best teams in Britain as their predecessors had done.

John Dawes, forever the realist, thought the All Blacks would prove to be far more formidable than most people imagined. He felt that British rugby had not absorbed the lessons of the 1971 Lions tour.

'If there was one lesson to be learned from that tour, it was the value of preparation,' he told me months before the arrival of the Seventh All Blacks. 'What are we doing about the forthcoming tour? Carwyn James and various Lions toured the country lecturing, and we are listening. But apart from London Counties, I don't know of any sides who have nominated team squads and started preparing for the All Blacks.'

More importantly, Dawes believed there was something wrong with the British rugby system. He saw the New Zealand system as the ideal, where club matches were played in one part of the season followed by representative matches. Under this system, there was no conflict between club and representative rugby, and players took part in no more than 36 matches a season. But in Britain the system was completely different. The club programme continued through the winter, with leading clubs playing as many as 50 matches a season. Then running side by side with the club matches, there were the representative games – the matches against touring sides, the county matches and the internationals. Leading players would find themselves attending training sessions held by their club and their county or national side in the same week. In England, the situation was particularly chaotic. In theory, the County Championship formed the natural stepping stone between club and Test rugby. But in reality, interest in the competition varied dramatically from region to region and in some groups, championship matches were played in midweek so they didn't conflict with the club fixtures. The demands on players were such that many refused to play county matches.

'The present system is a shambles,' Dawes told me. 'Instead of working together, you get the counties pulling against the clubs and then the conflicting demands of other representative matches such as Tests. All these matches cut across the club programmes. We said we were going to follow the example of the New Zealanders and so we introduced competitive rugby and coaching. But we forgot the main ingredient of the New Zealand season was a club programme of around 25 games followed by the representative matches afterwards. Until we get to this stage, I don't see how we can improve internationally. What might shoot me down on this coming All Blacks tour is the fact we have so many outstanding players at the moment – they might succeed in spite of the British system. But this won't improve our standards.

'We are very close to saturation point. The trouble is that

players are attending so many different training sessions that the basic skills of the game get neglected. The result is that when you attend a county or national squad training session, they assume the basics have been dealt with at club level. This is one of the biggest wrong assumptions. I remember when Wales started her national squad sessions, we found that more than fifty per cent of the players were not even match fit. New Zealand rugby is so strong in the basics of the game that she can put right the faults of her rugby almost overnight. But we cannot do that here as the present system is so chaotic. Don't believe the fault of British rugby lies either with the players or its technique – it is just a matter of practicing the basics. But there is no chance of this when you have conflicting programmes and players playing too many matches. It is rather like trying to play the piano when you cannot read music – you are just relying on ability. The gifted man will succeed, but the ordinary man will fail because he has to read the music.'

What Dawes wanted to see in Britain was a club programme of around 30 major matches that comes to a close by the end of January or the beginning of February. Then the county matches would be played, followed by the internationals.

'With this system, players would face the same demands,' says Dawes. 'They would train twice a week with their club, then later with their county and finally with their national squad. While leading players are playing representative matches, the clubs could fill out the remainder of the season playing their friendly matches, their less important games. If this system was adopted, I have no doubt the standard of British rugby would improve. But I cannot see it ever happening. As Bob Hiller says, the game is in the hands of the club treasurers – they are afraid of losing money. They haven't the vision to see that if you cut down your club programme, the quality of rugby will improve, your gates will get bigger and bar takings will increase. I think we ought to learn from the New Zealanders. The way we are going at the moment, we are cutting our own throats.'

Dawes' doubts about the ability of British rugby to

overcome the All Blacks were to prove justified. It was true that statistically the Seventh All Blacks were the worst New Zealand touring side ever to come to Britain. They played 26 matches and won 20 of them and were beaten four times (Llanelli 3–9, North West Counties 14–16, West Midlands 8–16 and the Barbarians 11–23). But disappointingly Ian Kirkpatrick's tourists were undefeated in their four international matches against the individual Home Union countries.

Dawes was in the London Counties team that were beaten 24–3 by the New Zealanders on November 11. Ironically, the Counties were the side that began preparing for their match against the tourists long before anyone else. A squad was announced and Dawes was appointed team coach at the end of the 1971–72 season. But for some inexplicable reason, the Welsh selectors decided to hold a trial on the day of the London Counties match. This was a severe blow for the Counties, as it meant leading London Welsh players such as John Williams, Gerald Davies and John Taylor could not play in the Twickenham game.

But, despite the comprehensive defeat of the London Counties team, the All Blacks' tour was to show the tremendous influence of John Dawes on British rugby. Wales were beaten 19–16 by the New Zealanders and one wondered if the Welsh might have won the match if Dawes had been there leading the team during the tremendous second-half rally they staged. In their next international, New Zealand beat Scotland 14–9. The absence of the skill of being able to pass the ball at the right time – the hallmark of Dawes' play – probably cost Scotland the match, for the Scottish centre, Renwick, fatally delayed his pass when right wing Billy Steele was running completely unmarked outside him. In the England match, it was the same story. The tourists won 9–0 and never looked like losing the match. But, on three occasions, the England backs wasted potential scoring situations when the overlap had been worked. The simple explanation was that players were unable to pass the ball correctly at the right time – the John Dawes hallmark.

The headline of the match report in *The Times* – 'England needed a Dawes among the backs' – said it all.

The reputation of British rugby was to some extent salvaged when Ireland drew 10–10 with the tourists. But the tour was a story of mounting frustration as far as the British rugby public was concerned. This All Blacks side had obvious deficiencies and they played unimaginative rugby. But the strength of their forwards, with the magnificent lineout jumping of Peter Whiting and the dominant back-row trio of Kirkpatrick, Sutherland and Wyllie, the play of Sid Going at scrum-half and the place-kicking of full-back Joe Karam, enabled them to go through these four Tests unbeaten. The tourists' midweek side had been beaten three times, but their strongest team was undefeated. It was against this background of disappointment that John Dawes, the man who led the 1971 Lions to victory in New Zealand, was summoned to lead the Barbarians against the All Blacks in the final match of the British tour.

By now Dawes was something of a legendary figure. He had retired from international rugby 18 months previously, but he was still playing well for London Welsh and at Old Deer Park he had the status of folk hero. Although now 32, there were no signs his talents were diminishing. The Barbarians were virtually a British Lions side and the match was regarded as the fifth Test match of the tour. The British public wanted to see the best New Zealand team humbled and it was in this context the Barbarians side, containing twelve of the 1971 British Lions, was chosen. The three exceptions were Phil Bennett, who was regarded as the best fly-half in Britain now that Barry John had retired, the dynamic Llanelli flanker Tom David, whose absence from the Wales team was something of a mystery, and the young Cambridge University lock, Chris Wilkinson, who had already distinguished himself against the tourists.

The Barbarians v New Zealanders match turned out to be one of the greatest games in rugby history. Carwyn James talked to the Barbarians before the match and, inspired by a capacity crowd of 51,000 singing Welsh battle hymns, John

Dawes' British Lions came to life again and the New Zealanders were simply torn apart by a brand of attacking rugby difficult to do justice to in print. The scale of the devastation was such that, at half-time the scoreboard read Barbarians 17 New Zealanders 0 and the All Blacks were simply aghast at the horror of such an experience.

After only three minutes play, the Barbarians scored as great an opening try as the game has seen. Half the team handled the ball in a 100-yard movement that demonstrated to perfection how the swift counterattack can manufacture a score from the most daunting defensive position. The move began after the New Zealand right-wing, Bryan Williams, cross-kicked deep into Barbarians territory. Phil Bennett gathered the ball 10 yards from his own line and then left three New Zealand sprawling on the ground with three rapier-like sidesteps off his right foot. Then he passed to John Williams on his left and, after being half-held in a high tackle, the Welsh full-back passed to Pullin. The English hooker then fed Dawes and the London Welshman gave the movement its incisive impact deceiving a cluster of defenders with a marvellous dummy in a surging 35-yard run up the left touchline. Dawes then delivered a perfect pass to Tom David who, in turn, fed Quinnell. Finally, it was scrum-half Gareth Edwards, seemingly coming from nowhere on the burst, taking a pass seemingly destined for wing Bevan and sprinting beyond the cover defence to score in the left-hand corner. The euphoria continued as the Barbarians added two further tries, a conversion and a penalty in a memorable first half.

It was too much to expect that such a tremendous pace could be sustained and, in the second half, the All Blacks rallied magnificently to reduce the deficit to 11–17. But towards the end of the match, the Barbarians raised their game to the heights again with a marvellous example of attacking rugby. The move started when David Duckham gathered a wayward kick and yet again set the crowd gasping as he sidestepped his way through the tourists' midfield defence and finally it was

John Williams who sidestepped past Joe Karam to score in the corner. Bennett added the conversion for what proved to be the final score 23–11.

SALUTE DAWES AND HIS LIONHEARTS
THIS WAS THE GREATEST
Daily Mail

Barbarians 23 New Zealanders 11
January 27, 1973 Cardiff Arms Park

Barbarians – JPR Williams (Wales) T); DJ Duckham (England), SJ Dawes (Wales) (Captain), CMH Gibson (Ireland), JC Bevan (Wales) (T); P Bennett (Wales) (2C, P), G Edwards (Wales) (T); RJ McLoughlin (Ireland), JV Pullin (England), AB Carmichael (Scotland); WJ McBride (Ireland), RM Wilkinson (Cambridge University); JF Slattery (Ireland), (T), DL Quinnell (Wales), T David (Llanelli)

New Zealanders – JP Karam (P); BG Williams, BJ Robertson, GB Batty (2T); IA Hurst, RE Burgess; SM Going; GJ Whiting, RA Urlich, K Lambert; HH Macdonald, PJ Whiting; AI Scown, AJ Wyllie, I Kirkpatrick (Captain)

Substitute for Going – GL Colling

Referee – MG Domercq (France)

The Barbarians had fulfilled the rugby doctrine of John Dawes even more decisively that the 1971 Lions. By swift passing, full use of the wings, the interventions of the full-back and the use of the counterattack, the Barbarians had torn gaps in a defence that had seemed extremely sound in previous months. For Dawes, his return to what was virtually international rugby was a great personal triumph. He played a vital part in three or the four Barbarians tries and the observant would have noted his qualities as a defender as well as an attacker. 'The influence of Dawes, with 11 of his old comrades in New Zealand under his command, brought into play all the generalship and wonderful timing of passes that he had showed on tour,' wrote Vivian Jenkins in *The Sunday Times*. Clem Thomas in *The Observer* simply said: 'Dawes again proved himself the finest passer and distributor of the ball in my lifetime.'

Dawes had come a long way since he played his first club game for Newbridge in 1959. His rise to fame is a remarkable story of a seemingly ordinary man accomplishing the extraordinary. Appearances can be deceptive and, meeting the man, it is difficult to realise the profound influence he has had on British rugby. A strongly built, sturdy-looking individual, he has a pleasant almost boyish-looking face, twinkling eyes and a soft-spoken voice. His clothes lack flamboyancy and he seems a pleasant-looking man with a pleasant voice and charming manner.

But beneath this façade of innocuous, John Dawes is a man with the rare gift of being able to separate the important from the unimportant. As Dick Ellis, the former London Welsh administrator, says: 'Everything is so clear-cut with Dawes. There are never any highfalutin discussions with Dawes. He simplifies everything and this is a sign of genius. He never panicked and his judgement never became warped in difficult situations. When John Dawes was playing, there were many other players who played much better because they felt they had nothing to worry about – they could leave it to John. He always had time for people and I don't think you could come across anyone more altruistic. I have never come across a chap who has found so much success and been so unaffected by it. He is the same man as he always was. I would say, without a shadow of doubt, he is the greatest rugby captain I have ever come across.'

Dawes has never been a shouter or a rouser of men by high invective. He ruled by respect. It is his qualities as a tactician and supreme ability as a reader of the game that explain his success as a leader. He inspired those around him through confidence. Players universally respect him and trust both the man and his judgements. This impression of perfection was increased by the fact Dawes remained completely calm on the field of play. Speak to rugby players and no one seems able to find fault with him. In the words of Barry John: 'I hope to Christ he has some faults – but God knows what they are!'

His ability to bring the best out of others is highlighted by the case of Barry John. John used to be known as a kicking fly-half and it was only under Dawes' leadership that his genius found full expression. Dawes knew how to handle John and the former Welsh fly-half remembers how during the Test series against New Zealand, Dawes was constantly cracking jokes with him on the field of play to ease the tension. 'I envy the players who have been able to play six years' rugby under John Dawes at London Welsh,' said John.

Dawes did not criticise top-class players when they made mistakes because he believed that any talented player knew when he was doing something wrong. He ruled by the power of suggestion – 'I think we should move the ball that way' – rather than direct command. And he was able to do this because of the instinctive trust players had in his judgements.

British rugby took a long time to make full use of Dawes' talents and his rugby philosophy. In his career, he only captained Wales in six international matches and he didn't lead the British Lions until he was 30. As the New Zealand critic Terry McLean wrote: 'For reasons totally beyond understanding, Dawes as a centre and captain took a long time to impress his countrymen, whose deputed representatives committed such idiosyncrasies as appointing Gareth Edwards and Brian Price to the captaincy of Wales when Dawes was already established as the most successful, if not the finest, club captain in the British Isles.'

The trouble was that Dawes never had the devastating break Welshmen expected of their centres. People were not astute enough to realise that this didn't matter a damn – it was an irrelevancy. They failed to see the London Welsh concept of the game evolved by Dawes, which saw centres in a completely different role.

As Dick Ellis said: 'Welshmen generally like to see a centre running down the middle of the field scoring tries. It is rather like people's attitude to cowboys. They say if you don't carry two guns, you can't be a cowboy.'

Quite apart from his talents as a leader and tactician, Dawes rated as an outstanding centre. Rugby has produced no finer passer of the ball. And it was this ability as a distributor who instinctively knew when to pass the ball that created so many tries. Dawes also scored many tries throughout his career through his ability as a support player, and there was never any doubt about his qualities as a defender. At London Welsh, they will tell you Dawes seemed to put yards on his speed to bring off crucial defensive tackles.

After his retirement from the game at the end of the 1972–73 season, Dawes was appointed London Welsh's official coach. But without his presence on the field, the Exiles stumbled through a mediocre season and it was obvious that a great era had come to an end. It was not an auspicious start to Dawes' career as an off-the-field coach. Few doubt he will continue to exert an important influence on the future of British rugby. But this has yet to be proved. In the 1973–74 winter, Dawes was appointed the coach of Wales, succeeding Clive Rowlands. Wales were clearly not the force they were when Dawes and Barry John were in the side, but now the London Welshman has the opportunity to re-establish Wales as European champions.

'The only ambition I ever had was that everyone would like to play the type of game we played at London Welsh,' says Dawes. 'And this happened. After years of criticising us, I find I get more satisfaction out of this than anything else.'

Whatever the future, Dawes' place in rugby history is assured. Britain now dominates the world rugby scene – a state of affairs that would have seemed inconceivable a decade ago. Without Dawes, it seemed doubtful that this would have happened. Many other players have made a more spectacular impression on the rugby public. But few of the game's great figures have matched the achievements of John Dawes, the quiet Welshman who enabled British rugby to end her long years in the rugby wilderness.

Ross Reyburn
Hampstead, London
1973

Postscript

(2013)

CHAPTER 1

How the 1971 Lions Changed the Rugby World

British rugby's Holy Grail still remains
winning a Test series in New Zealand.

TIME HAS NOT diminished the achievement.

The Test series victory in New Zealand by the 1971 Lions led by John Dawes ranks alongside Bobby Moore's England side winning the 1966 soccer World Cup, Martin Johnson guiding his England rugby side to their 2003 World Cup triumph in Sydney, the 2005 Ashes summer and the 2012 Olympics in the roll call of great British sporting deeds in the past 50 years.

Today British rugby's Holy Grail still remains winning a Test series in New Zealand and the measure of the sporting Everest conquered by Dawes and his fellow Lions in 1971 is reflected in the fact that four decades later they still remain the only British side to have achieved this feat in a battle that dates back to 1908. Subsequent Lions tours in 1977, 1983, 1993 and 2005 were all ultimately failures, producing a mere two wins v New Zealand in 14 Tests.

The achievement of the 1971 Lions is, in fact, unique for they are the only side in rugby history to have won a four-match Test series in New Zealand. And this record is likely to stand forever as the professionalism of the game has seen the end of the traditional long rugby tour involving as long as three months abroad. Only two other touring sides have won a Test series in New Zealand, but both those contests were of shorter duration. The legendary 1937 Springboks also lost just one tour game, defeating the All Blacks 2–1 playing three Tests, and in 1994 France won a two match series 2–0 in dramatic style with their wondrous 'Try from the End of the World' at Eden Park, Auckland, scored by full-back Jean-Luc Sadourny after winger Philippe Saint-André had started the move running a kick-ahead from his own 25.

Willie John McBride's 1974 Lions side outmatched their 1971 predecessors in result terms for they remained unbeaten, winning every tour match aside from the 13–13 draw in the fourth Test. But the 1971 party were the greatest of all Lions sides. Dawes' men beat a New Zealand team that had won 18 of their previous 21 Tests as well as defeating every provincial side they came across. The great All Blacks pack that dominated the world in the 1960s may have broken up with the retirement of The Prince of Props, Ken Gray, and the formidable try-scoring flanker Kel Tremain, while the legendary Colin 'Pinetree' Meads, the most feared rugby player of his generation, was nearing the end of his international career. But New Zealand were still a very formidable Test side on their own turf and winning every provincial game in that rugby-mad country was a phenomenal achievement. By contrast, three years later, South African rugby battered by the anti-apartheid movement was in such disarray that no less than 21 new caps played against the tourists in the four-match Test series.

Such was the state of Springbok rugby that, two years earlier in 1972, even John Pullin's England team, bottom of the 1971–72 International Championship losing all four games they played, travelled south to beat South Africa 18–9 at Ellis Park and remained unbeaten on their seven-match short tour with just a 13–13 draw against Northern Transvaal disrupting their one hundred per cent record. The forward dominated game played by McBride's 1974 Lions, coached by fellow Irishman Syd Millar, was a world away from the free-flowing rugby played by Dawes' men, despite the wealth of possession won by the 1974 forwards. To that most analytical of British rugby critics, John Reason, the 1974 tour was 'a betrayal of the traditions of British rugby with its great heritage of back play'.

There was no doubt which Lions side had the more dynamic backline. Two great backs from the 1971 tour, Gareth Edwards and JPR Williams, also starred on the 1974 tour. They were backed by some gifted players but none of the other Test backs in South Africa would have found a place in Dawes' side. Even so, such was the state of South African rugby the tourists were able to score ten tries in the four Tests despite forward domination being the basis of the tourists' game.

The 1971 Lions won 23, lost two and drew one of their 26 games, scoring 580 points with 231 against. In 1974, McBride's men boasted the more impressive record, winning 21 of their 22 games, scoring 729 points with 207 against. But, in terms of quality of opposition, the two tours were vastly different. And the try tallies backed Reason's argument that forward domination was the key feature of the 1974 tour while the 1971 Lions echoed the London Welsh attacking game. Dawes' men scored 95 tries on their tour and of these just 14 were scored by forwards. But the percentages were vastly different in South Africa where a total of 107 tries featured no less than 36 scored by forwards.

The most revealing insight into the depths the Springboks had sunk to was reflected after the Lions had won the first Test in Cape Town 12–3, when Scottish winger Billy Steele said of the match: 'It was like playing in a practice game.'

Even more dismissive were the cruel comments made by Dr Danie Craven, South Africa's Mr Rugby, presenting caps and blazers to the six new Springboks in the side at the post-match reception. In his vivid account of the tour, the *Daily Telegraph*'s rugby correspondent recalled how players of both sides were squirming with embarrassment when Craven described winger Chris Pope as 'the first Springbok ever to play for his country without touching the ball'. He said of the burly Kevin de Klerk: 'He looks like a big man here but he wasn't a big man on the field,' and on 'Boland' Coetzee's turn to be presented with his cap and blazer, he upped the insult level saying: 'He is the old man of the team and he played like one.'

Contrast this match with the epic Rorke's Drift rearguard action mounted by the 1971 Lions gaining an improbable 9–3 victory in their first Test in Dunedin. Directly compare these two celebrated Lions sides man for man and there is little doubt which is the stronger line-up. The 1971 backline was an unbroken line of great players and it is arguable that the formidable 1974 pack, which contained four 1971 Lions, was significantly superior to their predecessors.

Aside from the world-class England prop, Fran Cotton, it is difficult to think of any of the 1974 Lions newcomers that were superior to their 1971 equivalents. The Welsh winger, JJ Williams, master of the kick and chase, enjoyed a marvellous 1974 tour scoring four Test tries, but ball in hand the 1971 Lions wingers Gerald Davies, David Duckham and John Bevan were each a far more lethal threat. The Llanelli fly-half Phil Bennett was a key figure on the 1974 tour, adding three Test wins against South Africa to his key role in Llanelli's 9–3 victory, followed by that truly unforgettable display in the Barbarians win against the 1972–73 All Blacks. But he could hardly be chosen above Barry John. Captaining the 1977 Lions in New Zealand, Bennett was a shadow of the great player he was at his best, while John's 1971 New Zealand tour was a triumph. A winter of seemingly ceaseless rain on that ill-fated later tour providing the ultimate contrast to South Africa's sun-baked grounds was an awful handicap for a player possessing Bennett's gifts as a runner. But Barry John, with his masterful kicking ability, would have made good use of those conditions.

1971 Lions 9 New Zealand 3 Dunedin	1974 Lions 12 South Africa 3 Cape Town
JPR Williams (Wales)	JPR Williams (Wales)
TGR Davies (Wales)	WCC Steele (Scotland)
SJ Dawes (Wales, capt)	IR McGeechan (Scotland)
CMH Gibson (Ireland)	RA Milliken (Ireland)
JC Bevan (Wales)	JJ Williams (Wales)
B John (Wales) 2P	P Bennett (Wales) 3PG
GO Edwards (Wales)	GO Edwards (Wales) D-G
J McLauchlan (Scotland) T	J McLauchlan (Scotland)
JV Pullin (England)	RW Windsor (Wales)
JF Lynch (Ireland)	FE Cotton (England)
WD Thomas (Wales)	GL Brown (Scotland)
WJ McBride (Ireland)	WJ McBride (Ireland, capt)
PJ Dixon (England)	JF Slattery (Ireland)
TM Davies (Wales)	TM Davies (Wales)
J Taylor (Wales)	RM Uttley (England)

In his book on the 1974 tour, *The Unbeaten Lions*, John Reason derisively dismissed comparisons between the 1971 and 1974 Lions. He argued that in only one game was there a significant difference between the scores on England's short tour in 1972 and the same matches played by the Lions two years later.

'Despite the fact they had just lost all four matches in the International Championship for the first time in their history and despite the fact they were playing a better Springbok team, they achieved the same results as the Lions,' he wrote in his tour book.

'This would elevate the England team of 1972, complete with its wooden spoon, to the quite unexpected heights if the Lions team of 1974 was indeed "the greatest team in history".'

Reason's abrasive, somewhat joyless verdict on the 1974 Lions is extreme to say the least compared to the effusive tributes of other rugby writers. It is worth remembering the counter argument, for it took a formidable group of forwards to ensure not a single defeat occurred in a 22-match tour in one of the great rugby countries. Remember also England were on a short tour, playing a single Test, and winning a four-match Test series against the Springboks in their own country was a far more daunting task. The 1896 Lions are the only other touring side to have achieved this feat.

What the 1974 Lions achieved had been beyond the scope of even New Zealand, whose best effort was the 2–2 draw in the 1928 series. Twice in the 1970s they failed to match what the 1974 Lions achieved. In 1970, Brian Lochore's New Zealand team, handicapped by the fact Colin Meads in rampaging early tour form broke his forearm, lost the Test series 3–1. And it was the same scoreline in 1976 when Andy Leslie's All Blacks were deemed unfortunate to return home defeated in the Tests.

The 1974 Lions were a great touring side, but there is no doubt the 1971 Lions were the stronger side. Their tour was much more than a rugby triumph in a land where touring sides were routinely crushed by both the All Blacks and leading provincial sides. It represented the John Dawes vision of the game he had sensationally developed at club level as captain/coach with London Welsh at Old Deer Park, with its picturesque backdrop of the Chinese Pagoda in Kew Gardens, being translated successfully to the international stage in the toughest of all rugby environments. It had worldwide implications for the game, as it was also hugely influential in changing the New Zealand psyche, ultimately leading to a renaissance in back play that provided a throwback to the legendary early days of All Blacks rugby.

The first two All Blacks sides to tour Britain, Dave Gallagher's 1905–06 Originals and Cliff Porter's 1924–25 Invincibles, incredibly won all but one of their combined total of 60 games, with the sole reverse being the famous 3–0 win by Wales through winger Teddy Morgan's try at Cardiff Arms Park on December 16, 1905. And these two famous touring sides contained a host of great backs ranging from Billy Wallace,

Jimmy Hunter and Fred Roberts to Mark Nicholls, Bert Cooke and George Nepia.

Nearly 50 years later the All Blacks' supremacy was based on rather different battle lines and forward play was the key to that supremacy.

To John Dawes, the 1971 Lions tour was a Messianic journey preaching the London Welsh gospel. In rugby terms, he regarded New Zealand as foreign territory stuck in the Dark Ages, dangerously ignoring the virtues of rugby as an inspirational escape from the mundane and resorting too often to the dark arts of forward play.

More alarmingly he held the apocalyptic view that the future welfare of New Zealand rugby depended on the Lions winning the Test series. Should they fail and New Zealanders continue their slavish adherence to ten-man rugby, soccer would have far more appeal to future generations.

Etched on his memory was a school visit at New Plymouth during the 1969 Wales tour of New Zealand, when a teacher committed the ultimate heresy of berating a 12-year-old for selling an outrageous dummy and jinking past an opponent leaving him for dead rather than performing the standard drill of running into the defender and ensuring further ball for the forwards.

Recalling the incident, Dawes later told Welsh rugby writer David Parry-Jones: 'We began to clap before realizing suddenly that the master was hauling the youngster over the coals: "You will take the tackle," he howled wagging a finger under his nose, "You must take the tackle and make the ball available."'

Two years later, in 1971, Dawes was to discover this attitude was just as prevalent. In his book covering the tour, *The Victorious Lions*, John Reason recalled a clubhouse drink with Dawes in an Auckland suburb during which the Lions captain voiced his fears for the future of the game in the most rugby-mad country in the world.

'Who would want to be a back in New Zealand?' he asked.

'He is only there to stop the other side and return the ball to the forwards. They all look as if they come out of a machine.'

As a schoolmaster himself, he was a shrewd observer of changing attitudes, visiting schools in the towns they played. 'Look at the changes we have seen since we were here with Wales two years ago,' he told Reason.

'Soccer is on the increase everywhere... even schoolmasters are not supporting rugby in the way they did. And who can blame them? Rugby is this country is no fun for a schoolboy. He has no freedom of expression. He has to conform to the same dull pattern which you see right the way through the game. It is efficient, I grant you, but because it is so dull it contains the seeds of its own destruction.'

This may seem a harsh verdict in view of the fact that with ample possession in the Test series the All Blacks did try to run the ball in their backs not infrequently. But their inability to make decisive use of good ball was a damning indictment on the general standards of back play in New Zealand, in contrast to the frequently devastating displays of the gifted Lions backs defeating every New Zealand provincial side. Not for nothing was the exception, Bryan Williams, a gifted young wing three-quarter who proved a sensation on the All Blacks 1970 South Africa tour, dubbed 'The Conscience of New Zealand rugby'.

The worrying dependence on forward play and distrust of the running game and flair that was prevalent in New Zealand before the 1971 Lions brought about a sea change in philosophy, was summed up by the view of the great All Blacks flanker, Kel Tremain, after Gerald Davies had destroyed Hawke's Bay with a virtuoso four-try performance that combined elusiveness with blinding acceleration. Would Tremain have liked to have had Davies in the Hawke's Bay side he had coached? 'I'm not sure I would want him in my team,' came the bewildering reply. 'I am not sure he knows what he is doing!'

The Dawes prediction did indeed come to pass in a positive way, for that triumphant 1971 Lions tour was to convert New

Zealand coaches, players and public to the gospel of running rugby.

Among the converts was Graham Henry, later to become coach of one of the most dynamic sides in rugby history. His ultimate reward came when New Zealand again won the World Cup with an uncharacteristically dogged 8–7 victory against France at Eden Park, Auckland on October 23, 2011.

After the 1971 Lions tour, Dawes had staged a conference at the North London Polytechnic at which key members of his touring party, ranging from Dawes and the great Welsh coach Carwyn James to the Irish prop forward Ray McLoughlin, gave their views on rugby techniques, tactics, training and skills.

In 1972, Reason, who lived in Hampstead not far from the polytechnic, acting as the conference's Boswell published the results of this gathering of the men behind one of Britain's greatest sporting triumphs in a modest, slim 152-page paperback entitled *The Lions Speak*. It may have won no design awards but the publication voicing the combined wisdom of the 1971 touring party served as inspirational Bible for young coaches. Among them was 25-year-old Graham Henry.

'I wasn't the only young coach in New Zealand who seized on this book and its lessons,' Henry recalled in an interview with *Daily Telegraph* rugby writer Brendan Gallagher in 2001.

'The 1971 Lions tour was the biggest wake-up call in New Zealand rugby history.

'The Lions forwards were superbly organised and their backs were light years ahead of us. From feeling invincible in 1967, and again two years later when Wales toured, the All Blacks were suddenly a distant second. The game had moved on and changed. New Zealand rugby had to change. And we did.

'I would argue that the lessons imparted in this book provided the foundation for New Zealand's success in the 1987 World Cup, when we produced a multi-talented team with backs and forwards combining fluently and effectively.

'After '71 the coaching culture in New Zealand changed,

from the grass roots upwards – mini rugby, schools and youth. By the mid-'80s and going into the 1987 World Cup, New Zealand boasted a generation of outstanding modern-thinking, quick-witted players.

'It's a fascinating document. It represents a distillation of all that was good in British rugby during the greatest period they had ever known. You had the remarkable 1971 Lions team and very much the same players produced the definitive Barbarians performance against New Zealand in 1973. And then, a year later, the Lions destroyed the South Africans on their home patch.

'British and Irish coaches and the players set the agenda and were the cutting edge of thinking on the game. Time has rendered some sections obsolete. But some chapters are as meaningful as ever and you never tire of re-reading Carwyn.'

Interestingly Henry, talking in 2001, voiced the view that the genius of Carwyn James, as a coach who was shrewd enough to trust players rather than demanding they blindly adhered to preconceived game plans, had yet to be fully appreciated.

In a telling indictment of all those coaches who drill instinctiveness out of their charges, Henry said: 'Carwyn was on another planet – we're only just beginning to really fully embrace his philosophy. He empowered the players, trusted them, treated them as intelligent individuals.'

Sadly Carwyn James, rugby's Renaissance Man, died of a heart attack in his suite in an Amsterdam hotel in 1983 aged just 54 without ever coaching his country, due to the short-sightedness of Welsh Rugby Union officials unwilling to allow him total control of the national side.

Dawes affectionately recalled James' attributes: 'A chain-smoking, wine-drinking intellectual. A lover of classical music, a student of languages, a loner. Always well-dressed, hardly ever raised his voice, met every problem with another pack of cigarettes. In terms of planning and organisation, he was well ahead of his time. He was a motivator, but not in a drum-beating way. And he looked after his players like family.'

To defeat New Zealand at rugby motivation is a major requirement. As the late Clem Thomas, former Wales captain turned rugby writer, once commented: 'Any team which wants to triumph against the All Blacks must be prepared to die. But even that probably isn't enough.'

For a more recent insight into the scale of the feat the 1971 Lions accomplished, Brian Moore, the astute rugby critic who enjoyed a highly successful career as a combative England hooker in the Will Carling era, succinctly summed up the difficulties of achieving success in New Zealand.

In 1989 Moore was a member of the Lions side that beat Australia 2–1, but it was very different on his second Lions tour to New Zealand in 1993 when this same result was reversed.

'To understand the force of the silver fern you have to tour New Zealand and experience the unique claustrophobia that envelops international players around the time of the World Cup or the Lions tour,' Moore wrote in *The Daily Telegraph*. 'Unlike any other country on earth, rugby is in the soul of the country.'

It had not taken long for Dawes to experience this devotion to the sport in his first visit to New Zealand. The 10,000-strong crowd that had greeted the Welsh team on the balcony of the Criterion Hotel in New Plymouth in 1969 sufficed.

CHAPTER 2

The Greatest of All Rugby Tries

That 23 seconds of magic was rugby at its best.

As a young journalist and sports editor with the *Hampstead and Highgate Express*, I originally interviewed John Dawes in January 1972. At that time, Dawes was a £3,000 a year lecturer in recreational management and technical studies at the Polytechnic of North London in Kentish Town. The *Ham & High*, once memorably described as 'the only local newspaper in Britain with a foreign policy', decided to run a major feature on the man who changed the fortunes of British rugby on the Lions tour, as he had just taken up this new post in our circulation area.

Despite the considerable media interest in the 1971 Lions, Dawes was able to retain his anonymity in the capital aside from being recognised on the London Tube twice. An enterprising sub-editor headlined the article: 'The Unknown Giant of British Rugby'. As I wrote at the time: 'In Wales or New Zealand, people in the street would recognise him. But in London he is just another face in the crowd.'

Interviewing Dawes was a hugely enjoyable experience. He was a polite, immaculately mannered, unflappable character with a quietly-spoken Welsh accent.

The contact strip of shots of that interview taken by the *Ham & High* photographer all those years ago show Dawes,

153

with his rounded features, long sideburns and mop of dark hair reminiscent of the Welsh singer Tom Jones, conservatively dressed in a grey suit, white shirt and plain tie sitting arms folded on a desktop by my tape recorder in the somewhat drab room where the interview took place.

A sturdily-built figure 5ft 10in tall, he was someone with whom you felt instantly at ease. Initial impressions were not of a major figure in the world of sport. But views expressed with a quiet matter-of-fact clarity, a calm authority and no hint of arrogance left you in no doubt you were in the company of a rugby man of some vision.

I found Dawes such an impressive figure that after a publisher gave nominal backing to the project, he was good enough to let me continue interviewing him to write a book about his life and his key role as a tactician, player and leader ultimately ending New Zealand's domination of the world game.

After all the time Dawes had spent talking to me, it was a hugely disillusioning experience to find the biography I had written was rejected by a publisher who decided he was only prepared to accept an autobiography. So my manuscript remained in a folder untouched for four decades, as I was not willing to turn what I considered a balanced assessment of the achievements of Dawes and the sides he led so successfully into a personalised ghost-written account that by definition could not offer a truly objective assessment of the man and his life.

Although much older and in theory wiser, re-reading what I wrote some 40 years ago I was surprised to find nothing of any great significance I would change.

However, in retrospect, there is much I could have added to the narrative. For example, I could have emphasised the fact that it was a myth to think the famed 1971 Lions backline played a dominating attacking role throughout the series.

True, the Lions played some wondrous attacking rugby while losing the second Test, and their breathtaking display in the opening quarter of the third Test proved the decisive moment in the series. But it could be argued that the Lions could have ended the series putting the New Zealand defence to the sword in the final Test. The reality was that the All Blacks proved more adventurous that day. It was the home side, urged on by a capacity crowd of 56,000 at Eden Park, Auckland, anxious to avoid the unthinkable reality of a series defeat, which managed the final score of the game that levelled the match at 14–14. The score came via a Laurie Mains penalty goal after an act of gamesmanship involving a dummy run from a scrum that trapped the English back-row forward Peter Dixon offside. But it was the Lions, in their famous red jerseys, who dominated the final quarter of the game against the men in black. 'We had to win the series' was tour manager Doug Smith's verdict after the Lions fly-half Barry John was criticised for failing to pass the ball in promising situations some thirteen times.

Undoubtedly, it was a missed opportunity, for how many sides have New Zealand on the rack in a Test on their home soil? But Dawes commanded no change of direction as the Lions unsuccessfully resorted to the boot to pen their opponents in their own half and claim victory. Barry John narrowly hooked a 51-yard penalty wide of the posts and in the closing stages of the game both John and Edwards failed to land drop-kick attempts.

If the All Blacks had been ahead, instead of the scores being level, and the tourists faced the prospect of their potential triumph being downgraded into a drawn Test series, no doubt it would have been very different and the Lions would have put their foot down on the attacking accelerator, turning that final period when the field was theirs into points rather than seeking victory through kicking. But human nature being what it is there was a distinct air of end-of-tour malaise for the Lions as the minutes passed by nearer and nearer to that final whistle and a rugby Valhalla mission was accomplished. As Dawes acknowledged in David Parry-Jones' book *The Dawes Decades*: 'On that day we lacked spark... our half-backs both dropped for goal when scoring passes, in particular to Duckham, could have been given... that wouldn't have happened when the Test rubber stood at one-all. However it was not just those two, the whole team lacked the urgent desire to win.' Of course, the point was the Lions didn't have to win.

In 1996, twenty-five years later, in a television documentary recalling the tour, the great Welsh winger Gerald Davies, attacker supreme in a Lions backline of stellar ability and scorer of three tries in the Test series, was to voice with obvious mournful regret that the game at Auckland was a missed opportunity. 'Sadly,' he said, 'it became a close affair in the end, so close that it was only a draw we came away with instead of a convincing farewell victory of generous proportions... we should have accomplished that.'

Great though their attacking ability was with ball in hand, the all-round qualities of the Lions backs also had a crucial bearing on the series, viz. Barry John's masterful kicking in the first Test at Fergie McCormick's expense.

John's somewhat surreal ability to deceive opponents with ball in hand may have caught the eye, but he was also one of the game's great kickers. In 16 tour games in New Zealand, he blew apart previous Lions scoring records totalling 183 points, including 30 in the Test series. Ironically, he only became the side's main place-kicker by accident. Asked to kick to touch by Dawes from a mud-patch in the centre of the field while playing New South Wales in the Lions 14–12 win in the second match of the tour, John instead went with his intuitive nature and decided to have a kick at goal as his captain turned his back on him to rejoin his other backs. And, to everyone's surprise, he landed the kick. This left no doubt as to his capability as a place-kicker on either side of the field, and so he was instantly promoted to be the side's main penalty taker, unless the English full-back Bob Hiller, with his masterly orthodox style, was in the same side.

John's remarkable tour tally of 30 conversions, 26 penalties and eight dropped-goals, as well as six tries in New Zealand, came in the days when rugby was played with a leather ball that soaked up water in wet conditions, distorting its performance. John's success ratio was nowhere near matching the modern masters of the art of place-kicking, such as England's Jonny Wilkinson, New Zealand's Dan Carter or Wales's Neil Jenkins. While converting 30 tries, he missed 13 conversion attempts and, by modern standards, his penalty kicking was distinctly average with 25 misses in 51 attempts. Remember, though, the advantages today's players enjoy using laminated balls with dimpled surfaces and kicking tees which have made the art of place-kicking that much easier.

The defensive qualities of the Lions players were also a key feature in the series, notably in the first Test when the tourists survived wave upon wave of All Blacks attacks. Admittedly, in the second Test, New Zealand, inspired by a dynamic running performance by scrum-half Sid Going, decisively unlocked the Lions defence scoring four tries, but two of these tries came after JPR Williams, one of rugby's greatest defensive players, uncharacteristically missed two vital tackles. The explanation was that he was playing on after being concussed. In the final Test the speedy English winger, David Duckham, played a decisive role in securing the series victory with many try-saving tackles. The fact that the back play the Lions were capable of did not surface throughout the Test series does not change the fact that the 1971 tourists deserve legendary status for the way they captured the imagination of New Zealanders with their attacking play. Previously, the strongest provincial sides had daunting win records against touring sides but Dawes' men remarkably won all 20 of their encounters outside Tests.

Their 47–9 demolition of Wellington was rugby for the Gods that sent shock waves through New Zealand. The length-of-the-field try against Hawke's Bay, started by JPR Williams, and which gave the inspirational winger Gerald Davies one of his four scores, symbolised the heights this touring backline were capable of reaching. And the way Barry John ghosted his way through a New Zealand Universities' defence expecting the

Welsh fly-half to attempt a drop-kick at goal, was an uncanny act of elusiveness that left the crowd in a state of stunned silent disbelief.

So great was the public interest aroused by these popular tourists that some 750,000 spectators, in a country with a population of 2.8 million, paid to see their 24 matches.

My original biography also failed to pay due tribute to the coaching genius of Carwyn James. How many other coaches would have viewed the seemingly decisive second Test defeat as a game that offered the evidence that the Lions would win the series provided they negated the running threat posed by dynamic All Black scrum-half, Sid Going?

Carwyn also deserves praise for providing the tour's most amusing anecdote. Barry John avoided an arduous four-mile training run as the Lions prepared for the crucial third Test against the All Blacks by hiding in a wood and hitching a lift on a lorry filled with orange crates. Unfortunately he was spotted jumping from the lorry by a New Zealand journalist who thought he was in scoop territory.

How, he asked, was Lions coach Carwyn James going to discipline the team's main playmaker? What was his view of this flagrant act of disobedience?

'Well,' replied the masterful chain-smoking Welsh coach, aware of John's ankle trouble, puffing on a cigarette before turning on his heel and departing, 'I call it initiative.'

In a long tour, it is difficult to recall any serious misjudgements made by Dawes or James. True, Dawes arguably missed the chance of a memorable tour finale by not unleashing his backline at full throttle in the closing stages of the fourth Test. And Carwyn James had ignored logic in the provincial matches by misguidedly thinking the London Welsh lock forward Mike Roberts could be converted into an effective prop handling the intricacies of front row forward play. But these two decisions had no significant effect marring the success of the tour.

Dr Doug Smith, the third member of the hugely impressive

triumvirate running the tour, proved a master at baffling the media.

Smith, known as 'The Oracle of Orsett' after the Essex village where he practised as a GP, was seemingly equipped with uncanny predictive powers that could have bankrupted bookmakers. Did anyone really believe his outrageous assertion that the Lions would win the New Zealand Test series 2–1 with the other match drawn? Hell, didn't the man realise that from 1904, the Lions had played 20 tests on New Zealand soil and won two, just two, of these encounters in 1930 (6–3) and 1959 (9–6) and in each case the winning margin was a mere three points?

Less outrageously, but just as correctly, he also believed the Lions would lose their opening tour match against lowly Queensland. Why? 'Circadian dysrhythmia,' was Smith's explanation. This was translated for the benefit of baffled journalists as 'jet lag', for the game was being played just 48 hours after the party's arrival in Australia.

Later in the tour, Smith left New Zealand pressmen in a state of minor mental disarray with his unexplained but worrying assertion that the All Blacks were going to field 'a weak link' in their Test side. Their talisman Colin Meads, who was recovering from injured ribs, was a possible explanation but this was cleverly unacknowledged by the canny Smith.

The unity of the tour party could also have been dealt with in more detail. This was reflected in their frequent renderings of 'Sloop John B', the sea shanty that was a popular hit for the American West Coast group, The Beach Boys, which was adapted as the team theme song with Wales wing forward John Taylor as choirmaster. There was also the unlikely alliance of Chico Hopkins, the cheeky chappy from the Welsh valleys, with the urbane Londoner, Harlequins and England full-back Bob Hiller as the tour party's main comic double act.

Posterity has forgotten that Hopkins played an important part in the first Test defensive victory, for early in the game he replaced scrum-half Gareth Edwards, who had taken the field with thigh muscles jarred in training. Hiller also had a crucial tour role scoring 102 points, mainly through his mastery of the art of goal-kicking by the traditional toe-kicking method as opposed to John's round-the-corner style, which did much to ensure the formidable target of ensuring the tour's fixtures outside the Tests in New Zealand were won. Such was his kicking skill that, during the 39–6 win against West Coast and Buller (in which his England colleague Duckham scored six tries), he said he was too tired to run behind the posts while scoring a try of his own and so added the conversion from the touchline in far from ideal conditions.

The influence of the 1971 Lions on the rugby world did not end with the tour to New Zealand. In January 1973, the Dawes vision reached its ultimate pinnacle in his memorable farewell on the international stage when he and his fellow Lions reunited as the Barbarians, taking the field against the New Zealanders once more but this time on home ground.

In all but name this game was a fifth Test match for Ian Kirkpatrick's 1972–73 tourists. Disappointingly, from British rugby's viewpoint, the tourists had remained unbeaten playing the four Home Countries, beating Wales with no Dawes 19–16, England 9–0 and Scotland 14–9 with just a 10–10 draw against Ireland disrupting their winning record. But when the Barbarians selected a side captained by Dawes with eleven other 1971 Lions in their ranks, Kirkpatrick must have realised a battle royal beckoned.

Superficially, the amateur ethos of the Baa-Baas prevailed before the game. Dawes, who was now merely playing for London Welsh having retired from Test rugby after the Lions tour, received a telephone call the Sunday before the game. 'Can you play for the Barbarians against the All Blacks on Saturday?' said the voice at the other end of the phone. 'Oh yeah, and will you be captain as well?'

Dawes accepted the offer the following day. But the Barbarians management, paying undue heed to the game's amateur status, were not that keen to grant Dawes his wish that the coaching genius Carwyn James should be involved in the match preparations. Not only had James masterminded the 1971 Lions' triumph off the field but earlier in the tour, on October 31, 1972, he had guided his club Llanelli, in their centenary year, to a famous 9–3 win against the All Blacks at a Stradey Park packed with 28,000 spectators. Played beneath leaden skies, this match was no running carnival, for it was the rugby equivalent of a Roman Colosseum life and death struggle with fists and boots flying too often for comfort. The match's sole try was scored by centre Roy Bergiers charging down a clearance kick after a Bennett penalty had hit the crossbar, and the game was won by the passionate home side stopping the All Blacks in their tracks, halting their familiar back of the lineout drives and trademark rucks.

Welsh balladeer, Max Boyce, immortalised the victory with his song '9–3', writing:

> The shops were closed like Sunday and the streets were silent still,
> And those who chose to stay away were either dead or ill,
> But those who went to Stradey Park will remember 'till they die,
> How New Zealand were defeated and how the pubs ran dry.

From a New Zealand perspective, the defeat evoked a rather different emotional intensity. In his book on the tour, *The Winter Men*, Auckland-born writer, Wallace Reyburn, wrote:

> There is a look that comes over the face of touring All Blacks in the course of a match when it starts to become clear they are going to be beaten. It's not just disappointment. It is the look of shame that they have let their country down.
> I remember most vividly seeing it at Swansea in 1935 because it was the first time I had ever seen it. After a run of 36 victories here [in Britain] this was this new side going down 11–3 to Swansea... And again there was that look on the faces of these Seventh All Blacks as Andy Hill put over a 50-yard penalty to take Llanelli into the final minutes with a lead which there seemed no chance of wresting from a team playing like demons, urged on by a crowd so fervid that for these young new tourists Stradey Park reeked of

animosity. It was the Lions' coach Carwyn James, of course, who
was the architect of this triumph.

Come the morning of the Barbarians v All Blacks game
three months later on January 27, no Carwyn had been seen,
and the training sessions the team had held at Penarth RFC
during the week were little more than a reunion runaround for
the 1971 Lions joined by Wales fly-half Phil Bennett, his fellow
countryman the dynamic back-row forward Tommy David and
the uncapped English second-row forward Bob Wilkinson, who
had acquitted himself well playing for Cambridge University
against the tourists.

But at the eleventh hour, James did play a brief but key
role in the match build-up. Dawes invited the great man to his
hotel room at 11am for a coffee on match morning. 'Lo and
behold, when he walked in the whole of the team happened to
be jammed into that small room!' Dawes recalled.

His call to arms for the reincarnation of the 1971 Lions, with
him shaking every team-member's hand, proved inspirational.
The England winger, David Duckham, remembers Carwyn
asking him to repeat his deeds on the Lions tour with the words:
'Do it again, do it again for me.' And his advice to Phil Bennett,
the man with the daunting task of replacing the retired Barry
John in a Lions backline, proved prophetic: 'Go out and show
the world what Stradey knows. You can sidestep this lot off the
park.'

The judgement of Dawes in his playing days was rarely
widely off-target but an exception was his assertion, unwisely
voiced on the 1969 Wales tour, that given enough ball British
backs were capable of beating New Zealand by 30 points. No
one has ever even come near fulfilling that fantasy even in
the modern era of high-scoring matches – the New Zealand
Test side has never been a weak tackling unit whatever its
limitations and the All Blacks just don't lose by this margin.
The biggest defeat suffered by the New Zealanders in their
entire history of more than 400 Test matches was the 21-point

battering they suffered losing to Australia 28–7 in Sydney in 1999.

That afternoon in Cardiff the 1971 Lions were reborn as the Barbarians defeated the All Blacks 23–11 in one of the most memorable games in rugby history. It may have been a 12-point victory for the Barbarians, but the result could have been very different if the All Blacks captain, Ian Kirkpatrick, who had scored that sensational 70-yard try against the 1971 Lions at Christchurch, had not knocked-on with the tryline at his mercy. The Barbarians may have blitzed the tourists with that staggering opening try and been 17–0 ahead at half-time but Kirkpatrick's error cost his team what no doubt would have been a converted try levelling the scores during his side's impressive second-half comeback that saw the terrier-like wing Grant Batty scoring two fine tries.

However, that memorable afternoon in Cardiff the Barbarians backs did produce the ultimate attacking game Dawes always believed was possible against rugby's most formidable nation, and the crowd was treated to the rare sight of All Black defenders being continually beaten. The fact that the final victory margin was by no means vast was really a tribute to the resolve of the tourists refusing to be submerged by what was thrown at them.

This match will forever be remembered for what is regarded as the greatest of all rugby union tries. Climaxed by that turbo-charged sprint by Gareth Edwards along the left touchline when the game was only four minutes old, the seven-man move started with Phil Bennett racing back, picking up a well-directed kick-ahead from the New Zealand winger Bryan Williams, and turning around near his own line to produce three mind-blowing sidesteps that left three All Blacks grasping at thin air. Has there ever been a greater instant act of elusiveness in the game's top flight?

The 23 seconds of magic this created was rugby at its best. It elevated the game beyond a mere physical contact battle to a poetic level with flair, imagination and intuitiveness holding sway above the drawing board. In the words of Carwyn James writing in *The Guardian* after the match: 'You play at a level outside the conscious when everything is instinctive and sport achieves an art form. The try was a demonstration of a game at that almost super-conscious level.'

Appropriately, considering their country provided the major contribution to the success of both the Lions and Barbarians against the All Blacks, six of the seven involved in THE TRY were Welsh. And also, fittingly, it was the England hooker Pullin who, in his own words, 'gatecrashed the Welsh party'. His own record against the southern hemisphere giants even outmatched that of Dawes himself, for by the end of his impressive career he had captained England to home and away wins against South Africa, beaten Australia and also led his country to a national side's ultimate prize, a win against New Zealand at Auckland, as well as featuring in every 1971 Lions Test and the great Barbarians victory.

The Gloucestershire farmer's offbeat take on the Edwards try, provided for a *Daily Telegraph* article saluting the 40th anniversary of the game's 'greatest every try', is worth repeating:

> Phil Bennett got the ball and ran up his own backside and got lost as usual. He threw a typical hospital pass to JPR, who got a high tackle. I shouted for the ball – if he had seen it was me he probably wouldn't have given it to me.

And he added movingly in case anyone was deceived by his flippancy: 'In all seriousness, it was incredible. I've got the DVD but never watch it. Every second is seared on my mind forever.'

Pullin's England colleague, David Duckham, was equally in awe of what happened, saying of that climatic final Edwards run to the tryline: 'Gareth took the ball at full pace and not even a brick wall would have stopped him.'

The celebrated former Wales fly-half Cliff Morgan, who

later enjoyed a highly successful career in broadcasting, was behind the microphone for the television commentary as Bill McLaren was ill. The crowd singing 'Sosban Fach' and the All Blacks reviving their haka war dance indicated this was no ordinary game and, as Dawes led his side onto the field, Morgan paid a prophetic tribute to the London Welsh player with the words: 'Here [comes] the Barbarians captain John Dawes, the man who guided the destiny of the 1971 [Lions] side, a tactical genius, a man of immense talent, a superbly balanced player.'

Then a few minutes later came his famous commentary on the Edwards try:

> Kirkpatrick to Williams. This is great stuff. Phil Bennett covering, chased by Alistair Scown... Brilliant. Oh, that's brilliant... John Williams. Bryan Williams... Pullin. John Dawes. Great dummy. David, Tom David... The halfway line... Brilliant by Quinnell... This is Gareth Edwards. A dramatic start. What a score! Oh that fellow Edwards. Who can stop a man like that?
>
> If the greatest writer of the written word would have written that story, no one would have believed it.

Fittingly it was John Dawes himself who gave the move its vital impetus with that 30-yard break out of the Barbarians 25. The 'great dummy' hailed by Morgan was more an act of legerdemain than a feigned pass to winger Bevan on his left. His body language suggested he was about to pass to his powerful wing colleague and that amounted to a significant act of deception. As Derek Quinnell observed: 'Sydney John [Dawes] was known as a passer and everybody probably expected him to give it, so that "dummy" was probably him not passing straight away before he handed on to Tommy... We were beginning to rock and roll.'

Dawes himself recalled: 'I intended to put John Bevan clear but all of a sudden they [the All Blacks] disappeared. I wasn't conscious of doing anything although perhaps shaping slightly to pass to the left before I passed to Tommy [David].

Was it a dummy? If Cliff Morgan says it was a dummy, it was a dummy!'

No great euphoria amongst the players greeted the score. Edwards walked back to the halfway line alone, aside from Irish flanker Fergus Slattery giving him a quick tug on the shoulder as he arose from the ground after his touchdown dive, and Tom David briefly tapping his hand as they passed by each other. But the crowd left Edwards in no doubt what had been achieved: 'I remember then, going back [after scoring], this depth of sound. It's not up there in the stands, it's on top of you. I knew by the reaction of the crowd something special had happened.'

The game also saw the England winger David Duckham heeding Carwyn James' request by ripping the All Blacks defence apart with two devastating counterattacking runs as he carved his way through the opposing midfield. His last surge ultimately resulted in the wonderful final Barbarian try which featured superb support play from players from all four Home Countries in a 100-yard movement that was climaxed by JPR Williams sidestepping his way past full-back Joe Karam to the tryline. And the Welsh crowd gave the man from across the border the ultimate accolade, rechristening him 'Dai' Duckham.

Dawes and JPR Williams were the only two members of the London Welsh quintet who were key figures in the 1971 Test series on the field for the Barbarians. To their eternal regret, the injured winger Gerald Davies and No. 8 Mervyn Davies, laid low with a heavy cold, watched this magical display of attacking rugby from the stands. And 150 miles away in London, John Taylor was also absent but far from unfit, for he was playing for London Welsh in a RFU Club Knockout tie, scoring 15 points in his side's 22–7 win against London Scottish at the Richmond Athletic Ground. He was ruled out of the Cardiff encounter, as a Barbarians official displaying a laughable example of establishment political incorrectness, had decided the flanker could not play for the famous rugby club with the black and white hooped shirts after branding him a communist due to his anti-apartheid stance following his experiences on the 1968 Lions tour of South Africa.

Back in the real world, Dawes' theory that sublime back play could destroy New Zealand in scoreboard terms did not come to pass. Nevertheless Dawes' farewell to the international stage that afternoon was the ultimate vindication of the game he had developed at London Welsh.

Later he recalled this match as the best game of rugby he ever played in, not only because of his side's performance but also due to the attacking rugby played by the All Blacks that brought them back into the contest in the second half. 'The most remarkable thing about it to me was that I was part of a three-quarter line which never dropped the ball all afternoon. No fumbles, no stray passes, no knock-ons.'

CHAPTER 3

Dawes' Post-playing Career

'New Zealand did not win this Test series. We lost it.'

MY 1973 NARRATIVE did have the advantage of solely concentrating on Dawes' playing career with a welcome sense of immediacy as the Welshman was vividly recalling a rugby era in which his involvement as player at Test level had just ended.

It is an account that avoids being sidetracked by Dawes' post-playing career with its mixed results. As coach of Wales from 1974 to 1979, he had an impressive record, overseeing the national side as it won four successive Triple Crowns and two Grand Slams under his guidance in what was termed Wales' Third Golden Era which had begun with his own 1970–71 Grand Slam leading Wales on the field. Aside from Barry John, who decided to retire from rugby when only 27, Dawes was reunited with his Welsh Lions stars in his coaching role. His fellow London Welsh, Wales and Lions colleague, Mervyn Davies, was to captain his country with distinction with Dawes as national coach, while gifted newcomers included forwards Terry Cobner and the famed Pontypool front row, Graham Price, Bobby Windsor and Charlie Faulkner, plus the speedster JJ Williams in the backs.

But the success he had as a player against the All Blacks, three wins, two draws and three losses in eight encounters, was not to be repeated in his role as a coach. The Wales side he guided off the field for much of the 1970s failed to the halt his country's 'win' drought against the All Blacks and his return to New Zealand as coach of the 1977 Lions ultimately proved 'the one big regret' of his rugby career and a miserable contrast to the glories of 1971.

In 'The Bad News Tour', saddled with the most appalling weather conditions in a winter of seemingly ceaseless rain, the tourists also faced a hostile New Zealand press and public acutely worried that their national side might lose another series to the Lions. Unwisely, the tourists' management adopted a siege mentality after some lurid tabloid-style press coverage of their off-the-field activities had the Lions described as 'Lousy Lovers' and 'Louts and Animals'.

On paper the tour was far from a failure for, remarkably considering historical precedents, the Lions forwards outplayed their opponents and 21 of the 26 tour games were won. And these tourists matched the considerable achievement of their 1971 predecessors by winning every provincial game, although they surprisingly lost their match against New Zealand Universities 21–9. But from both a managerial and playing point of the view, the trip proved an unhappy contrast to 1971 as the forwards' superiority should have ensured a series victory.

The All Blacks were hardly short of quality forwards with men of the calibre of Tane Norton, Andy Haden, Ian Kirkpatrick and Graham Mourie to call on. But they were outplayed by the Lions forwards with their front row of Fran Cotton, Peter Wheeler and Graham Price, Gordon Brown and Bill Beaumont in the second row and a wealth of gifted back-row forwards in Willie Duggan, Terry Cobner, Derek Quinnell, Trefor Evans and Tony Neary. But forward supremacy failed to win the series as the Lions were beaten 16–12 in the first Test, won the second 13–9 and lost the third and fourth Tests 19–7 and 10–9.

Significantly, the large Welsh contingent in the tour party failed to match the deeds of their predecessors six years earlier.

Although Terry Cobner proved an inspirational pack leader, the tour captain, Welsh fly-half Phil Bennett, on rain-soaked surfaces, was unable to repeat his devastating form shown in the 1973 Barbarians game and the 1974 Lions tour of South Africa. High on the New Zealanders 'revenge' list, as the man who had played a key role in the famous Llanelli and Barbarians victories against the 1972–73 All Blacks, by the end of the tour Bennett was a demoralised figure, targeted by tacklers, and was unable to get the best out of a backline that scored just two tries in the Tests, and severely suffered from the Welsh trait for homesickness. It would have been a very different tour had the obvious candidate to lead the Lions, the successful Wales captain and great No. 8 Mervyn Davies, returned to the scene of his 1971 triumph, but sadly his playing career had ended when he suffered a brain haemorrhage during the Swansea v Pontypool Welsh Cup semi-final at Cardiff in 1976.

The Lions forwards dominated their opponents to such an extent that in the fourth Test the All Blacks eventually surrendered the scrum battle opting for a three-man scrum. But while they were outplayed, they were not out-thought as they disrupted their opponents placing their back row out in the backs.

Off the field Dawes' relations with the media, including former 1971 Lions colleagues covering the tour, turned distinctly sour. He also had the heavy disappointment of watching a backline he was ultimately responsible for as coach squander game situations that should have provided the Lions with more than a single Test victory.

Sadly Dawes' leadership and tactical skills as a player on the 1971 Lions tour were not so evident when he returned to New Zealand as coach of the 1977 Lions. Ironically his old personal Valhalla of gaining decent possession against the All Blacks was more than fulfilled but the backs were unable to take advantage of this forward supremacy.

In his 2009 autobiography, *Lion Man*, the Scottish centre,

Ian McGeechan, later to become one of the great Lions coaches, recalled his experience as a player on the ill-fated tour. He had a damning verdict on Dawes as a coach in New Zealand:

> He talked mostly in generalities, but he was never specific about what he wanted. He would sometimes call, quite gently, for "quick hands". But it was no more than a slogan. Before long, the backs had made up their minds to go off on their own and work on things.
> Perhaps John, a natural player and leader in his time, was just not so good at putting things across; perhaps in his heart he was telling himself that this '77 lot were not as good as the '71 team, that we couldn't do what they did then. I got the feeling there was a kind of "Oh well, I'll tell you this bit but you're not good enough to execute it" attitude about it all.

New Zealand veteran rugby journalist Terry McLean starkly highlighted the contrast between Dawes the player in 1971 and Dawes the coach in 1977 writing: 'John Dawes, of London Welsh, had looked ideal as captain and supportive midfield back, superb in judgement and timing of passes, with the great Lions side of 1971. Now he was revealed as a man of bitter attitudes.'

This volte-face on McLean's part, with the denigrating 'had looked' qualification assessing the Dawes of 1971 vintage, is somewhat extreme. True, the John Dawes portrayed by McGeechan and McLean in 1977 was a very different man from the quietly assured, approachable character I had interviewed five years earlier as his playing career was ending. In his early days with London Welsh when defeat was the norm, Dawes learnt from the gifted full-back Haydn Davies that 'the most important thing was to enjoy your rugby'. But there was little enjoyment on the 1977 tour and the calm authority that characterised Dawes' playing career seems to have deserted him.

In Dawes' defence it is worth pointing out that being an outstanding leader on the field of play, where you can have a direct influence on events, is a totally different discipline to coaching a side off the field.

At London Welsh, serving as both the club's captain and coach, this potential problem did not exist. As Gerald Davies, recalling his days at London Welsh in his 1979 autobiography, entitled simply, *Gerald Davies*, wrote:

> John Dawes had a perceptive eye on the essentials of coaching, he knew how to conduct training sessions, he knew what he wanted of his team and, at the same time, because he played, he had the sensitivity of a player.
>
> He knew ultimately his men's strengths and weaknesses and especially he knew the on-field pressures. Quite often a coach, sitting in the stands and looking objectively on the game, may not be fully aware of the problems on the field of play. Even a player who becomes a coach after his playing days are over can quite easily forget what it is actually like in the heat of action. This is why it is so essential that the captain has a strong rapport with the coach. With John Dawes as coach and captain the discrepancy did not exist... John Dawes also had, and this was one of his strongest points, a broad vision of how the game should be played.

In 1977 Dawes suffered the ultimate frustration. It is not hard to imagine the mental anguish Dawes, master of when to deliver a pass, must have endured when the Lions, 12–10 ahead in the first Test just before half-time, committed the ultimate heresy of squandering a three-man overlap and seemingly certain try. Worse followed, for the crucial misplaced pass from flanker Trefor Evans was intercepted by the impressive All Black wing, Grant Batty, who raced away to score what proved to be the match-winning try. Thus, the Lions were left trailing 12–16 when they should have been 18–10 ahead and this proved the final score.

There seems little doubt the series would have been won if the Dawes of the 1971 vintage had been captaining the 1977 Lions in the Tests. The reality was that Phil Bennett was not suited to the tour captaincy role. After the Lions lost the third

Test, he apologised to his forwards for kicking and passing 'like a novice' and later recalled: 'I felt a failure as captain and would willingly have given the responsibility to someone else at that stage.' And his tendency to crab across the pitch severely hampered the options available to the backline. This was a problem Dawes the coach didn't resolve and, taking the obvious but uncomfortable step of dropping the tour captain from the Test side and replacing him with the other gifted Welsh fly-half in the tour party, Aberavon's John Bevan, a player skilled at making best use of his three-quarter line, was a step too far for the tour management. With the fourth Test nearing the final whistle with the Lions winning 9–6, Bennett's disastrous tour reached its unhappy climax when he failed to find touch with an attempted clearance kick, instead sending the ball into the hands of Bill Osborne in midfield. The All Blacks centre then kicked ahead and in the defensive chaos that followed, No. 8 Lawrie Knight took advantage of a loose ball and a lucky bounce to score the try that deprived the Lions of the victory which would have drawn the series 2–2.

The bitter disappointment Dawes experienced that winter returning to the scene of his 1971 triumph was summed up by his view: 'New Zealand did not win this Test series. We lost it.' And this was a justified statement because the Lions, with their domination in the final Test, should have secured victory and had the touring party leaving New Zealand with honours even.

In the 1980s, Dawes was to spend a decade as the Welsh Rugby Union's coaching organiser, trying to create a framework to halt what proved a severe decline in Welsh rugby fortunes. Saddled with office duties that were not his forte, he also had the problem of contending with the inadequacies of the WRU administrative machine. When the next decade arrived Dawes, at the age of 50, found he was without a job after the Union's coaching committee asked for his resignation.

The unhappy end of his role with the WRU was not the only disappointment suffered by Dawes, for his decision to move back to his homeland from London to serve the Welsh rugby cause had resulted in the end of his marriage also.

However the highs and lows he was to experience in later life should not deflect from the fact that Dawes' deeds during his playing career alone justify his place among rugby's greatest figures.

Dawes was a success as coach of his country when Wales dominated the European rugby scene in the 1970s. And his relative failure as 1977 Lions coach should not diminish his great achievements during his playing career. It is almost like those who sagely bemoan the fact that the great American actor/director Orson Welles in his subsequent life was unable to match the brilliance of what he achieved with *Citizen Kane*. Whatever people's views on his later life, and it was hardly a failure, Welles was a genius who at the age of 26 happened to produce what many have rated the greatest film ever made.

Three decades after Dawes' triumph in New Zealand, Clive Woodward coached an England side captained by Martin Johnson to one of the most remarkable feats in rugby history, achieving 12 successive victories against the southern hemisphere giants, New Zealand, South Africa and Australia. This incredible sequence reached its climax on November 22, 2003, at the Telstra Stadium, Sydney, when England beat Australia 20–17 to win the Rugby World Cup after that famous extra-time dropped-goal by Jonny Wilkinson.

This England triumph has been one example of consistent northern hemisphere supremacy since the Dawes era. The southern hemisphere has not had everything its own way since the 1970s. Will Carling's England's side could well have won the 1991 Rugby World Cup final at Twickenham had it showed more tactical acumen and left the game's destiny in the hands of its superior pack rather than losing the game 12–6 trying to run the ball with previously under-employed backs. France went to New Zealand in 1994 winning the Test series 2–0, knocked New Zealand out of the 1999 and 2007 Rugby World Cups and were within a single score of preventing the All Blacks winning the 2011 Rugby World Cup final in Auckland, 8–7.

But Martin Johnson's England side could claim to be the best side in the world for several years, with a sequence that started with a 27–22 victory against South Africa in Bloemfontein on June 24, 2000 and ended as 2003 world champions. They may have lacked the flair displayed by the men Dawes commanded against the All Blacks, but no other Home Union side has come anywhere near matching this incredible sequence of victories over the game's giants. In pure rugby result terms, what Johnson and Woodward achieved outstripped the achievements of Dawes and Carwyn James. But that England sequence included just one game on New Zealand soil and didn't match the inspirational quality of the sides guided by Dawes. When the London Welsh, Wales, Lions and Barbarians teams he led turned on the afterburners, it was rugby for the Gods.

Woodward's post-Rugby World Cup return visits Down Under proved failures on a scale far beyond what happened with the '77 Lions who were, in all probability, just a decent touch-kick away from drawing the Test series 2–2 against the All Blacks and won every game against provincial sides that regularly claimed tourists' scalps. In 2004, England, with their inspirational captain Johnson and other key Rugby World Cup players retired, were hammered in New Zealand, losing the two Tests, 36–3 in Dunedin and 36–12 in Auckland. They were also slaughtered 51–15 by Australia in Brisbane. Then, far worse followed, when Woodward presided over a 3–0 series humiliation on the disastrous 2005 Lions tour to New Zealand. Should those subsequent failures be allowed to diminish Woodward's achievements masterminding an unprecedented sequence of victories against the major southern hemisphere rugby nations? It is also worth pointing out that unlike Woodward, Dawes in 1977 was in a different role compared to his 1971 and 1973 triumphs against the All Blacks, as he could no longer influence events as a player and captain. Greatness is not necessarily transferable from one discipline to another as is all too often evident in the world of sport. In the final judgment, Dawes, used to coaching an inspirational Welsh national team that virtually selected itself, was unable to master the far greater demands of the ultimate coaching challenge handling a Lions tour. In the most daunting of rugby environments with a winter of rain conspiring against his vision of how the game should be played, he was outmaneuvered by All Blacks coach Jack Gleeson.

CHAPTER 4

The Legacy of the Dawes Era

Brick wall rugby, substitutes galore and the gym
have limited appeal in the rugby philosophy of John Dawes.

IN THE WORLD of sport the past may be regarded as a foreign country by many, but the achievements of the 1971 Lions led by Dawes should not be forgotten.

Anyone who doubts the epic nature of this sporting odyssey in the Land of the Long White Cloud against the men aptly christened The Unsmiling Giants would do well to read *Lions Rampant* (1971), the classic account of the tour by the late Sir Terry McLean. Written in McLean's own distinctive idiosyncratic style, it deserves a place in any list of great sportsbooks and one has to go back to Denis Lalanne's *The Great Fight of the French XV*, memorably recording France's highly emotive 1958 triumph in South Africa, to recall a rugby tour book written with the same verve.

Some may regard McLean's assertion that you could 'almost hear' wingers benefiting from a Dawes wonder pass exultantly crying 'I gotta yard, I gotta yard, not all God's chillun gotta yard!' as somewhat over the top in Hunter S Thompson mode. But no rugby critic has summed up the understated genius of John Dawes better than McLean in that 1971 verdict unclouded by his later reassessment of the Welshman as coach of the 1977 Lions.

'It is impossible to recall an action, on the field or off it, which could have suggested he was momentarily out of control,' McLean wrote. He also highlighted Dawes' off-the-field qualities. At the end of the tour, twenty-four hours after the final Test, the Lions had promised to attend an afternoon party at Northcote Rugby Club in Auckland, centred on a meal cooked in traditional Maori fashion for touring teams. When departure time arrived at the hotel foyer, no Lions were to be seen to go to the function. But when told of the situation, Dawes said: 'Leave it to me' and gathered together some eighteen Lions to be conveyed to the party. 'That was Dawes,' recorded McLean. 'The Quiet One who got things done.'

The 1971 tour has retained its legendary aura. Interestingly, the highlight of Dawes' ultimate triumph with the 1973 Barbarians is regularly viewed by thousands, thanks to the wonders of the Internet. A clip of the BBC's film of the incredible Gareth Edwards try has been viewed more than 2.7 million times since it was posted on YouTube in 2006. Remember the game took place in the old Cardiff Arms Park, echoing to the sound of the Welsh battle hymns. It is easy to forget the devotion to rugby heroes of the past in south Wales. I can recall being told by my father, when he was covering the 1967 All Blacks tour, that he was guided to the hallowed spot on the Arms Park turf where winger Teddy Morgan scored his famous winning try inflicting the sole tour defeat on the formidable 1905 All Blacks.

By contrast, the various YouTube clips of the famous Geoff Hurst crossbar goal in the England football team's 1996 World Cup final win against West Germany, total around a million views despite soccer being England's main national sport. And the most popular posting of the famous Jonny Wilkinson drop-goal that won the Rugby World Cup for England in Sydney in 2003 has around 170,000 views, nowhere near the figure for the most celebrated of all rugby union tries.

The achievements of the 1971 Lions provides an example of the potential value of being aware of the past. Other spheres have shown that you can pay a heavy price for ignoring history. How different would the Western world be today if Hitler had acknowledged the futility of trying to conquer a country as vast as Russia with its inhospitable winter inhabited by a population seemingly immune to fear, as had Napolean? Would British troops have gone to Afghanistan if Tony Blair had heeded the lessons of the past? Didn't these illustrate that no one wins wars invading Afghanistan, something demonstrated by the recent Russian failure, and Britain disastrously losing not one but two Afghan Wars in the Victorian era.

Transferred to the world of sport, the value of history might seem largely irrelevant. But the 1971 Lions tour did illustrate that the virtues of rugby union, at its best, could be translated into a template to eradicate the more worrying downsides of modern rugby in the professional era.

Back in 1971 rugby union was an amateur sport but the Lions were virtually in a professional environment on their three-month tour of Australasia. In Doug Smith they had a manager who masterfully ensured they were not overburdened with functions and visits, who was also well capable of handling media pressures and was an accomplished after-dinner speaker. And in coach Carwyn James and the tour captain John Dawes, they had two incomparable readers of the game – one off the field and the other on the field – with the intellect to handle any potential tour problems.

This trio provided an object lesson in how to run a successful rugby tour worthy of translation into the professional era. But it was a lesson that came to be ignored with damning results in some instances, as coaches were given the financial leeway to do more or less as they wished in the pursuit of success in the years following the game's transition into a sport where leading players came to be paid far from insubstantial sums.

Contrast the simplicity and clarity of direction in 1971 with Clive Woodward's disastrous 2005 Lions tour, when the man who managed England's 2003 World Cup win headed to New Zealand with a ridiculous army of 26 backup staff.

Woodward's men, described as the best prepared Lions party ever assembled, were decisively outplayed, being beaten 21–3 in Christchurch, 48–18 in Wellington and 38–19 in Auckland in the final match of the three-Test series. Neither were they over impressive in their non-Test match fixtures, generally played against second-rate opposition compared to the full-strength provincial sides the 1971 Lions played and defeated.

This 2005 tour provided the ultimate debasement of rugby's old amateur ethos when Alastair Campbell, former spin doctor of Labour Prime Minister Tony Blair, was taken on tour as PR chief, parading around in a Lions tracksuit and doing his best to deflect attention from the on-the-field drubbings suffered in the Test matches.

Such was Dawes' own disillusionment with what he witnessed on the 2005 Lions tour that he thought Woodward's rugby philosophy could have had damaging implications for the future of the game, had the tour been a success.

'I was over there, actually, with the London Welsh rugby club choir,' he recalled. 'I shouldn't say that I was glad they lost but I was, because what Woodward seemed to be doing was against the whole tradition of Lions rugby: too many people, the way he selected teams, the itinerary, the whole spirit of it. And I felt that had he won, that could have become the norm.'

Interestingly, many thought the British and Irish Lions would be discarded as an out-of-date concept when rugby's professional era dawned in 1995, but their appeal has become greater than ever. The 2005 New Zealand tour saw Lions merchandise sales exceed 800,000 and incredibly this total included some 500,000 replica shirts. Even Real Madrid football club could not match these figures. After the hugely disappointing 2005 tour, the 2009 Lions tour to South Africa, with much-admired Lions veteran Ian McGeechan as chief coach and Dawes' old London Welsh, Wales and Lions comrade-in-arms Gerald Davies as manager, was hugely successful. An engrossing Test series saw the Lions narrowly defeated 2–1, with a return to old values eradicating the many unhappy memories of the 2005 tour. Such was the interest in the series that an estimated 50,000 British and Irish fans travelled to South Africa at various stages of the tour to see the Lions play.

What happened in 1971 not only changed New Zealand rugby for the better at the time. There are still lessons worth absorbing today. True, in many respects modern rugby can be viewed as superior to what was on view 40 years ago. For a start, the more violent aspects of the then amateur game have been largely, although not entirely, eradicated with the ten-minute sin bin and highly sophisticated camera coverage of games. In the fourth Test of the 1971 tour, Scottish lock Gordon Brown was knocked down by a lineout punch that split his right eyebrow, delivered by his opposite number schoolteacher Peter Whiting. The incident happened in front of John Pring, the New Zealand referee the Lions were happy to have handling all four Tests. Whiting remained on the field, as did Jas Muller, despite the front-row forward more than once blatantly kicking grounded Lions players. Today both players would have been sent off the field permanently with a red card. Had the referee or linesmen been unsighted, cameras would no doubt have caught these misdeeds and resulted in lengthy citing bans from playing the game.

Giving referees an effective alternative to the draconian penalty of sending a player off the field permanently has done wonders for rugby. The sin bin has greatly eased decision-making for officials, as they can now dismiss players from the field for ten minutes for minor acts of foul play and consistent penalty offences without ruining the match as a contest. Football's problems may be rather different but why hasn't professional soccer, contaminated by its widespread abuse of referees by players and its misguided tolerance of 'industrial language', adopted rugby's sin bin remains a mystery. Would soccer players swear at referees or packs of players dispute decisions – behaviour that sets an appalling example and is mimicked at grass roots level – if they knew it would mean they would be sent off the field for ten minutes?

Today the rugby's lawmakers, to their credit, have also transformed the lineout. It was such a shambles in Dawes' day that the Lions resorted to illegal tactics throughout the tour to counter New Zealand's skilled expertise in abusing the laws of the game in this area. Today, with lifting allowed, it has become less of a contest for possession, and you wonder what would happen if there was a return to straight jumping with forwards barred from physically confronting opponents until the ball was won. But at least the modern lineout is a clear-cut, quickly executed battle for possession.

However on the downside, the efforts by administrators and referees to ensure matches are free-flowing encounters with ball in hand have eradicated some of the game's finer skills by making rugby union more like rugby league, where players are constantly running into their opponents.

The electrifying back play of the 1971 Lions and the All Blacks forwards' inborn mastery of the ruck, offered inspirational examples of the rugby union game at its best. But today referees have made these two ideals less obtainable as rugby has become more and more a game of intense physical contact, with collision running rather than evasion becoming more prevalent. Brick wall rugby, substitutes galore and the gym may feature heavily in the modern rugby professional's life but they have limited appeal in the rugby philosophy of John Dawes. Asked for his views in an interview with *Independent* newspaper sports writer Brian Viner in 2006, he gave a perceptive verdict on the modern game stating:

> Since professionalism there has been an influx of rugby league influence and I find it unbelievable to see the players lined up across the field. You see a group of players fighting for the ball supposedly in a ruck or a maul, and outside them there's a six, a seven, an eight, a one, two or three. Not a back amongst them.
>
> Whereas professionalism has produced bigger, faster, stronger players, it hasn't improved the skill factor at all.

The misconception pervades that having the ball continually in play, as happens for most rugby league matches, makes the game more interesting. The reality is that the opposite can be the case, with too much emphasis on power and car crash tactics involving full-frontal contact with opponents, and teams retaining possession by monotonously, endlessly recycling the ball in phase after phase, making minimal forward progress sometimes for literally minutes.

Compare the average size of the 1971 Lions with the vital statistics of players in a modern Test side and the considerably widened gap emphasises how bulk and the gym have assumed increased importance. Whether this is progress is debatable, because the way modern rugby is refereed and played tactically has blurred the distinctive roles of forwards and backs, undermining rugby's rich heritage as a sport for a variety of sizes. Only four of the 32 members of the 1971 tour party weighed more than 16 stone. Today many backs weigh more than the majority of the 1971 Lions forwards.

Rugby union's undue respect for its less popular rival code has been to its detriment as the two games merge closer in outlook. Rugby league is a sport that fields some magnificent athletes – Will Carling's England side might well have won the Rugby World Cup in 1991 if the great Wigan trio of Ellery Hanley, Shaun Edwards and Martin Offiah had been in union colours. But it is a game without the complexities of the union code with its lineouts and meaningful scrums. For those in favour of the constant motion found in the 13-man game, it is worth asking the question that if rugby league is such a great sport why are relatively few people interested in the game? League only has a major following in Australia and the north of England (frequent attempts to colonise London have failed) and a mere three international sides, Australia, Great Britain and New Zealand, inhabit the game's top tier despite the fact that the game was created as a breakaway from rugby union in 1895 in the Victorian era.

For evidence of the relatively limited appeal of rugby league, just look at World Cup audience statistics. The 2007 Rugby Union World Cup hosted by France attracted 2.25 million spectators, an average match attendance of 47,000 across the 48 tournament matches. By contrast, in 2008, the Rugby League World Cup staged in the League code's heartland, Australia, attracted 290,000 spectators with the 18 fixtures averaging a 16,331 crowd. The global television audience for the League tournament as a whole was estimated at 19.2 million. By contrast, a single game in the 2007 Union World Cup – South Africa's 15–6 win against England in the final – was watched by 80,000 spectators at the Stade de France in Paris and attracted a worldwide audience of 33 million.

Ironically, the efforts of lawmakers to keep the game flowing have had the reverse effect and rugby union in the northern hemisphere, in many respects, has become a cumbersome version of rugby league. Top-flight referees with International Rugby Board approval, blatantly ignoring the law saying scrum-halves have to put in the ball straight, have turned scrums into chaotic pushing contests rather than a route to quick ball. Sadly this has significantly diluted the scrum as a battle enjoyed by that distinctive species, the front row union living in a world only they can fully understand. Is there another sport where officials are encouraged to turn such a blatant blind eye to the rule book?

Generally, today, the ball may be in play for long periods on the field but the breakdown and the tackle area have become a refereeing nightmare. It is hardly stimulating watching forwards engaged in tedious pile-ups. The object is to run directly into an opponent for the ball to be recycled, and all too often players remain unpenalised by over lenient referees for failing to release the ball immediately. This gives the team in possession a huge advantage as it has become increasingly difficult to secure possession with a turnover.

The 2013 Six Nations tournament was a largely disappointing spectacle, with games being shorn of creativity by collapsing scrums being re-set and the ball continually being lost from sight among forwards engaged in possession phases that in the past would be regarded as pile-ups warranting penalties.

These trends are the antithesis of the free-flowing London Welsh style masterminded by Dawes which was to have a worldwide influence in the 1970s. 'What the game has developed into now is physicality,' said Dawes, speaking in his Cardiff home after Wales had memorably won the 2013 Six Nations. 'In my day the backs were never considered physical – they were the prima donnas.

'These days the first thing you look at in a player is how big he is, how strong he is. This is best exemplified by the current Welsh team that has just won the Six Nations – their back division is huge.

'You don't see the ball go down the line from set pieces. When did you last see the top of the lineout ball go straight down the line to the wing?

'They don't see a scrum or a lineout as a means of scoring. All the teams have pace but they don't use it. It is not their priority. They move the ball after X phases and X phases means physicality.

'You have to have four or five pile-ups before you score a try. What you see is just a mess.

'With a ruck you could see the ball on the floor and the forwards were pushing over it, binding together much like a scrum. A maul was the same except the ball was in the hands. Nowadays it's a pile-up. You would be penalised in our day for a pile-up. But now they just dive in, jumping on each other. I can't understand how the referee allows it. It's a mess and it should be tidied up.

'Where the game has become a little more dangerous is in the size of people. There is more emphasis on fitness and weight training. Playing the game as physically as they do now, injuries will increase and I think that's happening.

'I find it a bit sad. What I'd like to see is someone take it on, and movement of the ball. The laws haven't changed. They have the same amount of forwards in the scrum, the distance between three-quarter lines is the same. I would return to straight put-ins and the ruck and the maul as they used to be.'

The role of the coach has dramatically changed since Dawes' day when coaching was in its infancy.

'When we were playing, the game was for the players, about the players. Now the game is totally dominated by the coach and his team. If you pass it out to the wing from a set piece, you get into a row with the coach. If you do it twice you are dropped!

'I don't think Carwyn James ever told me how to play. We just talked. It was just a natural relationship. Carwyn did a lot of consultation, far more than coaches would these days. He would sit down at dinner with a player and have what you and I would call a chat. He was a listener rather than a teller. He would glean a lot from talking to Barry or Gareth.

'He would select guys for a particular skill. If they perform that skill you are happy. If they don't you have to think why. It is a selection rather than a coaching problem.'

Dawes also feels the current problems involving scrums need to be resolved.

'These days they don't even strike for the ball in scrums. You don't get one against the head unless a scrum is out-shoved.

'The other thing is replacements. The front row battle used to be determined in the last twenty minutes of a match. There was a degree of pride between who won that battle. But now, with substitutes, when that period comes they take players off. It's a different game.'

Rugby's clear division between backs and forwards has been severely undermined by the fact that open spaces are now continually inhabited by forwards spread across the field to provide sequences of recycled ball. How often do you see modern sides matching the speed of the 1971 Lions and Welsh sides of the 1970s, passing the ball across the field to set their wingers free?

In 1971, Dawes' Lions side in the second Test at Christchurch were at the receiving end of a classic example of how hooking skill could counter being out-shoved. While the Lions forwards were driving the All Blacks pack back yards, New Zealand were scoring a blindside corner try through the ever-dangerous scrum-half Sid Going, after his forwards produced a quick heel despite being out-shoved.

The physicality of the modern game has also concerned Dawes' rugby contemporaries. In his autobiography, *Shadow*, the much-admired Wales back row forward, Dai Morris, a mineworker who was one of the finest products of the hard school of Welsh valleys rugby despite being just 13 stone, described how modern rugby, with players taking out rather than flooring opponents in a tackle, is like 'American football without the padding'.

The legendary Lions forward, Willie John McBride, a big man in every sense of the word, speaking to a Birmingham sporting lunch as the 2012–13 British season ended, said of modern rugby: 'It's all about big men bulking up. I know kids of 16 or 17 who are a funny shape. It concerns me. The human body is being asked to take something it is not built to take.'

The fact that the skill/brawn factor in rugby union has become out of kilter has attracted considerable media criticism. *Daily Telegraph* rugby columnist and television match analyst, Brian Moore, an outstanding England hooker in his playing days, has waged a high-profile crusade for years against officialdom ruining the traditional rugby scrum. He views the modern scrum as dangerous because top referees are ignoring the straight put-in law and turning scrums into a frequently chaotic shoving contest as players try to outmanoeuvre rivals, often illegally.

'Because of the demise of proper hooking, most beaten packs cannot find a way to resist annihilation,' he has said.

'When scrums were refereed properly and there was a skill to hooking, it was always possible for the ball to be struck quickly into channel one. Any modern players unaware of this now mythical passage should ask their grandfathers.'

Sunday Times rugby correspondent Stephen Jones is equally withering in his condemnation of the way the IRB encourages referees to blatantly ignore the laws of the game. After watching Harlequins win their Aviva Premiership match 23–9 against Bath at The Stoop on April 14, 2013, before a 14,326 crowd, he wrote:

> I calculated that from 18 scrums, the ball emerged for play to continue four times. All the other scrums ended in a penalty, a free kick or a reset. It was a ghastly affair – a crabbing, cheating mass, beyond frustration and for a professional sport deeply embarrassing.
>
> The culprits? None were present at The Stoop. The scrum has been a disaster for years, chiefly because the International Rugby Board has disgracefully allowed referees to ignore the law. Instead of ensuring that the referee penalises pushing before the ball is put in and the blatantly crooked feed, the IRB has allowed the game to invent a range of other offences to stop play.

Despite these reservations, rugby union's appeal in the professional era has been ever increasing. Traditionally, internationals have always attracted full grounds with club rugby a relatively minor attraction in spectator terms compared to football. But this has vastly changed, notably in England, Ireland and France. On March 31, 2012, a world record crowd of 83,761 for a club rugby match watched Harlequins beat Saracens 24–19 in England's Premiership Leauge at Wembley. The previous record was the 82,208 audience witnessing Leinster defeat Munster 24–6 in a Heineken Cup semi-final at Croke Park in Dublin on May 2, 2009. Twickenham has also had more than 80,000 for a club Premiership match, while French club rugby has attracted crowds of more than 79,000 at the Stade de France in Paris.

Long gone from rugby union are the dreary, low-scoring games that characterised the 1950s and 1960s, and you no longer see matches dominated by safety first touch kicking. Modern rugby finds teams in their own 22 often prefer running the ball from defensive scrums or lineouts through their forwards, rather than escaping downfield by kicking away possession to the other side.

Backline skills remain a key element of the game, as was shown when Wales won the 2013 Six Nations title inflicting a devastating 30–3 defeat on Chris Robshaw's England side. Key moments in the match showed that while the game may have changed much since the 1970s, the art of catching and passing a rugby ball effectively remains as important as ever. Twice, when the game was theoretically in the balance, England's bulldozing outside centre Manu Tuilagi – whose running and passing had destroyed the All Blacks backline in December – squandered golden try-scoring chances. Firstly, while running into the Welsh 22 he dropped a pass when faced with a huge inviting gap and no opponent marking him. Later, he ignored a glaring overlap, running straight into a tackle rather than passing the ball. Then came the game's most skilful act of 'centre play', when flanker Justin Tipuric created Alex Cuthbert's second try by deceiving an English defender with a dummy before delivering a perfectly judged pass to the huge winger outside him.

It wouldn't take that much imagination for the lawmakers controlling the game to ensure referees enforce the traditional values of the scrum as a contest. This would allow the return of the ruck and the maul so that backline skills, rather than brute force, have a higher priority. Forwards spending more time on the game's coalface would leave more space on the field. And the dominance of forwards, who are fitter than ever, could be further reduced by simply extending game time from 80 minutes to football's 90 minutes of play, limiting substitute numbers, or stopping the match clock when penalties are awarded until the ball is in play again.

John Dawes was a key figure in what arguably ranks as the greatest back division in rugby union history. It is true that the buccaneering 1955 Lions backline, with Welsh fly-half Cliff Morgan, England centre Jeff Butterfield and the Irish teenage wing Tony O'Reilly, scored seven Test tries. And that the gifted 1959 Lions backs, with England's mesmeric running genius Peter Jackson on one wing and the record breaking O'Reilly on the other wing, scored nine series tries compared to the four scored by Dawes' fellow backs against New Zealand. But they didn't win the series, whereas the 1971 Lions achieved a historic victory that has remained unequalled.

That 1971 Lions backline was unique in the fact that all its seven members – half-backs Gareth Edwards and Barry John, centres Mike Gibson and John Dawes, wingers Gerald Davies and David Duckham and full-back JPR Williams – were indisputably great players. And their defensive qualities and the kicking ability of Barry John added to their attacking prowess – all were important factors in the series victory.

The team's best performances, and their reunion as the 1973 Barbarians side, serve as a reminder of rugby union at its best. Today's lawmakers would do well to ensure that features of the game then are not lost.

CHAPTER 5

Dawes' Place in Rugby History

Remember also he had no easy path to fame.

JOHN DAWES SHOULD be remembered not just as tactician and leader. Just note how many times overlaps in the modern game are squandered because players adopt the wrong running lines, or fail to pass the ball correctly or at the right time, and you realise why Dawes' unmatched ambidextrous skill as a pass master justified his rating as a great player. How many modern players do you see taking and passing the ball accurately in one motion? In action he had neither the Rolls-Royce grace of England centre Jeremy Guscott nor the seemingly ceaseless, highly productive energy in attack and defence of the great Irish centre Brian O'Driscoll. By contrast Dawes was the quiet man with the pass that created scoring opportunities for others, while he was also a superb defender, putting to good use his strong physique honed in the hard school of valleys rugby. But it was his qualities as a leader that enabled those around him to fulfil their potential, translating his visionary attacking rugby style into a reality.

Dawes had exceptional, gifted players in his ranks when his playing career reached its memorable climax. But that was no sure guarantee of success. It was not only dynamic wingers such as Maurice Richards, Gerald Davies and David Duckham who realised their potential with Dawes in midfield. On the

1969 Welsh tour of New Zealand, despite the high praise in advance publicity, Gareth Edwards and Barry John made little impact. John was then regarded as predominantly a kicking fly-half and it was only later that he realised his full potential, earning the nickname 'The King'. Edwards also achieved greatness under Dawes' leadership of Wales, the Lions and the Barbarians.

When the 1972–73 All Blacks toured Britain there was a telling tribute to Dawes as the result of a game he never even took part in. That winter England were beaten 9–0 at Twickenham by the tourists in a match of squandered try-scoring opportunities by the home side. And, as I recalled in my original manuscript, *The Times* headline over the newspaper's match report read: 'England needed a Dawes among the backs'. Scotland, being beaten 14–9, could also have done with Dawes in midfield, as the Scottish centre Jim Renwick squandered a certain try by fatally delaying his pass to the unmarked winger Billy Steele poised outside him for an uninterrupted run to the tryline from halfway. More surprisingly Wales, with their much vaunted side on home ground, were unable to down the tourists, losing 16–19 with Dawes absent, despite dominating the latter stages of the match. Finally, the tourists remained unbeaten playing the Home Union countries in Tests, drawing 10–10 with Ireland in a game they would have lost if the wind had not deflected a Barry McGann conversion off target after winger Tom Grace won a touchdown race by kicking over full-back Joe Karam's head. Thus, it was left to the former Lions leader to return as captain of the Barbarians to provide the massed choirs at Cardiff Arms Park with the victory they craved against the men in black.

Remember also that Dawes had no easy path to fame. When he became captain of London Welsh in the winter of 1965–66, he was in charge of a mediocre rugby club. But from these humble beginnings he was adventurous enough to adopt a concept of rugby that revolved around skill rather than brawn, something that was regarded by many as laughable in a sport of often intense physical demands. And even when he established the Exiles as the most glamorous rugby club in Britain, excitingly highlighting the value of the swift counterattack from defence and the full-back creating overlaps, the Welsh selectors for years failed to realise the significance of the smoke signals coming out of Old Deer Park. They were to prove long overdue in giving him a free reign as captain of his country, a move that resulted in five successive victories heralding what came to be revered as another Golden Era for Welsh rugby.

No doubt, the fact that Dawes has been an unobtrusive character has contributed to the odd state of affairs in which he is a largely unremembered today outside Wales, aside from London's oasis of Welsh rugby nationalism at Old Deer Park where he justly remains an exalted figure.

But, the achievements of the sides he led are far from forgotten. When the 2011 Rugby World Cup was being staged in New Zealand, BBC Wales screened a memorably evocative hour-long documentary titled *The Lions – New Zealand 1971*, narrated by *Guardian* rugby writer Eddie Butler, with some dazzling footage of the Lions backs putting the All Blacks and the country's leading provincial sides to the sword.

The Rugby World Cup may have been reaching its climax when the film was screened but, in a masterful witty tribute to the documentary, fellow *Guardian* writer Martin Kelner wrote of 'a week when the best rugby action was 40 years old' with those 'magical black and white images of Barry John, Gareth Edwards, Mike Gibson, Gerald Davies et al. in full attacking flow'.

In the column neatly headlined 'When New Zealand hosted fantasy rugby', Kelner viewed the great Lions coach Carwyn James as very much the hero of the story: 'James was way ahead of his time in that amateur era, studying professional coaching methods at Manchester United and also at Wigan rugby league club – which may have been punishable by death at the time.'

In his intriguing narrative Eddie Butler ('mysteriously

rechristened Edward Butler in the credits' observed Kelner) paid a memorable tribute to James. 'Complex Carwyn,' said the former Welsh international, 'brought simplicity to rugby: weapon of choice, the brain.'

Oddly, while the playing footage revealed to the observant Dawes' gifts as a player, scant homage was paid to the man who ultimately deserves the main credit for the sea change in British rugby's fortunes in the early 1970s.

The Lions success was not backtracked to its origins at Old Deer Park. Fittingly there were no less than seven London Welsh players in the tour party – Dawes and fellow key players in the Test series, Gerald Davies, JPR Williams, Mervyn Davies and John Taylor plus Mike Roberts and late replacement Geoff Evans.

As the tour film illustrated, British rugby's debt to John Dawes has been all too easily forgotten while his more flamboyant contemporaries remain revered. This reality was amusingly highlighted by Mark Reason, son of the most perceptive British writer covering the 1971 odyssey, in an article on the greatest Lions players in which he wrote: 'John Dawes, the Welshman who captained the Lions in 1971, was almost a mythical person. It would be no great surprise to find out that he actually didn't exist.'

John Dawes did very much more than exist. It was his generalship that enabled Wales to achieve their memorable last-ditch 19–18 win against Scotland in Murrayfield in February 1971, the Lions to gain an improbable 9–3 first Test victory at Dunedin against New Zealand with a heroic defensive effort that would have been beyond most teams in June 1971, and destroy the All Blacks in a memorable opening quarter of the third Test at Wellington the following month. Then, finally, it was he who guided his Lions side, reunited as the Barbarians, to that famous victory against the Seventh All Blacks in Cardiff in January 1973. Superior firepower alone is no guarantee of success – it has to be used effectively. For the benefit of those who believe great players alone are enough to win Tests, Terry

McLean neatly summed up the qualities of Dawes the captain and player with the verdict that his unflappable presence was 'absolutely essential' for the supremely talented Lions backline to function at its best.

Many Welshmen may regard the view as heresy, but the reality is that John Dawes is a more important figure in rugby history terms than Welsh legends such as Gareth Edwards, Barry John, Gerald Davies, JPR Williams and Mervyn Davies.

There has been a minor avalanche of books on the achievements of the Welsh sides of the 1970s after Dawes retired from Test rugby. But what Dawes achieved with the 1971 British Lions and the 1973 Barbarians was more significant than what followed in the 1970s when he coached Wales. And the 1970–71 Welsh side he led to his country's first Grand Slam for 19 years was arguably the best of all Welsh sides in that decade because, unlike the later tournament-winning Welsh sides, it contained not only Dawes but also the rugby magician Barry John.

The Welsh produced some wonderful sides dominating European rugby in that era, playing with flair that captured the imagination of the public. In terms of excitement, they were rugby union's equivalent of the Brazilian football team. But the Five Nations tournament was no reliable barometer of greatness. There is some truth in Brian Moore's somewhat cruel observation that the Welsh can be 'emotionally incontinent' celebrating their rugby triumphs. The Wales national sides of the 1970s weren't world beaters but this didn't prevent David Tossell, an Englishman caught up in the adulation, writing *Nobody Beats Us – The Inside Story of the 1970s Welsh Team*. This book title, borrowing the New Zealand observation 'Nobody beats Wales – you just score more points than they do', neatly captured the charisma of the Welsh sides of the 1970s.

The reality was that while their rugby was something to behold, their record against southern hemisphere sides was in fact a disappointment. After Dawes retired from Test rugby following the Lions tour, Wales played the All Blacks three times on home turf in 1972, 1974 and 1978, losing every game. They beat a weak Australia convincingly at Cardiff 24–0 in 1973 and 28–3 in 1975, but touring Down Under in 1978 they were beaten 18–8 and 19–17 in the two Tests against the Wallabies. In 1970 they had begun the decade by keeping intact the Welsh record of never beating South Africa, by drawing 6–6 in the mud at Cardiff.

Poor old England, routinely humbled by Wales throughout most of the decade had, in fact, a far more impressive record against southern hemisphere nations in that era. In December 1969, on a dry day at Twickenham, John Pullin's side, with the hooker himself dropping on the ball for a crucial try, beat the South African touring side 11–8. Wales later drew with the tourists 6–6. As already mentioned, not only did Pullin feature in all the 1971 Lions Tests and the 1973 Barbarians triumph against the New Zealanders, but his remarkable sequence of featuring in wins against the southern hemisphere giants continued when he led England, in June 1972, to an 18–9 victory against South Africa in Johannesburg. And then on another short tour in September 1973, Pullin's men sensationally beat New Zealand 16–10 in Auckland. Wales may have been the glamorous European side, making headline news throughout the 1970s, but in their entire history they have never beaten New Zealand or South Africa when these two great rugby nations have had home advantage.

That elusive Wales victory against New Zealand, last achieved in 1953, was the one great benchmark missing from Welsh rugby's Golden Era in the 1970s. Three times they played the All Blacks on home ground at Cardiff Arms Park backed by their Welsh choral legions and thrice they fell (1972: 16–19, 1974: 3–12 and 1978: 12–13). But although the Welsh team were surprisingly subdued in the 1974 match that was somewhat oddly deemed an unofficial Test, they could well have won the other two encounters.

In 1972 the All Blacks, with just 83 Test caps compared to the 227 Welsh and Lions caps in the Wales team, needed all their gamesmanship ploys to survive a heavy attacking onslaught by a Welsh side fielding eight 1971 Lions. As Wallace Reyburn recalled in *The Winter Men*, Wales were 'going like a bomb', roared on by the crowd in the second half and 'The All Blacks seemed to have no answer but obstruction and late tackles'. Fast-forward to the present era and the persistent illegal tactics the tourists used to prevent the Welsh scoring tries that afternoon would have, in all probability, justly resulted in sin bin penalties that would have ensured a Wales victory.

In the 1978 Test, the somewhat unsavoury gamesmanship tactics the All Blacks were quite prepared to resort to when a match was in the balance were again in evidence. Graham Mourie's tourists won the match with a nervelessly-taken late Brian McKechnie penalty, while the crowd raged after All Black locks, Frank Oliver and Andy Haden, had taken Hollywood dives out of a lineout, a facet of play in which they had been consistently out-jumped by the Welsh. It was little consolation that the English referee, Roger Quittenton, later pointed out that Geoff Wheel placing his hand on Oliver's shoulder, rather than the theatricals staged by two All Blacks, was the reason for the penalty.

Nevertheless, the Six Nations, or Five Nations as it was during Welsh rugby's Golden Era in the 1970s, ranks as the best of all rugby tournaments. Its huge appeal is demonstrated by the fact that every Test is invariably a sell-out and the good-natured rivalry among national supporters when legions of away fans make their annual rugby pilgrimages to London, Cardiff, Edinburgh, Dublin, Paris and Rome testifies to the sense of comradeship evoked by the sport. Its popularity has been unmatched by the southern hemisphere's equivalent, the Tri Nations (now the Rugby Championship with the inclusion of Argentina), and even the Rugby World Cup has failed to equal its appeal as a spectacle and social event.

Anyone who has experienced the Six Nations regularly has happy memories of the spirit of the tournament. Inevitably rugby club quotas of tickets never satisfy the demand. In

1970, scrum-half Chico Hopkins replaced the injured Gareth Edwards to inspire a memorable 17–13 victory at Twickenham after England seemingly were heading for a certain win. Twenty minutes before kick-off I was without a ticket standing among thousands queuing to get into the ground asking somewhat optimistically: 'Has anyone got a spare ticket?' I was offered a South Terrace ticket that gave me a grandstand view of the Hopkins tour de force by a kindly elderly Welshman from the valleys who simply asked if I was a rugby player. Before the arrival of corporate hospitality, invariably one could spend the lunchtime before the game among rugby followers at the atmospheric White Cross Hotel pub, with its distinctive huge Georgian windows picturesquely placed alongside the Thames in Richmond, and find a party of friends with a spare ticket after one of their number had failed to make it on time. And no one would dream of asking a penny more than the price on the ticket. Sadly, times have changed, with professionalism and the increased commercialisation of the sport lowering the ticket numbers available to genuine rugby followers. Not that long ago, my brother and I were offered £500 for our two tickets for an England v France match as we dashed towards the entrance gate as kick-off neared. The logical explanation for this desperate last-ditch hunt for match tickets was a corporate hospitality package promising more than it could deliver.

The good-natured exchanges between rival fans, who never have to be separated watching the game, remain in the mind. Most of the Twickenham international crowd would no doubt fail the breathalyser test, but no one need fear for their own safety in a rugby crowd. In decades of viewing Twickenham internationals, I can only remember one relatively trivial example of yobbish crowd behaviour that verged on the violent. A few feet from where I was standing watching an England v Scotland match before Twickenham became an all-seater stadium, a spectator threw an empty beer can at a steward. The can missed its target but the culprit was told, 'You're not at Millwall now', as those nearby turned on him.

Another vivid recollection was a Tube journey back into central London after Carling's England had slaughtered Wales 34–6 at Twickenham in 1990. I found England supporters happily singing the lyrically-challenged football chant 'Here we go, here we go' and inviting some neighbouring Welsh lads to join in. 'Sorry, boyo, don't know the words' was the reply. And then an admiring silence enveloped the compartment as the group of Welsh youngsters, too young to have seen Gareth, Barry, JPR or Gerald in their heyday, movingly sang 'Bread of Heaven'.

After the Five Nations turned into the Six Nations with Italy's entry in 2000, rugby supporters had the enjoyable prospect of a weekend in Rome to watch a rugby Test. A friend who travelled with fellow Saracens members to the Italian capital to witness the first Italy v England game in the tournament recalled how, while among a large crowd of English supporters cheerfully consuming great amounts of alcohol in a city square, they were faced with a line of Italian policemen stationed to prevent any trouble. My friend decided to have a friendly chat with the inspector in charge. 'You don't have to be here you know; there'll be no trouble. We're not football fans,' he told him. And back came the reply: 'I anno that, you anno that, but we're onna double time!'

In the 1970s on the field of play in the Five Nations, Wales were the flair side that captured the imagination, producing some unforgettable passages of play: a memorable Gerald Davies try, when the great winger in a thrilling, arcing run outflanked the Scottish defence and a superbly struck John Taylor conversion from out wide labelled 'the greatest conversion since St Paul' as Dawes led Wales to the Grand Slam in Murrayfield in the 1970–71 season; the stunning Gareth Edwards kick and chase try against Scotland at Cardiff Arms Park in 1972 when he broke at full throttle from his 25, prompting BBC commentator Bill McLaren to excitedly tell viewers: 'It'll be a miracle if he scores'; the unprecedented try by prop Graham Price after he finally collected the ball after a run of 75 yards when Wales, coached by Dawes in the Five Nations for the first time, fielded six new caps and a new captain in Mervyn Davies beat France 25–10 in Paris in the 1974–75 season ; the shuddering, match-winning shoulder charge by JPR Williams that bundled French winger Gourdon over the touchline as he was about to score a corner try in the 1975–76 Grand Slam season when Wales beat the Tricolours 19–13 in Cardiff; and, when Wales again won another Triple Crown in the 1976–77 winter, that imperious try against Scotland at Murrayfield that ended with Bennett sidestepping his way to the posts after JPR Williams has started a counterattack in his own 25.

However, the ultimate judgement is that Wales, in a wonderful era for Welsh rugby and with home advantage, fielded a host of gifted individuals and an impressive quota of great players, yet could not get the better of the men in black. Tellingly, it was only with Dawes as their leader for the Lions and the Barbarians that any of those famous Welsh household names – Gareth, Barry, Gerald, JPR and Merve the Swerve – defeated the All Blacks.

Wonderful as it is, the Six Nations, in rugby terms, needs to be put in context. Martin Johnston's England are the only Six Nations winners who have had a consistent run of victories against the trio of major southern hemisphere sides. Wales won Grand Slams in 2005, 2008 and 2012 and then another Six Nations title in 2013 with a record-breaking 30–3 win against Robshaw's England seeking the Grand Slam in Cardiff. But during this eight-year period their record against New Zealand, South Africa and Australia is a sorry procession of defeats, with just two wins in 2005 and 2008 and a draw in 2006 against Australia interrupting a tally of 27 defeats in 30 games by the time 2012 drew to a close.

In the 2011 Rugby World Cup, Sam Warburton's Welsh side captured the public imagination, valiantly failing to reach the final against New Zealand by a narrowly off-target long-range Leigh Halfpenny penalty attempt against France with 14 men.

They then won the Grand Slam after returning home. But when 2012 came to an end Wales had yet to beat any of the great southern hemisphere trio, losing six closely-contested matches against Australia in the space of a year, as well as being beaten 26–19 by Samoa, 26–12 by Argentina and 33–10 by New Zealand in the autumn internationals at the Millennium Stadium. However England, in a surreal end to their 2012 campaign, shocked the rugby world with a humiliating 38–21 defeat at Twickenham of a New Zealand side that had been undefeated for 20 Tests.

So Welsh rugby still remains haunted by the fact its national side has not beaten New Zealand since 1953. Although recent decades may have offered little comfort for Wales as defeats have invariably been heavy, the past was very different. It is worth remembering Wales v New Zealand encounters have a celebrated history and it took the All Blacks more than 60 years to get the better of the Welsh when they met in internationals.

The victory over the 1905 All Blacks at Cardiff owed much to Welsh ingenuity. They countered the problems posed by the 2-3-2 scrum used by the tourists by adopting the same formation themselves and it was a cleverly engineered switch move by scrum-half Dicky Owen from a set scrum that produced Morgan's decisive try.

Cliff Porter's 1924–25 Invincibles silenced a 50,000 crowd, defeating Wales 19–0 in Swansea but the Welsh, playing back at Cardiff Arms Park, went ahead 3–1 in the series, famously defeating the 1935–36 All Blacks 13–12, and the 1953–54 All Blacks 13–8, with tries in the closing minutes of each match.

Playing the major Welsh clubs was always the hardest section of All Blacks tours of Britain before short tours became the vogue. The First All Blacks demolished most sides they encountered in the rest of the UK but there were single score victories against the three famous Welsh clubs: Newport, 6–3; Cardiff, 10–8; and Swansea, 4–3. Later Swansea (1935: 11–3), Cardiff (1953: 8–3), Newport (1963: 3–0) and Llanelli (1972: 9–3) each recorded wins against the New Zealanders. Other setbacks against the Welsh were Swansea drawing 6–6 with the 1953–54 tourists, while an East Wales XV with a backline featuring Edwards, John, Dawes and Gerald Davies were judged unfortunate not to have ended the unbeaten record of Brian Lochore's 1967 All Blacks. That game ended in a 3–3 draw at Cardiff Arms Park before a 40,000 crowd, after a Barry John drop-kick grazed the right upright just before the final whistle. It was the only match Lochore's much-admired touring team, who had added a welcome degree of back play to forward power under their influential coach Fred 'The Needle' Allen, failed to win on their 15-match tour of Britain and France.

Swansea's 1935 victory against the tourists highlighted the Welsh ability to produce backs with flair. The half-back combination that played such a key role in that win were teenage schoolboys Haydn Tanner at scrum-half and his cousin Willie Davies at fly-half. Interestingly, Dawes was the fourth Welsh centre three-quarter to distinguish himself as a victorious captain against the New Zealand in internationals. Wales in their three Test wins against New Zealand were led by centres – the Prince of Centres, Gwyn Nicholls (1905), the celebrated crash tackler, Claude Davey (1935) and the great Bleddyn Williams (1953), who also captained Cardiff to their victory against the same tourists.

For Wales, though, no victory has come since the 57,000 crowd at the old Cardiff Arms Park erupted when Olympic sprinter Ken Jones gathered a cross-kick on the burst to score the winning try against Bob Stuart's Fourth All Blacks on December 19, 1953. In the 1960s, when the All Blacks dominated world rugby with their great pack, Wilson Whineray's 1963–64 All Blacks beat Wales 6–0 and the proud Welsh record of bettering New Zealand in Test matches finally ended after 62 years when Lochore's side three years later levelled the win count at 3–3 by defeating Wales 13–6. After two conclusive defeats when Wales toured New Zealand for the first time in 1969, Welsh honour was restored, after a fashion, through the 1971 Lions. But the national side suffered the anguish of witnessing its stars of the 1970s twice narrowly fail to halt what developed into a seemingly endless series of reverses. Since 1953, the two countries have met 25 times and Wales have lost every match, with heavy defeats occurring depressingly often after the end of the Third Welsh Golden Era in the 1970s.

What would today's Welsh rugby followers, movingly reciting those evocative battle hymns of old at the Millennium Stadium, give to witness their compatriots repeating the achievements of Dawes' Wales and Carwyn James' Lions and Barbarians with victory against the All Blacks?

Of the many rugby books in print covering that era, none, including the hugely-detailed David Parry-Jones book, *The Dawes Decades*, pay due tribute to Dawes as the key figure in British rugby's renaissance in the early 1970s, nor is there any book in print devoted to the greatest of all Lions tours.

What John Dawes achieved at London Welsh was eventually to have a worldwide influence through the success of the 1971 Lions. For an insight into just how dreary rugby could be in the pre-Dawes era, when you could kick directly into touch from anywhere, just recall the notorious match at Murrayfield in 1963 when Wales beat Scotland 6–0. During that game, Welsh captain Clive Rowlands at scrum-half spent the game kicking the ball directly into touch and the result was 111 lineouts in one of the dullest matches in the game's history.

Admittedly, this was an extreme case of negative rugby, but the 1958–59 International Championship that has today become the Six Nations tournament offered another vivid illustration of the game's limitations as a spectator sport in the decades immediately after World War II.

That winter England failed to score a solitary try in four matches which ended with soccer-style scorelines. They drew 3–3 with Scotland at Twickenham, with each side scoring a penalty goal, followed by a 5–0 loss to Wales in Cardiff, with the hosts scoring a converted try, then in Dublin they beat Ireland

203

3–0 through a penalty goal, and finally against France they drew 3–3 at Twickenham, with each side scoring a penalty. Thankfully the following season provided a sharp contrast when, inspired by the arrival of the gifted Oxford University attacking fly-half Richard Sharp on the Test scene, England scored seven tries in their campaign, sharing the International Championship title with France.

The British and Irish Lions were hugely popular as, primed with the best backs produced by the four Home Unions, they offered an escape from the negativity that characterised so many of the post-war rugby years as they played attacking rugby to counter the superior forward strength of the All Blacks and Springboks. In 1955, the Lions, boasting a great buccaneering backline that included Welsh fly-half Cliff Morgan, England centres Jeff Butterfield and Phil Davies, and 19-year-old Irish winger Tony O'Reilly, drew their Test series 2–2. While the 1958–59 International Championship produced just 11 tries in 10 matches, the 1959 British Lions in New Zealand, with a dazzling array of gifted backs including English fly-half Bev Risman, Ireland's David Hewitt in the centre, O'Reilly and the mesmeric Englishman Peter Jackson on the wings and Scotland's Ken Scotland at full-back, averaged more than four tries a match. And in the first Test against New Zealand they even had the home crowd, with a commendable sense of justice, chanting 'Red, Red, Red' when they scored four tries, only to be defeated 18–17 as the New Zealand full-back Don Clarke kicked six penalty goals.

The All Blacks were used to being outplayed by Lions backs but they remained in their comfort zone as their forwards invariably produced victory. But in 1971 it was different, as the nightmare realisation dawned that producing world-class forwards was no longer enough to ensure success. That defeat inflicted a huge scar on the New Zealand psyche. And so future years were to see a sea change in tactics throughout New Zealand rugby, with backs no longer in a straightjacket acting primarily as servants of their forwards and this led directly to the All Blacks convincingly winning the first Rugby World Cup in 1987.

The tour was not only a success in result terms, for the deeds of the Lions captured people's imagination. Forty years later, Dawes still remembered the sheer enjoyment of that long visit to a rugby obsessed country:

'The New Zealand people became very affectionate towards us. Not to the extent they wanted us to win the series but when we did win the series they accepted it.

'We became quite a popular team. Everything became pleasurable, the tour, meeting people, the travel, the scenery. Above all the rugby became very enjoyable, hard but enjoyable. The popularity of the Lions grew enormously and wherever we went they turned out and lined the streets. It was like a coronation. That made for the whole ambience of the tour.

'The other thing which was vital that not many people appreciate is the weather. We never played in the rain and I can only remember one pitch that was wet.'

The *joie de vivre* of the 1971 Lions side surfaced throughout the 1970s in Dawes' exciting Wales side that dominated the Five Nations with running rugby and captured the public imagination. Rugby players may be fitter and stronger than their predecessors in the amateur era but how often do you see modern sides matching the speed of pass and handling skills that were the hallmark of the 1971 Lions side and the Wales teams of the 1970s?

The changes for the better on the worldwide rugby scene inspired by the success of the 1971 Lions can be backtracked to Old Deer Park in the late 1960s when Dawes became captain and coach of London Welsh.

For much of the history of the sport, the full-back position was almost totally defensive as the ball could be kicked directly into touch from any spot on the field, with a lineout then following at the spot where the ball went into touch. This effectively placed a premium on the skill of a full-back kicking from hand.

The fact the full-back was primarily a defender was highlighted by the statistic that prior to 1969, a mere three tries were scored from that position in the International Championship (now the Six Nations) created in the 1883–84 season. Rare exceptions to the norm at Test level were provided by the gifted Scottish full-back Ken Scotland playing for the 1959 Lions, and then in the late 1960s France fielded another hugely gifted attacking full-back in Pierre Villepreux (34 caps, 1967–72), remembered by those lucky enough to see him for his elegant entries into the Tricolours backline and distinctive flip pass.

But it was John Dawes at London Welsh who fully exploited the full-back as an attacker as a crucial ingredient of the counterattacking philosophy that was at the heart of his rugby vision. Appropriately it was his club colleague John Williams who became the first Test full-back to score tries with any regularity. As well as creating many tries for others with his counterattacks from defensive positions and well-timed entries into orthodox backline producing overlaps, JPR, as he was known, crossed the tryline six times in Welsh colours.

In September 1968, one of the game's most inspirational law changes, devised by the Australians, was adopted worldwide and players were only able to kick directly into touch from inside their own 25-yard line. As well as elevating the art of touch-finding to a new level as players had to bounce-kick the ball out of play from outside their 25, it also shifted the game's emphasis more towards keeping the ball in hand.

But Dawes didn't need this rule change to create a rugby philosophy based on footballing skills rather than brute strength. The full-back entering the backline to create the overlap was a key feature of the Exiles' game. Dawes also realised that the best attacking options could frequently be found in what seemed defensive situations. The accepted wisdom when he joined London Welsh in 1963 was: from inside the 25 the ball should be cleared to safety with a kick to touch. But Dawes realised that in this area of the field, possession in the hands of talented counterattacking backs offered try-scoring opportunities with potential overlaps as man-to-man marking ended in broken field play.

The counterattacking philosophy Dawes encouraged was symbolised by that sensational try scored by the Exiles in their away fixture with Bristol in the 1966–67 season. This was the game in which the Exiles speed merchant, Colin Gibbons, playing at full-back, fielded the ball ten yards from his own tryline and sidestepped his way through the midfield rather than kicking to touch. The move ended with Dawes himself scoring and turning around to see that the nearest players behind him were all members of his own side.

Fast-forward six years from Bristol to Cardiff Arms Park on January 27, 1973 and the famous Gareth Edwards Barbarians try offered a similar decidedly unpromising situation and then the ultimate realisation of the Dawes rugby philosophy against the most feared rugby side in the world when Phil Bennett running towards his own line retrieved a kick ahead and turned to face the All Blacks.

The evidence that Dawes deserves to be rated above his Welsh playing contemporaries is not hard to find. Before Dawes was given his reign as leader of his country and then the Lions, the great Edwards and John partnership was on the losing side for Wales against the 1967 All Blacks. They made little impact on the disastrous 1969 Wales tour of New Zealand either and Edwards was no great success as captain of Wales. And it wasn't until they played with Dawes in the Lions and Barbarians that the multi-talented Irishman Mike Gibson, hampered by playing in an average Ireland side, and the dashing David Duckham, starved of decent ball on the England wing, realised their destinies as great players and finished on winning sides against the All Blacks.

It took the perfect sporting partnership of a great on-the-field leader, John Dawes, and a great off-the-field coach, Carwyn James, to create history in New Zealand in 1971. It is difficult to separate these two great rugby figures in terms of importance. British rugby had so many gifted players in the Dawes era you could argue no single player was indispensable in simple rugby playing terms. Had not the Lions won that vital first Test against New Zealand at Dunedin with Chico Hopkins at the helm for the majority of the match at scrum-half after Edwards went off injured? Without the benefit of his celebrated partner's famous long pass, didn't Barry John still manage to destroy the All Blacks' full-back McCormick with a masterful example of precision kicking? And was not that memorable 1973 Barbarians victory achieved with Phil Bennett rather than Barry John at fly-half? But take away either Dawes or James from the 1971 Lions tour and it's hard to imagine the All Blacks would have fallen. Neither should the role of Scottish tour manager Doug Smith be forgotten for, as a confidence booster with a sense of destiny, he was in the same league as Dawes and James. After the Lions had won the notorious Canterbury match, the game dominated by rugby thuggery that saw the Lions lose their two first-choice prop forwards to injury, veteran Lions player Willie John McBride recalled: 'I remember Doug Smith coming on the bus after the game and saying to me, "The King is dead, long live the King – we'll beat the All Blacks next week" as half of our team had gone to hospital. I'm sitting looking around me and saying "I'm needing a lot of convincing here".'

Quietly-spoken persuaders rather than shouters, Dawes and James were very much brothers-in-arms, two sons of the valleys whose fathers worked in the coal mines, two teachers with the same national heritage who graduated from UCW, Aberystwyth and played rugby for Wales, and two visionaries capable of elevating the sport they were devoted to far beyond the mundane to an inspirational level best summed up by the Welsh word for which there is no true English equivalent, *hwyl*.

Carwyn James was on his own as a coach, treating rugby as a sport of intellect. He had the intuitive gift of being able to inspire his charges with that most vital of all qualities needed for success – self-belief.

To realise that Carwyn James was no ordinary mortal one just needs to recall what he told the 1971 Lions when they gathered at London's Park Lane Hotel before heading for a few days practice together at Eastbourne prior to flying Down Under. That most brilliant of sports writers, the late Frank Keating, in an article in *The Guardian* on May 11, 2011 celebrating the 40th anniversary of the Lions tour, repeated the 'unforgettable statement of landmark philosophy' delivered that evening after dinner: 'Look here, I want each one of you to be your own man,' James apparently told the mix of nations before him. 'Express yourself not as you would at the office for the next three months, but as you would at home.

'I don't want you Irishmen to pretend to be English, or you English to think you are Celts, or for Scotsmen to be anything less than Scottish to the core. You Irish must continue to be the supreme ideologists off the field, and on it, fighters like Kilkenny cats. Let you English stiffen those upper lips and simply continue to be superior. And the conservative traditionalism of you Scots – strong, dour, humourless in phoney caricature – let it be seen as colourfully fired up these next 90 days by the oil of your country's new-found radicalism. As well, I demand that all of you make sure you let us Welsh continue to be bloody-minded and swaggeringly over-cocky in our triple-clowning, triple-crowning arrogance.'

And then on the field of play James had John Dawes' inspirational leadership and ability as a master passer guiding the best players in Britain. Carwyn James justly remains revered as one of the greatest figures in rugby history while, by comparison, the true debt the game owes to Dawes has been largely forgotten. As an off-the-field coach he did not match James' genius and it is interesting to speculate how the 1977 Lions would have fared if James had revisited New Zealand once again in charge of the British tourists. But neither did James match Dawes' attributes as a great rugby captain gifted enough as a player to translate his rugby vision into a reality at the highest level on the field of play, for his career as a player brought just two Welsh caps as he was overshadowed by the great Welsh fly-half of the 1950s, Cliff Morgan.

Remember also there was no Carwyn James with Dawes in the six years preceding the Lions tour when he memorably realised his vision of how rugby should be played.

What Dawes, James and their fellow Welshmen achieved with the Lions and Barbarians was far more significant than the later Wales Five Nations triumphs. In terms of attacking brilliance and significance, the Lions' amazing 47–9 demolition of Wellington, the magical 13–0 points blitz in the opening 20 minutes of the third Test in 1971 and the awesome display of rugby by the Barbarians against the All Blacks in 1973 were a level above the deeds of the Wales sides that later dominated the European scene.

London has played a significant role in rugby history. Despite the shift of the game's power axis on the field of play to the southern hemisphere, Twickenham has remained the acknowledged headquarters of the sport despite, in recent times, the all too frequent administrative inadequacies of the Rugby Football Union and the impressive claims of the Millennium Stadium in Cardiff as the best rugby amphitheatre in the UK.

England's capital has also provided the traditional HQ for not only the game's lawmakers but also the operating base for some of the game's great innovators. In England's rugby Golden Era from 1913–24, five Grand Slams in seven seasons were won. Tactically two men played key roles in this achievement. Before World War I, Adrian Stoop famously revolutionised the art of back play while, after the conflict, fellow Harlequin Sir Wavell Wakefield pioneered mobile forward play at a time when forwards in Britain were regarded, in his own words, as 'little more than pushing machines'. To this celebrated English duo of rugby visionaries operating at the most famous rugby club in the capital, should be added the name of John Dawes who moved to London in August 1963 and remained at Old Deer Park with London Welsh for the rest of his playing career.

There, in the late 1960s, in the relatively humble setting of a rugby field overlooked by that pagoda in Kew Gardens not far from Richmond Station, Dawes in floodlit winter evening training sessions, guiding fellow club members who had earlier finished their day's work, developed the style that was to change the rugby world.

The London Welsh philosophy developed naturally. As a centre Dawes viewed his prime task as getting decent ball to rugby's fastest runners, the wing three-quarters. And Haydn Davies had showed the value of an attacking full-back. There was another crucial part of the jigsaw puzzle in place when Dawes, as he had been at Loughborough Colleges, was given the job of coaching as well as captaining the Exiles.

'There were a lot of PE men in the club and therefore our fitness levels were better than most clubs. When I became responsible for the training and selection, we deliberately chose people who were footballers. It is what I wanted to do. Teachers like to play running rugby. It was easy to convince people this was the way forward. "Let the ball do the work" was our philosophy.'

By the time the game turned professional three decades later, the glory days of London Welsh had long gone and it wasn't until June 2012 that the club emerged from relative obscurity, absurdly having to win a legal battle to gain its justified promotion to the Aviva Premiership, English rugby's showcase club league.

At that time, *Sunday Times* rugby correspondent Stephen Jones neatly highlighted the debt rugby owed the Exiles, writing:

> If you lumped together most of the current Aviva Premiership clubs they would not in aggregate have been as important to the development of rugby as London Welsh have.
> Younger followers may have no idea that the club was the

driving force behind a colossal expansion of rugby. John Dawes, a clever yet unspectacular centre, became club captain. He may not have been pyrotechnic with his hands and feet but he was a cutting-edge professor of the game and he helped transform it.

The London Welsh team of the Dawes era not only played spectacular rugby at a time when the sport was leaden, but catapulted forward seven great players who were at the heart of Grand Slams in Wales' Golden Era, and of the triumph of the 1971 Lions in New Zealand. Dawes led that celebrated party, the first and so far the only Lions team to win a series in New Zealand in almost 128 years of trying.

That tour galvanized rugby in Britain and Ireland clean out of sight.

The 1970s were christened 'The Dawes Era' but this is barely acknowledged in the many publications about Welsh deeds in this decade. Dawes never acquired rugby superstar status but the reality is that he was a far more influential figure than any of his fellow players. He was the catalyst who inspired British rugby's revival, through his leadership of three exceptional sides who by coincidence all played in red shirts.

Those who doubt John Dawes was the key player behind the unrepeated success of the 1971 Lions should heed the views of Barry John, the most charismatic of all the rugby superstars in Welsh rugby's Golden Era in the 1970s. John, who rated Dawes 'the greatest captain I have seen' wrote in his 2000 autobiography, *Barry John – The King*:

It is somewhat ironic that the Welsh back who rarely grabbed the spotlight just happened to be the one who held everything together. That man was John Dawes in the centre, perhaps best described as a player's player.

The best way I can describe the Dawes factor is this. If, before matches, the public address man announced a sudden change to the Welsh line-up, and either JPR or myself was missing through injury, you could hear the moans and groans reverberate around the ground. In the dressing room, however, it would not worry us because these things happen in sport and we had good backup players anyway. If, on the other hand, the public address man announced John Dawes was missing through injury, the crowd would not bat an eyelid. In the dressing room, however, there would be a mood of panic because we knew just how important his presence was to the way we played.

Syd, as we called John, was simply brilliant in the way he encouraged us. "Don't worry about it," he would say if a pass had gone astray. "Keep trying things." His attitude meant the rest of us had the confidence to play with panache and style, to attempt the off-the-cuff moves. A truly great captain. What is more, to this day, I believe Syd had never received enough credit for his own playing ability, for he was a master of passing superbly under pressure and had a big hand to play in many of our famous tries.

Dawes was the key figure who enabled the supremely gifted generation of British players to finally end the dominance of the southern hemisphere nations, New Zealand and South Africa, which had lasted for nearly seven decades. In the second half of the 20th century, no other rugby player matched his influence on the game, for his achievements transformed not only British rugby but also significantly changed perceptions of the sport for the better in New Zealand, countering what had been the increasing appeal of soccer.

When Sydney John Dawes came to command the game's high stage there was frequently – to quote a Welshman I once knew – 'magic in the air' and The Quiet Welshman from Chapel of Ease deserves a place among the game's immortals as one of the most influential figures in rugby union history.

Ross Reyburn
Moseley, Birmingham
2013

Appendix

British and Irish Lions Tours

THE BRITISH AND Irish Lions, consisting of players from England, Wales, Scotland, Northern Ireland and the Republic of Ireland, are one of the world's most popular sports teams. But their success has been limited in breaking the dominance of the two great southern hemisphere rugby nations New Zealand and South Africa.

The Lions have undertaken 28 tours from 1888 to 2009. In ten Test series in New Zealand, the 1971 Lions triumph is their only success and they have won just six, drawn three and lost 29 of their 38 Tests against the All Blacks.

In South Africa their record is far better, with four wins and one drawn encounter in 13 series and 17 wins, six draws and 22 defeats in 45 Tests. And generally they have had the better of Australia, winning 15 and losing just five of 20 Tests, but it has to be remembered that it is only in the past thirty years the Australians have emerged as a major rugby power rivalling the All Blacks and Springboks.

The Rugby World Cup has also reflected the strength of southern hemisphere rugby with only England's win against Australia in Sydney in 2003 disrupting the trophy wins by New Zealand (1987, 2011) South Africa (1995, 2007) and Australia (1991, 1999).

The 1971 Lions are the only touring side to have won a four-Test series in New Zealand as South Africa's sole away series win against the All Blacks was a 2–1 victory in a three-match contest in 1937.

* Lions Test wins are highlighted in grey.

1888 Australia and New Zealand
P 35 W 27 D 6 L 2 For: 292 Against: 98
Managers: A Shaw (England) & A Shrewsbury (England)
Captain: RL Seddon (Swinton & England)

1891 South Africa
P 20 W 20 For: 226 Against: 1
Manager: E Ash (England) Captain: WE MacLagan (Scotland)

British Isles	4	South Africa	0	Port Elizabeth
British Isles	3	South Africa	0	Kimberley
British Isles	4	South Africa	0	Cape Town

1896 South Africa
P21 W19 D1 L1 For: 320 Against: 45
Manager: R Walker (England) Captain: J Hammond (England)

British Isles	8	South Africa	0	Port Elizabeth
British Isles	17	South Africa	8	Johannesburg
British Isles	9	South Africa	3	Kimberley
British Isles	0	South Africa	5	Cape Town

1899 Australia
P 21 W 18 L 3 For: 333 Against: 90
Manager & Captain: Rev. MM Mullineux (England)
British Isles 3 Australia 13 Sydney

British Isles	11	Australia	0	Brisbane
British Isles	11	Australia	10	Sydney
British Isles	13	Australia	0	Sydney

1903 South Africa
P22 W11 D3 L8 For: 229 Against: 138
Manager: J Hammond (England) Captain: MM Morrison (Scotland)

British Isles	10	South Africa	10	Johannesburg
British Isles	0	South Africa	0	Kimberley
British Isles	0	South Africa	8	Cape Town

1904 Australia & New Zealand
P19 W16 D1 L2 For: 287 Against: 84
Manager: AB O'Brien (New Zealand) Captain: DR Bedell-Sivright (Scotland)

British Isles	17	Australia	0	Sydney
British Isles	17	Australia	3	Brisbane
British Isles	16	Australia	0	Sydney
British Isles	3	New Zealand	9	Wellington

1908 New Zealand

P 26 W 16 D 1 L 9 For 323 Against: 201

Manager: GH Harnett (England) Captain: AF Harding (Wales)

British Isles	5	New Zealand	32	Dunedin
British Isles	3	New Zealand	3	Wellington
British Isles	0	New Zealand	29	Auckland

1910 South Africa

P 24 W 13 D 3 L 8 For: 290 Against: 236

Managers: W Cail (England) & WE Rees (Wales)

Captain: Dr T Smyth (Ireland)

British Isles	10	South Africa	14	Johannesburg
British Isles	8	South Africa	3	Port Elizabeth
British Isles	5	South Africa	21	Cape Town

1924 South Africa

P 21 W 9 D 3 L 9 For: 175 Against: 155

Manager: H Packer (Wales) Captain: R Cove-Smith (England)

British Isles	3	South Africa	7	Durban
British Isles	0	South Africa	17	Johannesburg
British Isles	3	South Africa	3	Port Elizabeth
British Isles	9	South Africa	16	Cape Town

1930 New Zealand & Australia

P 28 W 20 L 8 For: 624 Against: 318

Manager: J Baxter (England) Captain: D Prentice (England)

British Isles	6	New Zealand	3	Dunedin
British Isles	10	New Zealand	13	Christchurch
British Isles	10	New Zealand	15	Auckland
British Isles	8	New Zealand	22	Wellington
British Isles	5	Australia	6	Sydney

1938 South Africa

P 24 W 17 L 7 For: 414 Against: 284

Manager: Col. BC Hartley (England) Captain: S Walker (Ireland)

British Isles	12	South Africa	26	Johannesburg
British Isles	3	South Africa	19	Port Elizabeth
British Isles	21	South Africa	16	Cape Town

1950 New Zealand & Australia
P 29 W 22 D 1 L 6 For: 570 Against: 214
Manager: LB Osborne (England) Captain: KD Mullen (Ireland)

British Isles	9	New Zealand	9	Dunedin
British Isles	0	New Zealand	8	Christchurch
British Isles	3	New Zealand	6	Wellington
British Isles	8	New Zealand	11	Auckland
British Isles	19	Australia	6	Brisbane
British Isles	24	Australia	3	Sydney

1955 South Africa
P 25 W 19 D 1 L 5 For: 457 Against: 283
Manager: JAE Siggins (Ireland) Captain R Thompson (Ireland)

British Isles	23	South Africa	22	Johannesburg
British Isles	9	South Africa	25	Cape Town
British Isles	9	South Africa	6	Pretoria
British Isles	8	South Africa	22	Port Elizabeth

1959 Australia, New Zealand and Canada
P 33 W 27 L 6 For: 842 Against: 353
Manager: AW Wilson (Scotland) Captain: Ronnie Dawson (Ireland)

British Isles	17	Australia	6	Brisbane
British Isles	24	Australia	3	Sydney
British Isles	17	New Zealand	18	Dunedin
British Isles	8	New Zealand	11	Wellington
British Isles	8	New Zealand	22	Christchurch
British Isles	9	New Zealand	6	Auckland

1962 South Africa
P 25 W 16 D 4 L 5 For: 401 Against: 208
Manager: Cmdr DB Vaughan (England) Captain: A Smith (Scotland)

British Isles	3	South Africa	3	Johannesburg
British Isles	0	South Africa	3	Durban
British Isles	3	South Africa	8	Cape Town
British Isles	14	South Africa	34	Bloemfontein

1966 New Zealand, Australia & Canada

P 35 W 23 D 3 L 9 For: 524 Against: 345

Manager: DJ O'Brien (Ireland) Coach: JD Robins (Wales)

Captain: MJ Campbell-Lamerton (Scotland)

British Isles	11	Australia	8	Sydney
British Isles	31	Australia	0	Brisbane
British Isles	3	New Zealand	20	Dunedin
British Isles	12	New Zealand	16	Wellington
British Isles	6	New Zealand	19	Christchurch
British Isles	11	New Zealand	24	Auckland
British Isles	19	Canada	8	Toronto

1968 South Africa

P 20 W 15 D 1 L 4 For: 377 Against 181

Manager: DK Brooks (England) Coach: AR Dawson (Ireland)

Captain: T Kiernan (Ireland)

British Isles	20	South Africa	25	Pretoria
British Isles	6	South Africa	6	Port Elizabeth
British Isles	6	South Africa	11	Cape Town
British Isles	6	South Africa	19	Johannesburg

1971 Australia and New Zealand

P 26 W 23 D 1 L 2 For: 580 Against: 231

Manager: Dr DWC Smith (Scotland) Coach: CR James (Wales)

Captain: SJ Dawes (Wales)

British Isles	9	New Zealand	3	Dunedin
British Isles	12	New Zealand	22	Christchurch
British Isles	13	New Zealand	3	Wellington
British Isles	14	New Zealand	14	Auckland

1974 South Africa

P 22 W 21 D 1 For: 729 Against: 207

Manager: AG Thomas (Wales) Coach: S Millar (Ireland) Captain: WJ McBride (Ireland)

British Isles	12	South Africa	3	Cape Town
British Isles	28	South Africa	9	Pretoria
British Isles	26	South Africa	9	Port Elizabeth
British Isles	13	South Africa	13	Johannesburg

1977 New Zealand and Fiji

P 26 W 21 L 5 For: 607 Against: 320

Manager: G Burrell (Scotland) Coach: SJ Dawes (Wales) Captain: P Bennett (Wales)

British Isles	12	New Zealand	16	Wellington
British Isles	13	New Zealand	9	Christchurch
British Isles	7	New Zealand	19	Dunedin
British Isles	9	New Zealand	10	Auckland
British Isles	21	Fiji	25	Savu

1980 South Africa

P 18 W 15 L 3 For: 401 Against: 244

Manager: S Millar (Ireland) Coach: Noel Murphy (Ireland)

Captain: WB Beaumont (England)

British Isles	22	South Africa	26	Cape Town
British Isles	19	South Africa	26	Bloemfontein
British Isles	10	South Africa	12	Port Elizabeth
British Isles	17	South Africa	13	Pretoria

1983 New Zealand

P 18 W 12 L6 For: 478 Against: 276

Manager: WJ McBride (Ireland) Coach: JW Telfer (Scotland)

Captain: CF Fitzgerald (Ireland)

British Isles	12	New Zealand	16	Christchurch
British Isles	0	New Zealand	9	Wellington
British Isles	8	New Zealand	15	Dunedin
British Isles	6	New Zealand	38	Auckland

1989 Australia

P 12 W 11 L 1 For: 360 Against: 182

Manager: DCT Rowlands (Wales)

Coaches: IR McGeechan (Scotland) & RM Uttley (England)

Captain: F Calder (Scotland)

British Isles	12	Australia	30	Sydney
British Isles	19	Australia	12	Brisbane
British Isles	19	Australia	18	Sydney

1993 New Zealand

P 13 W 7 L 6 For: 314 Against: 285

Manager: G Cooke (England) Coaches: I McGeechan (Scotland) & D Best (England)

Captain: AG Hastings (Scotland)

British Isles	18	New Zealand	20	Christchurch
British isles	20	New Zealand	7	Wellington
British Isles	13	New Zealand	30	Auckland

1997 South Africa

P 13 W 11 L 2 For: 480 Against: 278

Manager: F Cotton (England) Coach: I McGeechan & J Telfer (Scotland)

Captain: M Johnson (England)

British Isles	25	South Africa	16	Cape Town
British isles	18	South Africa	15	Durban
British Isles	16	South Africa	35	Johannesburg

2001 Australia

Manager: D Lenihan (Ireland) Coaches: G Henry (New Zealand) & A Robinson (England)

Captain: M Johnson (England)

P 10 W 7 L 3 For: 449 Against: 184

British Isles	29	Australia	13	Brisbane
British Isles	14	Australia	35	Melbourne
British Isles	23	Australia	29	Sydney

2005 New Zealand

P 12 W 7 D 1 L: 4 For: 353 Against: 245

Manager: WB Beaumont (England) Head Coach: Sir C Woodward (England)

Captain: B O'Driscoll (Ireland)

British Isles	25	Argentina	25	Cardiff
British Isles	3	New Zealand	21	Christchurch
British Isles	18	New Zealand	48	Wellington
British Isles	19	New Zealand	38	Auckland

2009 South Africa

Manager: TGR Davies (Wales) Head coach: I McGeechan (Scotland)

Captain: P O'Connell (Ireland)

P 10 W 7 D 1 L 2 For: 309 Against: 169

British Isles	21	South Africa	26	Durban
British Isles	25	South Africa	28	Pretoria
British Isles	28	South Africa	9	Johannesburg

Bibliography

The All Blacks. TP McLean (Sidgwick & Jackson, 1991).

All Black Power – The story of the 1968 All Blacks in Australia and the 1968 French Team in New Zealand and Australia. Terry Mclean (AH & AW Reed, 1968).

Barry John, The King. Barry John with Paul Abbandonato (Mainstream Publishing, 2000).

Behind the Lions – Playing rugby for the British & Irish Lions. Stephen Jones. Tom English, Nick Cain & David Barnes (Polaris Publishing & Birlinn, 2012).

The British & Irish Lions Miscellany. Richard Bath (Vision Sports Publishing, 2008).

British Lions. John Griffiths (Crowood Press, 1990).

Cliff Morgan – The Autobiography. Cliff Morgan with Geoffrey Nicholson (Hodder & Stoughton, 1996).

The Dawes Decades – John Dawes and the Third Golden Era of Welsh Rugby. David Parry-Jones (Seren, 2005).

The Encyclopedia of New Zealand Rugby. Rod Chester, Ron Palenski, Neville McMillan (Hodder Moa Beckett, 1981).

England Rugby – A History of the National Side, 1871–1976. Barry Bowker (Cassell, 1976).

Everywhere for Wales. Phil Bennett with Martyn Williams (Stanley Paul, 1981).

Fred Allen on Rugby. Fred Allen & Terry McLean (Cassell, 1970).

Gareth Edwards – The Autobiography. Gareth Edwards with Peter Bills (Headline, 1999).

Gerald Davies – An Autobiography. Gerald Davies (George Allen & Unwin, 1979).

The Great Fight of the French XV. Denis Lalanne (AH & AW Reed, 1960).

The Greatest Lions – The Story of the British Lions Tour of South Africa, 1974. JBG Thomas (Pelham Books, 1974).

The Greatest Welsh XV Ever. Eddie Butler (Gomer Press, 2011).

Haka! The All Blacks Story. Winston McCarthy (Pelham Books, 1968).

The History of the British Lions. Clem Thomas updated by Greg Thomas (Mainstream Publishing, 1996).

JPR: Given the Breaks – My Life in Rugby. JPR Williams (Hodder & Stoughton, 2007).

Lion Man. Ian McGeechan with Stephen Jones ((Pocket Books, 2009).

The Lions. Wallace Reyburn (Stanley Paul, 1967).

Lions Down Under: The British Isles Rugby Tour of Australia and New Zealand, 1959. Vivian Jenkins (Cassell, 1960).

Lions Rampant. Terry McLean (AH & AW Reed, 1971).

The Lions Speak. Edited by John Reason (Rugby Books, 1972).

Men in Black – 75 Years of New Zealand International Rugby. H Chester & NAC McMillan (Pelham books, 1978).

The Men in White – The Story of English Rugby. Wallace Reyburn (Pelham Books, 1975).

More Thoughts of Chairman Moore – The Wit and Wisdom of Brian Moore Vol. II. Brian Moore (Simon & Schuster, 2011).

Mourie's Men – The All Blacks Tour 1978. Wallace Reyburn (Cassell, 1979).

The Official England Rugby Miscellany. Stuart Farmer (Vision Sports Publishing, 2008).

On the Ball – The Centennial Book of New Zealand Rugby. Gordon Slatter (Whitcombe & Tombs, 1970).

Playfair Rugby Football Annual 1970–71, 1971–72 & 1972–73. Edited by Gordon Ross (Dickens Press, 1971, 1972 & 1973).

The Red Dragons of Rugby – Welsh–All Black encounters from 1905–1969. Terry McLean (AH & AW Reed, 1969).

Rothmans Rugby Yearbook 1978–79. Editor: Vivian Jenkins (Macdonald & Jane's, 1978).

Rugger. WW Wakefield & HP Marshall (Longmans, Green & Co, 1930).

Rugger: The Man's Game. EHD Sewell (Hollis & Carter, 1950).

Shadow – The Dai Morris Story. Dai Morris with Martyn Williams (Y Lolfa, 2012).

The Unbeaten Lions – The 1974 British Isles Rugby Union Tour of South Africa. John Reason (Rugby Books, 1974).

The Unsmiling Giants. Wallace Reyburn (Stanley Paul, 1967).

The Victorious Lions – The 1971 British Isles Rugby Union Tour of Australia & New Zealand. John Reason (Rugby Books, 1971).

The Wales Rugby Miscellany. Rob Cole & Stuart Farmer (Vision Sports Publishing, 2008).

Wallace Reyburn's World of Rugby – The complete illustrated history of the international game. Wallace Reyburn with Ross Reyburn (Elek Books, 1967).

Who Beat The All Blacks? – The story behind the most famous club victory in Welsh History. Alun Gibbard (Y Lolfa, 2012).

The Winter Men – The Seventh All Blacks Tour. Wallace Reyburn (Stanley Paul, 1973).

The Man who changed the world of Rugby
is just one of a whole range of publications
from Y Lolfa. For a full list of books currently
in print, send now for your free copy of
our new full-colour catalogue.
Or simply surf into our website

www.ylolfa.com

for secure on-line ordering.

TALYBONT CEREDIGION CYMRU SY24 5HE
e-mail ylolfa@ylolfa.com
website www.ylolfa.com
phone (01970) 832 304
fax 832 782